INTERCULTURAL SCREEN ADAPTATION

INTERCULTURAL SCREEN ADAPTATION

British and Global Case Studies

Edited by Michael Stewart and Robert Munro

EDINBURGH
University Press

Edinburgh University Press is one of the leading university presses in the UK.
We publish academic books and journals in our selected subject areas across the
humanities and social sciences, combining cutting-edge scholarship with high editorial
and production values to produce academic works of lasting importance. For more
information visit our website: edinburghuniversitypress.com

© editorial matter and organisation Michael Stewart and Robert Munro, 2020, 2022
© the chapters their several authors, 2020, 2022

Edinburgh University Press Ltd
The Tun – Holyrood Road
12 (2f) Jackson's Entry
Edinburgh EH8 8PJ

First published in hardback by Edinburgh University Press 2020

Typeset in 10/12.5 Adobe Sabon by
IDSUK (DataConnection) Ltd, and

A CIP record for this book is available from the British Library

ISBN 978 1 4744 5203 8 (hardback)
ISBN 978 1 4744 5204 5 (paperback)
ISBN 978 1 4744 5205 2 (webready PDF)
ISBN 978 1 4744 5206 9 (epub)

The right of the contributors to be identified as authors of this work has been asserted
in accordance with the Copyright, Designs and Patents Act 1988 and the Copyright
and Related Rights Regulations 2003 (SI No. 2498).

CONTENTS

List of Illustrations   vii
Acknowledgements   viii
List of Contributors   x

   Introduction   1
   Michael Stewart and Robert Munro

PART I   NOSTALGIA, HERITAGE AND THE TOURIST GAZE

1. Adapting Pagnol and Provence   11
   Jeremy Strong
2. 'A Tourist in Your Own Youth': Spatialised Nostalgia in *T2: Trainspotting*   26
   Douglas McNaughton
3. '200 Miles Outside London': The Tourist Gaze of *Far from the Madding Crowd*   46
   Shelley Anne Galpin

PART II   RADICAL CONTINGENCIES: NEGLECTED FIGURES AND TEXTS

4. Reframing Performance: The British New Wave on Stage and Screen   67
   Victoria Lowe
5. Why We Do Not Adapt Jean Rhys   84
   Sarah Artt

CONTENTS

PART III RE-ENVISIONING THE NATIONAL IMAGINARY

6. 'To see oursels as ithers see us': Textual, Individual and National Other-selves in *Under the Skin*   101
   Robert Munro

7. Back to the Future: Recalcitrance and Fidelity in *Julieta*   120
   Michael Stewart

PART IV THE LOCAL, THE GLOBAL AND THE COSMOPOLITAN

8. *El Patrón Del Mal*: A National Adaptation and *Narcos* Precedent   141
   Ernesto Pérez Morán

9. Constructing Nationhood in a Transnational Context: BBC's 2016 *War and Peace*   155
   Carol Poole and Ruxandra Trandafoiu

10. *The Beautiful Lie*: Radical Recalibration and Nationhood   172
    Yvonne Griggs

PART V REMAKING, TRANSLATING: DIALOGUES ACROSS BORDERS

11. In Another Time and Place: Translating Gothic Romance in *The Handmaiden*   191
    Chi-Yun Shin

12. Chains of Adaptation: From *D'entre les morts* to *Vertigo*, *La Jetée* and *Twelve Monkeys*   206
    Jonathan Evans

13. A 'Double Take' on the Nation(al) in the Dutch-Flemish Monolingual Film Remake   222
    Eduard Cuelenaere

Index   241

ILLUSTRATIONS

Figures

3.1	Gabriel surveys his dead flock in *Far from the Madding Crowd*	53
3.2	Early shots of the landscape setting the mood for the film to come in *Far from the Madding Crowd*	59
6.1	Projecting the eye in *Under the Skin*	106
6.2	Screaming children in *Under the Skin*	108
6.3	From 'an "it" to a "she"' in *Under the Skin*	109

Table

13.1	Complete list of Dutch-Flemish source films and subsequent remakes	224

ACKNOWLEDGEMENTS

This collection came out of a symposium we organised at Queen Margaret University, Edinburgh, in June 2017. For supporting the symposium, we'd like to thank QMU, and in particular our head of department, David Stevenson. For helping us to organise and host the symposium, we thank Liz Suttie and her Events colleagues, as well as our Media Services team.

For her support of and attendance at the symposium, and for her ongoing enthusiasm and advice as it turned itself into a book, we'd like to thank Gillian Leslie at Edinburgh University Press. We'd also like to thank Richard Strachan at EUP for taking the reins from Gillian and being a constant and invaluable source of help and advice. We'd also like to thank readers and committee members at EUP for their very helpful criticisms and suggestions on the proposal we submitted to them.

For allowing Jeremy Strong and us to re-publish Jeremy's chapter on Pagnol, we'd like to thank Homer B. Pettey and R. Barton Palmer (editors of *French Literature on Screen*, 2019) and Manchester University Press. We're also grateful to Taylor and Francis for allowing us to re-publish Chi-Yun Shin's article on *The Handmaiden*. Chi-Yun's article originally appeared in *Journal of Japanese and Korean Cinema*, Volume 11 number 1.

We'd like to thank all of the 2017 symposium's participants, who travelled from various parts of the world and contributed to a hugely enjoyable and informative day – and then stuck with us to help put together this valuable work. The memory of the symposium is tinged a little by the recent death of Laurence Raw. Laurence came with his wife from Turkey to Edinburgh and had useful and interesting things to say about all the papers presented. As a major figure in the field of adaptation studies, and as someone always glad to help others with their work and ideas, he will be greatly missed.

We'd like to thank Yvonne Griggs and Jonathan Evans for agreeing to contribute to this book despite not being with us at the Edinburgh symposium. Their chapters, very clearly, make a strong collection stronger still.

Robert would like to thank his co-editor Michael for his sage words of wisdom throughout the process, and his wife Jenni for her unyielding patience and support, particularly as the undertaking of editing this collection began shortly before they welcomed their daughter – a bundle of joy and sleepless nights – Eilidh into the world.

Michael echoes these sentiments – generally speaking! – in that sharing this project with Robert has been a pleasure and relief, and his family, as ever, have been too generous in allowing him to hide himself away at points in order to get it done!

CONTRIBUTORS

Sarah Artt is Lecturer in English and Film at Edinburgh Napier University. Her recent publications concern images of nineteenth-century prostitution on screen, in *Neo-Victorian Villains* (2017) and *Transforming Cities* (2018). She has also written about bodies, Frankenstein and Black Mirror in Science Fiction Film and Television. She is working on a book about women and silence in the cinema.

Eduard Cuelenaere is a PhD researcher at the Department of Communication Sciences at Ghent University and is also affiliated with University of Antwerp (Belgium). His research interests focus on adaptation/remake studies, European cinema, cultural studies and audience studies. The FWO-funded research project he is working on aims to critically investigate the emerging practice of monolingual film remakes in the Low Countries. Eduard has published with *European Journal of Cultural Studies* and *Tijdschrift voor Communicatiewetenschap*, guest-edited the special issue 'Current trends in remaking European screen cultures' with *Communications: The European Journal of Communication Research*, and is, together with Dr Gertjan Willems and Dr Stijn Joye, preparing an edited volume *(European Film Remakes)* with Edinburgh University Press (forthcoming).

Jonathan Evans is Senior Lecturer in Translation Studies at the University of Portsmouth. He is the author of *The Many Voices of Lydia Davis* (2016) and co-editor of the *Routledge Handbook of Translation and Politics* (2018).

He is currently co-investigator on the AHRC funded project 'Translating for Change' which investigates the use of Anglophone queer cinema by Chinese LGBT+ groups. His research interests include film remakes, transcultural fandom and the circulation of political ideas.

Shelley Anne Galpin is a PhD candidate at the University of York, where her thesis explores the ways in which teenagers engage with period dramas. Shelley's work engages with the relationship between the past and film and television, as well as questions of literary adaptation. She has been published in *Journal of British Cinema and Television* and *Studies in European Cinema*.

Yvonne Griggs is a Lecturer in Media and Communications at the University of New England. She specialises in adaptation studies and has published monographs, articles and chapters in edited collections in her specific research area. She is the author of *Adaptable TV: Rewiring the Text* (2018), *The Bloomsbury Introduction to Adaptation Studies: Adapting the Canon in Film, TV, Novels and Popular Culture* (2017) and *King Lear on Screen* (2007). Her articles on screen adaptations have appeared in leading adaptations journals (*Adaptation, Journal of Film and Performance*, and *Literature Film Quarterly*), and her recent work on Nordic Noir television is published in *The Routledge Companion to Adaptation* (edited collection, 2018). She is currently a Contributing Editor for *Literature Film Quarterly*.

Victoria Lowe is a Lecturer in Drama and Screen Studies at the University of Manchester. Her research interests lie in British cinema history, specifically the connections between film aesthetics and practices and Western theatrical traditions. She has published articles in the *Journal of Film and Video* on the relationship between performance and stardom in British cinema in the 1930s, with Robert Donat as a case study; in *Scope* on Hitchcock and performance; in the *Journal of British Cinema and Television* on stardom and the voice; and in *Studies in Theatre and Performance* on stage and screen acting in British cinema in the 1930s.

Douglas McNaughton is a Senior Lecturer in Film and Screen Studies at the University of Brighton. His research interests include British television drama, telefantasy, screen technologies and the sociology of space. His research focus is on the intersection of space, technology and labour in television production. His publications include work on the historical influence of the actors' union Equity on British television production in *Journal of British Cinema and Television* and research on experimental multi-camera film technologies in *Historical Journal of Film, Radio and Television*. His recent publications include articles and book chapters on camerawork as performance, and on film and television representations of Cold War spaces. He is co-editor of a 2019 special issue of *Film Criticism* focusing on on-screenspaces, places and identities.

Robert Munro is Lecturer in Digital Media and Communication at Queen Margaret University. His research focuses on Scottish cinema, the video essay, screen industries and film genre. Robert is preparing a monograph titled: *Adapting Scotland: Screen Adaptation, Visual Culture and the Image of Scotland in the Twenty-first Century*. Robert is also currently leading a research project funded by Screen Scotland to explore Scotland's moving image archive in primary schools.

Ernesto Pérez Morán is a Spanish PhD. He is Associate Professor at Complutense University, Spain. His research concerns Cultural Studies, Film History, Audiovisual Languages and Fiction Narratives in TV. He has published five books, several papers in ISI/Scopus journals and he has participated in several Research Projects about Spanish Cinema. Nowadays he teaches History of Art and TV Screenplay.

Carol Poole was seconded to Ambassador to MediaCityUK in 2012 from her substantive post of Head of Media at Edge Hill University, where from 1997 she established and led the Media subject area. Her research areas are documentary, film and adaptations. As producer, recent credits include *Exclaim!* (2012), Lowry Theatre, Salford Quays; *Journey to the Land of Cando* (2013) BBC; *A Kiss of Frost* (2013); *Exclaim* (2014), Everyman Theatre, Liverpool. Her consultancy work includes chairing international student film festivals, such as the Hong Kong and Chinese Region International Student Film Festival, and work with prestigious film schools, such as the Russian National Film and Television School, the Polish National Film Television and Theatre School, Lodz, Poland, and the Film Academy of Miroslav Ondříček, Pizek, Czech Republic. Together with Ruxandra Trandafoiu she has written on the screen adaptation of *Death Comes to Pemberley*, soon to be published in the *Routledge Companion to Adaptation*, and on the craft of Andrew Davies as adaptor in the *Midwest Quarterly Journal*.

Chi-Yun Shin is Principal Lecturer in Film Studies at Sheffield Hallam University. She is co-editor of *New Korean Cinema* (Edinburgh University Press, 2005) and *East Asian Film Noir* (2015). Her articles on contemporary East Asian cinema (of gender, genre, remake and reception) and diaspora films in Britain have been published in a range of journals and edited volumes as well as an encyclopaedia. She is on the editorial boards of the *Journal of Japanese and Korean Cinema* and *East Asian Journal of Popular Culture*. She also organised the 3rd Korean Screen Culture conference in 2014.

Michael Stewart is senior lecturer in film at Queen Margaret University, Edinburgh. His key area of interest is film melodrama. He has published articles on this topic in various journals, including *Cinema Journal* and *Journal of British Cinema and Television*. His most recently published articles are on *Father of My Children* (2009 – in *Studies in French Cinema*) and *Calvary* (2014 – in *Studies in European Cinema*). He also edited a collection of essays entitled *Melodrama in Contemporary Film and Television* (2014), and is a member of the editorial board of *Film Criticism*.

Jeremy Strong is Professor of Literature and Film and the University of West London. Chair of the Association of Adaptation Studies from 2010 to 2016, he is widely published in literature on screen as well as on movies, books, culture and food. His books include *Educated Tastes: Food, Drink and Connoisseur Culture* (2011), *James Bond Uncovered* (2018) and the novel *Mean Business* (2013). He recently guest-edited a special issue of *Adaptation* on 'Adaptation and History' (2019).

Ruxandra Trandafoiu is Reader in Communication at Edge Hill University. Her research interests include nationalism, migration and diasporas; minority politics; visual art, communication and representation; the socio-historical contextualisation of novel to screen adaptations. She is the author of *Diaspora Online: Identity Politics and Romanian Migrants* (2013) and the co-editor of *The Globalization of Musics in Transit: Music Migration and Tourism* (2013) and *Media and Cosmopolitanism* (2014).

INTRODUCTION

Michael Stewart and Robert Munro

This collection comes out of a one day symposium held at Queen Margaret University, Edinburgh, in June 2017. Broadly speaking, the symposium brought together scholars working in the area of adaptation and nationhood. The film and television texts examined during the day were produced in France, Belgium, the Netherlands, UK, South Korea, Spain, USA and Colombia – though even this attempt to begin to fix the texts' national status could easily be undone. Various prefixes (trans, inter, post) and adjectives are used by contributors to this volume – which we're delighted to say includes two new colleagues who weren't able to attend the symposium: Yvonne Griggs and Jonathan Evans. On a sadder note, while the symposium benefited from the participation of a well-kent and highly regarded figure in the field, we were very sorry to hear of the passing away of Laurence Raw in 2018. Laurence's chapter would have considered a particular period and type of UK film production, the significance of these films (e.g. *I Know Where I'm Going!* (Powell and Pressburger 1945) and *Whisky Galore!* (Mackendrick 1949)) as adaptations, and their continued meaning and resonance in contemporary cultures. While the collection, regrettably, doesn't contain Laurence's chapter, his interests (and enthusiasm!) endure across all the chapters here, most specifically in the work of Munro, Lowe, McNaughton and Galpin. For example, Vicky Lowe also looks at films from a distinctive moment in UK filmmaking. In so doing, she revisits questions of history and nationhood. A key part of Lowe's argument is that the historical, aesthetic, and to some extent social impact of films like

The Entertainer (Richardson 1960) cannot be grasped outside of their close relations with their theatrical counterparts; and, moreover, that this has been a neglected part of the study of these films. In this respect, Lowe's chapter supports the argument of Della Coletta that texts must be examined within their '*own* historical, institutional and cultural environments' (2012: 24, Della Coletta's emphasis) if their 'density' (2012: 16) is to be restored. What scholars have tended to overlook, Lowe argues, is the deeply inter-medial and geographically local nature of these texts' cultural formation. By being faithful to these films' historical complexity, Lowe helps us to look not only at these 1960s films in new ways, but also to reconsider what really characterised their theatrical progenitors.

Key here is a notion of performance and a moving away from entrenched dualities – in particular the literary (theatre)/non-literary (film) dichotomy. The argument or desire to look at texts and adaptations as particular types of performance, staging, encounter, and to move beyond binary thinking, is evident across the chapters collected here. Munro, for example, examines *Under the Skin* (Glazer 2013) as a studied, post-human performance of the national and post-national. In considering the film's playing out of national and individual selves and others, Munro's study underscores Kamilla Elliott's looking glass theory of adaptation as an expression of excess where 'absence is always "already inverse inherent presence"' (Della Coletta 2012: 20, quoting Elliott). *Under the Skin* is the strong vision of an auteur-director who wanted to keep the film in the country (Scotland) of the novel *Under the Skin* (Faber 2000), but also make key paradigmatic (e.g. casting, setting) choices and changes, and in some ways move as far away from the novel as possible. What we end up with, Munro argues, is a film which re-inscribes and perhaps transcends the national.

Under the Skin is interpreted and categorised variously, and was also promoted on a number of fronts, including but not limited to nation and auteur. The film Shelley Galpin's chapter examines, *Far from the Madding Crowd* (Vinterberg 2015), was also promoted strongly via nation and auteur; but more than *Under the Skin*, it was the transnational treatment of a markedly English story that was emphasised in the promotion of *Far from the Madding Crowd*. What opened up, then, Galpin's study indicates, was an apparent disjunction between transnational, outward-looking aspirations, and a film which reproduces England and Englishness in mostly conservative and familiar ways. Galpin's findings support Rawle's (2018) argument that we should be cautious in our application of transnational, a term and practice open to multiple meanings and appropriations. Similarly, in our opening chapter, Jeremy Strong looks at the relationship between screen adaptations, tourism and the marketing of place along familiar and easily digestible lines. All of the film and television texts examined in this volume can be argued to be transnational in one way or another, and the various definitions and schemata of the transnational provided by Rawle (2018) in his introduction help us to identify how. As Rawle indicates, transnational can mean little more than major players maximising economic potential; but alongside this, film and television texts will always in some way be 'indiginiz(ed)' (Rawle 2018: 12, quoting Iwabuchi) by and within their sites of production and consumption.

The ways in which the film and television examples examined in this collection do this – indiginise – are fascinating and varied. Galpin's example arguably looks inwards and backwards in the belief that this might maximise British and international consumption. Stewart's example – *Julieta* (Almodóvar 2016) – would seem to be inward looking to the point of retreat. Stewart argues, though, that the film's adaptation of Alice Munro's work (no brief encounter for *Julieta*'s director) produces an indiginisation and confrontation with history that is no less productive for its backwardness and inwardness. Shin and Griggs also examine texts which have been local or indiginised in powerful ways. Shin looks at the way *The Handmaiden* (Park 2016) transports a story set in Victorian England to 1930s Korea. Not only are elements of genre and sexuality expanded and re-routed by the film, Shin shows, but *The Handmaiden* also articulates specific questions of history which continue to resonate in Korea and beyond. Griggs's example, *The Beautiful Lie* (2015), shows how a classic Russian and international story can be produced to speak directly and in complex ways to contemporary Australian audiences about their cultural identities and residual and changing senses of nationhood.

Both of these texts, then – *The Handmaiden* and *The Beautiful Lie* – as well as being clearly and variously intercultural, also engage in nuanced ways with questions of Europeanness. These questions and inflections of Eurocentricism, Rawle (2018: 9) argues, are hard to avoid in globalised media cultures. This certainly is given evidence by the texts and cultures examined in this volume, though questions of Europe and Europeanness are more prominent in some of the studies than others. Poole and Trandafoiu, for example, examine the ways in which *War and Peace* (Davies 2016) effectively reworks discourses of Europeanness, both historically and in the context of contemporary neoliberalism and cultural tourism. The extent to which *War and Peace* is able to give new form to Europe is dependent to at least some degree, Poole and Trandafoiu discuss, on who we consider to be the text's primary adaptor – in this case, Andrew Davies. To understand Davies' oeuvre, his passions and his values, is to understand the journey *War and Peace* attempts to take its viewers on – as well as, as we've noted, the ways in which this journey can be circumscribed by factors frequently beyond Davies' control. Journeying, Della Coletta (2012) notes, is a useful way of thinking about adapted texts. Journeys, Stewart notes, are at the heart both of Almodóvar's work and the writer (Alice Munro) he draws on in making *Julieta*. Applying the ideas of Bruce Isaacs (2016), Stewart argues that these two writers or artists can be thought of as sharing a method; and that this again helps us to move beyond some residual oppositions and better understand the intensity and complexity of particular adaptive encounters.

Encounter, journey, method – thinking of adaptation in these ways might explain the evident frustration in Sarah Artt's compelling study of Jean Rhys. It is not that filmmakers till now have failed to be faithful to Rhys's work or its spirit. It is – at the risk of invoking Conrad – that they haven't quite gone into that place yet; fully faced that challenge or grasped that method. If Pedro Almodóvar would recognise what we mean here, then so we're sure would all of the film and television makers studied in this volume – Jonathan Glazer's fascinating and complicated journey, as Munro shows, being another that immediately comes to mind. We shouldn't imagine too that scholars are not going into this place in an attempt to understand and to some extent get inside a complicated encounter. This is daunting as well as exciting; and all of the chapters here have worked hard to develop methods appropriate to, or sharp enough for, their subjects and their aims. The chapters are also joined by a shared methodology and philosophy, some of which we've referred to above. They share Rawle's 'critical transnationalism' (2018: 18) in their approaches – locating the transnational on the uneven terrain of the historical, the geographic, the economic and the social – and always in a close and complicated relation to the national. The chapters conceive of adaptation as a dialogic, frequently lateral and spatial process (Della Coletta 2012: 5ff); a series of what Della Coletta calls 'principled mistranslations' (2012: 5).

This dialogic and spatial process of adaptation features in Douglas McNaughton's chapter on *T2: Trainspotting* (Boyle 2017), which offers an invigorating discussion of the film's complex adaptive nature, where its relationship to its supposed progenitor text, Irvine Welsh's novel *Porno* (2002), is barely even fleeting. Instead *T2* is far more interested in what McNaughton calls 'embodied' and 'spatialised' nostalgia, made evident by the film's excavation of loss, memory and time. The film plays with the audience's expectations, and their own memories of *Trainspotting* (Boyle 1996), Cool Britannia and their youth, and McNaughton shows how the well-known and loved characters from Boyle's earlier film are themselves wrestling with how unkind the passing of time has been. We are again through the looking glass of adaptation here, and the film's conceit is frequently to show the characters seeing their former selves in Edinburgh's spaces, only to find that their present selves are unfaithful adaptations of those cinematic memories. McNaughton's work here can be read in conjunction with Berghahn's analysis of exoticism and nostalgia in transnational cinema, where she finds a compulsion to long for the energy of 'significant historical junctures' (2019: 34–5). In the case of *T2*, McNaughton shows that this longing for the high watermark of British culture in the mid-90s is powerfully contrasted with the story of Veronika, the Bulgarian sex worker, and a subplot involving funding from the European Union, a telling narrative device for Brexit Britain.

Another of the collection's most methodologically ambitious chapters is Jonathan Evans' analysis of a transnational and translational chain of adaptations, which includes but is not restricted to *La Jetée* (Marker 1962) and *Twelve Monkeys* (Gilliam 1995). Evans's ideas are close to those of Della Coletta (2012), and both theorists might agree with Chan (2012) that adaptation is by definition and in different ways translation. The chapters collected here, certainly, support Chan's argument that adaptation is a 'quintessentially intercultural project' (2012: 413). Chan argues that one of the best methodological routes for avoiding binary thinking in intercultural analysis is to theorise adaptation as a process of translation and as part of translation studies. In this respect, Chan draws on Venuti's (2007) critique of adaptation studies, and appeal for a more rigorous, and in Venuti's case hermeneutic, methodology. There isn't space to look at the detail of Venuti's argument here. One of his most interesting concepts, though, is 'abusive fidelity' (2007: 39), which 'zeroes in . . . (on) . . . clusters of textual energy' (ibid.). The most effective, or abusively faithful, translation, Venuti argues, 'will . . . abuse . . . the source text, exposing linguistic and cultural conditions that remain implicit' (2007: 39); and furthermore, will direct 'a critical thrust back toward the text that it translates and in relation to which it becomes a kind of unsettling aftermath' (ibid. – Venuti here quoting Philip Lewis).

In her study of Australian cinema, Anne Rutherford also tries to think through difficult questions of 'foreignisation' (Chan 2012: 415) and fidelity. In formulating her dialogic theory of 'intercultural membrane' (Rutherford 2013: 138), Rutherford argues that scholars should not aim to uncover a text's fidelity to a pre-colonial or pristine past. Instead they should consider a text's capacity to be faithful in some way, to show fidelity to the complexity of the present. In this respect, Rutherford theorises de-colonisation as an ongoing and uneven process – 'a negotiation embedded in the local, the contextual and the contingent in the present, as much as it is in the national, the global and the historical' (2013: 149). In different ways, the chapters in this volume ask to what extent adaptations make these negotiations visible, and if the processes of film and television adaptation are embedded within cultural hierarchies, making a dialogic relationship with national imaginaries more apparent, perhaps, than in non-adaptations. In this respect, and as we note above, the collection responds to Hutcheon's (2013: 174) argument that adaptations display the ability 'to be at once both self and Other', and asks how this might be so not only in aesthetic, narrative and thematic ways, but also in terms of cultural appropriation and the national imaginary. This may be most apparent in examples which exhibit cross-cultural adaptation, such as Shin's study of *The Handmaiden*, but this self/Other dynamic extends to those adaptations which, in the first instance, do not cross national borders, but which nonetheless operate within a dialogic relationship with an imaginary or idealised past, and the contingency of the present, as Rutherford (2013) suggests.

The ideological underpinnings frequently found in cross-national adaptations is analysed by Ernesto Pérez Morán in his examination of *Narcos* (Netflix 2015–), which, he argues, reproduces an imperialist perspective in its retelling of the story of Colombian drug lord Pablo Escobar. Contrasting the American production with *El Patrón del Mal* (Caracol TV 2012), a Colombian telenovela itself an adaptation of Alonso Salazar's *La Parabola de Pablo* (2001), Morán finds a colonialist process of Othering apparent in Netflix's version of the story. The argument here is that not only does Netflix fashion the narrative events of Escobar's story to fit a Western perspective, but that the aesthetic of its show also presents a hegemonic televisual language at odds with that found in *El Patrón del Mal*. These shifts in emphasis between adaptations across borders are also the subject of Eduard Cuelenaere's study of Dutch-Flemish remakes, albeit the differences between productions here are more nuanced. Cuelenaere's chapter shows that one way in which small, non-anglophone, national film industries seek viability is by faithfully remaking films for local audiences. Here we see the productive tension between the transnational and localised approaches, as the films analysed are often co-productions between Flemish and Dutch production companies, but the shift in language and in localised details in the remakes shows the extent to which filmmakers still seek to make connections with local audiences. As we suggested above, transnationalism within screen studies has previously perhaps been too willing to iron out difference in seeking to locate cultures of production with global flows. However, Lim argues that tensions between the global and regional remain evident and frequently unexpected in their consequences, and calls for the continued development of 'transnational cinema as a conceptual framework that can be both inescapably national and inadvertently nation-less' (2019: 2).

It is in these areas that we believe this collection can prove of significant interest. The chapters contained in this volume offer methodological approaches for thinking through processes of adaptation within and across national borders, through localised histories and globalised flows of production. Here we might think of Foucault's (1998) theory of the author-function and try to extend it into the field of national and intercultural adaptation. We might, for example, speak of a nation-function, through which the idea of the nation is crucial to the 'mode of existence, circulation and functioning of certain discourses in society' (Foucault 1998: 211). This then will invite us to ask how adaptations make use of this nation-function, in efforts, for example, after certain types of authenticity and cultural legitimacy, or instead to unsettle certain imaginaries and discourses via free or complicated movements across time, space and cultures. We have avoided trying to pin down the study of screen adaptations through any dominant method, keeping faith with adaptation studies' renowned dexterity, once perhaps seen as an indicator of the discipline's lack of rigour but now, rightly we would argue, more commonly seen as indicative of its relevance to contemporary cultures. In this respect, this collection's focus might seem quite traditional, with literature to screen adaptations dominating, even if all chapters question such linear readings or relations. While we might have welcomed contributions which looked at adaptations in terms of convergent and transmedia storytelling, though Strong's opening chapter looks at Pagnol through this lens, there is abundant evidence throughout the volume of exploratory thinking, adopting approaches from cultural studies, philosophy, translation studies and beyond. Indeed, what we hope becomes apparent as the reader weaves their way through the collection, is that while the chapters may be organised around apparently conventional case studies, they are interested in processes of adaptation which go well beyond the texts in question. What is evident is the consideration of the adaptation of specific national, historical and cultural junctures, and the ways in which the respective texts can be read through these fragmented, hierarchical and contested perspectives, and what doing so might tell us, to paraphrase Dudley Andrew (1984: 106), about the societies from which they come and the ones to which they point.

References

Andrew, D. (1984). *Concepts in Film Theory*, Oxford: Oxford University Press.
Berghahn, D. (2019), '"The past is a foreign country": exoticism and nostalgia in contemporary transnational cinema', *Transnational Screens*, 10: 1, 34–52.
Chan, L. (2012), 'A survey of the "new" discipline of adaptation studies: between translation and interculturalism', *Perspectives: Studies in Translatology*, 20: 4, 411–18.
Della Coletta, C. (2012), *When Stories Travel: Cross-Cultural Encounters between Fiction and Film*, Baltimore: Johns Hopkins University Press.
Foucault, M. (1998), 'What is an author?' In *Michel Foucault: Aesthetics, Method, and Epistemology (Essential Works of Foucault, 1954–1984, Vol. 2)*, New York: New Press, pp. 205–22.
Hutcheon, L. (2013), *Theory of Adaptation* (2nd edn), London: Routledge.
Lim, S. H. (2019), 'Concepts of transnational cinema revisited', *Transnational Screens*, 10: 1, 1–12.
Rawle, S. (2018), *Transnational Cinema: An Introduction*, Basingstoke: Palgrave Macmillan.
Rutherford, A. (2013), '*Ten Canoes* as "inter-cultural membrane"', *Studies in Australasian Cinema*, 7: 2–3, 137–51.
Venuti, L. (2007), 'Adaptation, translation, critique', *Journal of Visual Culture*, 6: 1, 25–43.

PART I

NOSTALGIA, HERITAGE AND THE TOURIST GAZE

1. ADAPTING PAGNOL AND PROVENCE

Jeremy Strong

INTRODUCTION

It is nearly impossible to commence this chapter without remarking upon the coincidence that Marcel Pagnol's birth in 1895 in Aubagne, Provence, occurred in the same year that his countrymen Auguste and Louis Lumière held the first public screenings of their cinematograph in Paris. Yet Brett Bowles reminds readers that this pleasing accident of chronology was not necessarily 'a sign that Pagnol's fate was somehow cosmically intertwined with cinema' (2012a: 10). Bowles indicates that while Pagnol's family history did not readily suggest a nascent facility for any particular art form, including the newest, what was to prove remarkable was his success across *several* media and roles. For Pagnol would achieve acclaim as a novelist, playwright, film producer and director, becoming one of France's leading cultural figures of the twentieth century. Unusually for an instance of adaptation, the films examined in this chapter have not followed the familiar trajectory of novel-film, but rather *film*-novel-film; an adaptive journey that reflects Pagnol's identity as a multimedia author. Responding to Pagnol's original 1952 film, itself a version edited down significantly from his desired vision of the story, André Bazin wrote that 'in *Manon of the Springs*, with his inspiration finally at its peak – he gave Provence its universal epic' (1995: 204). Hence, even before the novels that gave rise to the adaptations examined here, Pagnol and this story were inextricably associated with Provence. Pagnol later novelised his own *Manon* into *L'eau des collines* (*The Water of the Hills*) in 1962. Finally, in 1986 – eleven years after his death – the constituent stories of *L'eau des collines* were adapted as the films *Jean de Florette* and *Manon des Sources*. They achieved both critical and commercial success, nationally and internationally, though it was domestically that they achieved their greatest box office success, running for seventy and fifty-eight weeks respectively, and selling 7.2 and 6.6 million tickets, making them the most popular films of that year (Bowles 2012a: 237). Importantly, the films were also a notable example of a concerted effort on the part of the French government of the time to support and promote cinema that foregrounded French history and culture, especially in the face of competition from anglophone filmmakers.

The opening credits of both films emphasise their place in a national cultural and literary tradition. 'D'après l'oeuvre de MARCEL PAGNOL de l'Académie Française' precedes any of the other major acknowledgements and works to assert the films' credentials as quality adaptations, and – in turn – vouchsafes the adaptive source with the imprimatur of his being one of 'les Immortels'; a member of a preeminent French cultural institution that has included such major literary figures as Voltaire, Alexandre Dumas and Victor Hugo. Equally, it should be noted that Pagnol's election to the Academy in 1946 rested essentially on his achievements as a filmmaker and playwright; the first filmmaker ever elected to the Academy, at that time his work in the forms of the novel and the memoir were still to come. Bowles argues that Pagnol's 'legacy as a French cultural icon depends largely on the enduring appeal of his trilogy of films set in Marseille – *Marius* (1931), *Fanny* (1932) and *César* (1936), the first two co-directed adaptations of his hit plays of the same name' (2012b: 371). In the context of this particular chapter it is also worth noting the Academy's role in policing the French language, in particular its opposition to English loanwords, to the use of feminine equivalents for conventionally masculine nouns, and to the affording of constitutional protection for regional languages. In defending its own rightness, the Academy has frequently revealed itself as unfriendly to neighbours and new arrivals.

The extent to which the films are further anchored in a context of national structures, and work to promulgate a politically endorsed version of cultural patrimony, is further revealed by the credit 'avec la participation du CENTRE NATIONAL DE LA CINEMATOGRAPHIE et du MINISTERE DE LA CULTURE'. Through funding and other forms of promotion and acknowledgement – for example the attendance of Minister of Culture, Jack Lang, at a special pre-release screening – the French state stood squarely behind what was at the time the nation's most costly film project. Governmental involvement continued into the year after the films' release in the shape of a large project to screen them in schools and colleges across France (Frodon and Loiseau 1987: 218). Italy's broadcaster RAI may have been one of the movies' co-funders, but the credit given to Guiseppe Verdi as the original composer of the 'theme de Jean de Florette' scarcely diluted the Gallic heft of what audiences were offered. Indeed, for British audiences the Italian connotations of the musical theme were further diminished through the 1990s by a series of award-winning television adverts for Stella Artois beer inspired by *Jean de Florette* that used the Verdi leitmotif and were set in an idyllic French countryside that was closely modelled on the films. The first advertisement was titled 'Jacques de Florette'.

The Story

A brief summary of the events of *L'eau des collines*, common to the book and films, is germane to the discussion that follows. In *Jean de Florette*, Ugolin Soubeyran conspires with his uncle César to obtain the property 'Les Romarins' where Ugolin intends to grow carnations. Although the land in question ostensibly lacks a water source, there is a neglected spring known to César and other older villagers. Ugolin and his uncle approach the owner Pique-Bouffigue to buy 'Les Romarins', whose angry refusal sparks a fight in which he is accidentally killed. Leaving the body so it appears the result of a fall, Ugolin and César plug and cover the spring, intending to purchase the property for a depressed price. However it is inherited by Jean Cadoret, a hunch-backed tax-collector from another village, Crespin. Jean is the son of Florette, a childhood friend of César's and fellow villager. According to the local custom he would be called Jean de Florette, but the Soubeyrans deliberately do not reveal his connection to Florette, and to their own village, telling other locals that he is simply from Crespin. This manoeuvre is intended to ensure that the villagers are motivated not to help him, but to treat him with the indifference or outright antipathy traditionally afforded to outsiders. Arriving at 'Les Romarins' with his wife and young daughter Manon, Jean reveals that he intends to farm the land himself despite his inexperience. Although he experiences initial success, with Ugolin presenting himself as a friendly neighbour, Jean's enterprise fails because of the lack of water. He takes out a mortgage and is eventually killed when he attempts to dynamite a new well. Finally acquiring the property, a gleeful Ugolin and César unplug the spring as the family are leaving. Unseen by them, this act is witnessed by Manon.

Manon des Sources takes up events several years later. Ugolin's carnation business is thriving, while Manon has become a beautiful young woman, living half-wild as a shepherdess in the countryside around 'Les Romarins'. After glimpsing her bathing in a pool Ugolin becomes infatuated with Manon and hopes to marry her. She is disgusted by his clumsy approaches and, of course, recalls his role in deceiving her father. At the same time a new schoolteacher, Bernard, arrives in the village and a mutual attraction develops. Overhearing a conversation between two villagers Manon realises that others knew of the spring but did not help her father by telling him. This coincides with her accidental discovery, high in the hills, of the source of the water that serves the whole village and its surrounding farms. She takes her revenge by secretly blocking the source and driving the village to near collapse. César and Ugolin's crime is exposed by another villager and the pair are publicly shamed. Rejected by Manon, Ugolin hangs himself and seemingly ends the Soubeyran family line. Bernard persuades Manon to unblock the source. They marry and she becomes pregnant. A childhood friend of César's returns to the village and reveals that Jean was in fact César's son, conceived before he went on military service in Africa. The letter in which Florette told him of her pregnancy had gone missing in Africa and went unanswered, leading her to marry the blacksmith in Crespin, though only after taking dreadful measures to lose her unborn child; measures which, though unsuccessful, result in his being born hunch-backed. Broken, César dies in his sleep, leaving his property to Manon, his granddaughter.

Hence the narrative of *L'eau des collines* builds towards the revelation of a dreadful irony – generations in the making – that caps the successive tragedies of Jean's failed labours and death, and of Ugolin's doomed love and suicide. Believing himself childless, César has treated Ugolin as a substitute son and made him the vessel of his prideful hopes for the continuation of the Soubeyrans, assisting him in his business and encouraging him to marry and have heirs. The scheme to obtain 'Les Romarins' could never be conceived by the hapless Ugolin, but is the brainchild of the crafty uncle who, throughout the lengthy process of bringing about Jean's failure, deliberately keeps his distance from the family, using Ugolin to bring him reports. Not knowing that the man he systematically torments and whose death he precipitates is his own son, César at first experiences the success of his scheme – a thriving carnation business for his nephew, and the possibility of Soubeyran successors – but sees his hopes dashed in the loss of Ugolin, in public humiliation and ultimately in the discovery of his enormous mistake. The narrative device of the 'incomer', used by many nineteenth-century writers, is here deployed and adapted to great effect. Whilst César is fully aware that Jean is not quite so much of an incomer as he wishes the village to believe, he is wholly ignorant of the extent to which he is not an incomer at all. Although this bald summary elides many other features of the story – including the close observation of peasant life (by turns affectionate and critical), moments of comedy (though these are reduced in adaptation), and the developing romance between Manon and Bernard – it does little to explain why the story's countryside setting should figure so prominently and positively in critical and public responses, and why it should have played a part in making the region a popular destination for visitors. Considered purely in terms of *what* happens, *L'eau des collines* would induce readers/viewers to visit Provence to much the same extent that the events of Hardy's *Jude the Obscure* would prompt anyone to visit Dorset. Which is to say, not at all. The explanation for the story's success in conjuring a desirable image of Provence evidently resides elsewhere.

A Sense of Place

In the novel, Jean Cadoret's affection for 'Les Romarins' and its surroundings is expressed strongly in the phases soon after their arrival, before his dream of a country existence has begun to be seriously thwarted:

> For the first time in his life he had great pleasure in living. His mother had been born on this lonely farm. In her youth she had gathered the almonds of these almond trees, and dried her sheets on the grass under those olive trees that her forefathers had planted two or three centuries ago . . . He loved these pine woods, these junipers, these turpentine trees, the cuckoos in the morning. (Pagnol 1988: 105–6)

Jean's delight in the place reflects a couple of decidedly contemporary responses to the countryside; both the holidaymaker's happiness in being away from the regular routine and the second home owner's nostalgic desire to connect with the lives and places of rural forebears. Connections with 'places of childhood and family origin' (Hall and Muller 2004: 10) are understood as common motivations for modern second home ownership; ownership that often endeavours to 'ground' modern mobile urban-dwellers through a location that is perceived to have a more enduringly significant bond. Although the novel and the adaptations develop the theme of how Jean's prior life experience and his bookish approach to farming do not serve him well in his agricultural ambitions, it is clear that the films invite us to share his view of the setting as essentially idyllic. When Jean's family arrive at 'Les Romarins' and the upstairs shutters are thrown open to expose the vista – the musical theme swelling in the background – character point of view and omniscient perspective are collapsed into an unalloyed celebration of the beautiful landscape. By contrast, the view of César tasting a purloined pinch of soil from 'Les Romarins', moistened with a little water from a carafe, is presented as meanly utilitarian, an appreciation of the land arising from very different motives. The desire of Ugolin and César for the land – for its productivity (when allied with the crucial spring), for the generation of wealth, for the restoration and continuation of a family name – is very different to Jean's, who explains his motives to a perplexed Ugolin:

> I need air, I need space to crystallize my thoughts . . . I want to live in communion with Nature. I want to eat the vegetables of my garden, the oil of my olive trees . . . (Pagnol 1988: 75)

Although Jean's grandiloquent account of an 'authentic' existence and Ugolin's bafflement (believing 'orthentics' to be a new-fangled crop Jean seeks to cultivate!) are ripe for a comic interpretation on page and screen alike, it is clear that Jean's dreams largely anticipate popular urban fantasies of decades later; of escaping the rat-race, of returning to nature and of engagement in a type of Utopian agriculture that will not prove back-breaking or precarious. In their study of contemporary second home ownership Hall and Muller observe that 'removal or inversion from everyday urban life appears to be a main attraction of second homes' (2004: 12) and it is apparent that Jean too seeks not merely a relocation in this move to his mother's childhood home, but a transformation. Whilst the term 'lifestyle' is not anachronistically deployed within the text(s), what Jean rhapsodises about is recognisable to any modern reader or viewer as just that. Texts as varied as the cookery-focused *River Cottage* series of books and television programmes (1998–2012), the property programme *Escape to the Country* (2002–present) or – far more closely connected to the specific Provençal setting of *L'eau des collines*, Peter Mayle's *A Year in Provence* (1989, adapted for TV in 1993) – would seek to seduce readers and audiences with accounts of the rejection of city lives and the adoption of new lifestyles in attractive rural settings; lifestyles in which local foods and customs, seasonality and landscape would loom large. Jill Forbes discerned other intertextual chimes in the adaptations of *L'eau des collines*; finding in 'the lush colour, the sounds and scents of the countryside before it was destroyed by intensive farming, the peculiar mix of Van Gogh and Elizabeth David that so excites the British middle classes' (Forbes 2001: 105–6). In identifying a familiarity with British cookery writer Elizabeth David – author of *A Book of Mediterranean Food* (1950), and *French Country Cooking* (1951) – as a likely shared connection between UK viewers of *Jean de Florette* and *Manon des sources*, Forbes also served to emphasise the connection between the adaptations and Mayle's works, given the extent to which Mayle's francophilia and his rapturous accounts of meals and associated lifestyles appear influenced by David. In the opening sentence of *Mediterranean Food*, David's reference to, and enthusiasm for, the 'colour and flavour of the South' (David 1950: 1) seems a phrase equally applicable to Mayle (one could easily imagine this on a book jacket quotation!), to Pagnol or to Berri's adaptations. As David's biographer, Lisa Chaney, observes, the writer 'was gifted with a consummate ability to evoke time and place and – significantly for the English, enticed by it for centuries – this place was the Mediterranean' (Chaney 1998: xviii).

Whilst the adaptations were especially notable for their pictorial qualities, with Bruno Nuytten's BAFTA-winning cinematography attracting particular acclaim, it would be inaccurate to interpret this aspect of the films as simply an adaptive invention. Pagnol's lyrical, nostalgic rendering of the Provençal landscape is strongly present in his autobiographical account of his childhood, *My Father's Glory & My Mother's Castle*, first published in 1960 before the publication of *L'eau des collines* but after the original film. With many of its incidents and locations clearly identifiable as the inspiration for parts of *L'eau des collines*, *My Father's Glory & My Mother's Castle* offers the reader a view of the country landscape as seen by Pagnol as a child that maps in many respects onto the idealising vision of his character Jean. Described by Pagnol as 'the most beautiful days of my life' (1991: 83) his holidays there are marked by a close and sustained engagement with the landscape – walking, watching, listening, picking – and his account pays close attention to topography, geology, flora and fauna. Summarising the influence of those holidays on Pagnol, Bowles observes that 'the young Marcel's vacations in the countryside instilled in him a strong sense of regional identity and underscored the contrast between rural and urban culture' (2012a: 11). Those same Provençal landscapes would also be used by Pagnol as a filmmaker, along with performers with marked regional accents, in many of the films he made through the 1930s. The inherently scenic potential of Pagnol's Provence, and of *L'eau des collines* in particular, comprised an opportunity and challenge for Berri to 'faire du spectacle', rather than merely a village comedy, as the director announced in *Cahiers du Cinéma*, (quoted in Ostria 1986: 62).

One outcome of the massively successful adaptations of *L'eau des collines* was an increased interest in Provence as a tourist destination, particularly for British visitors. Abetted by Peter Mayle's *A Year in Provence* and its TV adaptation, which both centred on the rural and culinary charm of the region and emphasised a cast of quaint local characters, the effect of a type of tourism and property ownership inspired in part by literary and screen influences was becoming apparent by the early 1990s. Writing in *The Times* in 1992 Dominic Tonner observed how wealthy and trend-setting Britons were eschewing Tuscany – a perennially popular destination – for France; 'forsaking chianti for champagne'. In particular he noted that 'the burgeoning popularity of Provence is thanks, in part, to Peter Mayle-inspired fantasies of summer months spent sipping pastis in a café in Menerbes' (Tonner 1992). A year later, French writer Philippe Seel would explicitly link Pagnol and Mayle in a strident article in *The Guardian*, adapting the figure of the ubiquitous French aperitif to characterise Mayle in Provence as 'the happy Englishman who floats there like a blob of crème anglaise on a pool of pastis'. Responding angrily to the phenomenon of many local properties being snapped up by British buyers, renovated and profitably let to other UK holidaymakers, Seel's criticisms centred on the inauthenticity of Mayle's view of Provence and its people. In particular, he pointedly described Mayle's Provence as an incompetent ersatz of that originally rendered by Pagnol:

> Mr Mayle, your Provence, so touching in its simplicity, is on the verge of being ridiculous. It does not exist. No more than the Provence of Brigitte Bardot and her likes in Saint-Tropez, or this pastoral Provence of Marcel Pagnol that you so clumsily try to recreate. Please understand that Provence is not for sale, and neither are we. (Seel 1993)

Describing relations between the transplanted English and locals, Seel asserts that 'it must be said that relations have slowly deteriorated and we are doing nothing to repair them: beneath our friendly and welcoming appearance, we southerners are in fact naturally suspicious' (Seel 1993). It does not require any great leap of imagination to discern, in this account, echoes of the relationships between villagers and the family of Jean Cadoret in *L'eau des collines*. Ugolin's mixture of friendly overtures and sabotage, and the village's studied silence in the face of Jean's travails – when a hint of local knowledge would make all the difference – may be traced in Seel's description (1993) of wily Provençal contractors who factor into their costs the time they may spend feigning friendliness or sharing a drink with their English clients. Hall and Muller observe that antipathy to second home households, who may be perceived as 'outsiders and even as invaders' (2004: 3), is not uncommon, and Seel's pointed reference to the Hundred Years War between England and France works to place the matter in a specifically adversarial context of conflict, conquest and occupation.

These intersecting, and sometimes clashing, interpretations of Provence reveal the extent to which what is at stake here is a 'cultural landscape' socially constructed out of textual representations. In *Society of the Spectacle* (1983, originally published in 1967), Guy Debord argued that real social life has been displaced by the 'spectacle', a social relationship between people that is profoundly mediated by images. Employing Debord's concept in the context of forms of tourism motivated by moving image texts, Joanne Connell argues that a 'distinguishing feature of film tourism is spectacle, and a landscape or setting made into a spectacle through film transforms into a cultural landscape that may be created, manipulated, reinforced, and contested' (2012: 1013). Equally, the construction of conceptions of landscapes and of the desire to visit them may also be identified in pre-film media, including, but not limited to, the novel. Jewell and Mckinnon (2008) point to the creation of new cultural landscapes through 'literary tourism' that both prompted the intention to visit and shaped the very identity of the place visited. Connell (2012: 1010–11) gives the example of Walter Scott's narrative poem *The Lady of the Lake* (first published 1810) as an early instance of a text prompting literary tourism. Selling 25,000 copies – a record-breaking figure at the time for a work of poetry – the work was popular both in the UK and the US and is credited with launching commercial tourism in the Trossachs in central Scotland.

The 'film tourism' connection postulated here between the viewing experience of *Jean de Florette* and *Manon des Sources* (and/or of *A Year in Provence*) and the desire to visit or purchase property there is not proposed along the lines of a 'magic bullet' effect. Rather, the texts are seen to be operating in a busy media landscape, along with other competing and complementary forces, to generate both awareness and a positive impression of a place greater than that which existed previously. Fernandez-Young and Young contend that the 'binary classification of visitors into film tourists or non-film tourists' (2008: 208) is not an especially helpful way to understand how films may encourage us to visit a particular place. A whole spectrum of activities with greater and lesser degrees of connection to film may fall under the rubric of film tourism. A visit to Disneyland, with its many film-specific attractions, may be said to be more deeply imbricated in the phenomenon than, for example, tossing a coin into Rome's Trevi fountain (which might, or might not, be done with an awareness of the 1954 picture *Three Coins in The Fountain*[1]).

Film tourism, it is suggested here, exists – to varying degrees – in an amalgam with other forms of tourism, enacted as a cultural practice in ways that commonly do not reveal distinct fault-lines. Equally, it is clear that since the 1986 Berri-directed adaptations the intervening years have seen a more explicit acknowledgement by the tourist industry internationally of the capacity of film (and in many cases its antecedent literature) to develop a propensity to visit. In 1990 Butler argued that the influence of screen-related tourism would increase (Butler 1990) and those expectations have largely been met. The *Lord of the Rings* trilogy (2001–3) saw explicit endeavours to encourage travel to New Zealand in the years following, emphasising the country's unspoiled natural landscapes as the setting for Tolkien's fictional Middle Earth, and resulting in an increase in overseas tourist visitors approaching 23 per cent from 2001–4 (Phillips, in Fish 2007: 150). The 'Braveheart Country' tag sought to promote Scottish tourism on the basis of the success of the 1995 film, while Cephallonia was the beneficiary of increased visitor interest following the publication of Louis de Bernieres' *Captain Corelli's Mandolin* (1994) and its adaptation in 2001. Given the number of movies associated with film tourism that derive from literary sources, one might also speak plausibly of the phenomenon of 'adaptation tourism', in which visiting is allied to the experience of both a book and a film. If film and literary tourism are understood as the desire to re-experience aspects of a favoured text, then adaptations afford the opportunity for its triangulation, including – for example – the opportunity to connect with places/locations that may have been elided in the inevitable compressing of events that occurs in most instances of the transit from page to screen. A corollary of this understanding is that film and literary tourism may themselves be understood as inherently adaptive; a deliberate engagement – like cosplay and fan fiction – that takes a source text as the inspiration for a new experience. Adaptation tourism might also be taken to encompass other forms of inter-medial activity. *Brunetti's Cookbook* (Pianaro 2010), a compendium of dishes from Donna Leon's Venetian detective novels (1992–present), is precisely the type of text that could operate in the context of the Leon aficionado seeking to extend and augment their pleasure from the crime novels through a process that might involve 'primary' reading (the novels), 'secondary'/peripheral reading (the cookbook) and visits to specific Venetian restaurants, bars and markets named in the texts. Equally, the multitextual and transmedia experiences afforded by spin-out texts allied to long-running series (for example Andrea Camilleri's Montalbano crime novels (1994–present), their Italian TV adaptations (1999–present) and the now-predictable cookbook[2]) may also be said to be so comprehensive as to afford a type of 'virtual' adaptation tourism experience, similar to the non-visit to London undertaken by the narrator of Huysmans' *A Rebours* (2008, originally published 1884).

The concept of 'mental', as opposed to actual, travel is firmly associated with Xavier de Maistre's late eighteenth-century book, *A Journey around My Room* (2004), written while under house arrest, as well as with the verb 'robinsonner', invented by Arthur Rimbaud and referring, in turn, to Daniel Defoe's *Robinson Crusoe*. Incorporated into the inchoate field of psycho-geography –a domain associated, though not exclusively, with Guy Debord – the figure of the endlessly re-invented Robinson summons both the concept of the mental traveller on an imaginary adventure as well as the actual *flâneur*, or urban wanderer, traversing Paris or London. I. Q. Hunter specifically invokes psychogeography in his account of fan responses to the cult film *The Wicker Man* (1972) in which devotees visit numerous locations around Scotland that comprised the movie's fictional setting. 'The film has inspired considerable such cult tourism or psychogeography, by which fans invoke the ghostly historical valences of the film' (Hunter 2016: 15). In an earlier paper Hunter had also acknowledged the potential dual nature of the psychogeographical 'visit', in which participants' involvement may be as either a 'sofanaut' or could actually involve 'taking our cue from online guides to the film's locations, reading up on some Iain Sinclair and J. G. Ballard, and scooting off to the M3' (Hunter 2013). Relatedly, Douglas Cunningham refers to the 'cinephilic pilgrimage [that] is born of love (for the diegetic world of the film), loss (the apparent absence of that diegetic world within the realm of the real) and a longing to occupy/influence a space-time somewhere between the index and the referent' (2008: 123). Evidently the type of responses to films discussed above, and especially the desire to experience film locations, intersect (if only to a degree) with the practices of tourism and second home ownership analysed in this chapter. They share a sense of being an 'excessive' response, one that – in seeking a deeper grounding in a physical site – transgresses the bounds of viewer involvement planned by the makers of the texts. Equally, significant differences may also be observed. In terms of ideological orientation it seems likely that a not inconsiderable gulf would separate the second home owner motivated in part by the Berri films, and the edgier peregrinations of the cult film psychogeographer drawn to grittier locations and frequently (though not always) to the elevation of relatively ephemeral or obscure movies.

Nostalgia and Heritage

A many-faceted nostalgia is at work in the 1986 Berri adaptations, in the audience responses they stimulated, and in the phenomenon of increased touristic interest and second home ownership in Provence that they – in part – encouraged. Beyond the general cinematic tendency in which 'the countryside is outside of, and lost to, modernity' (Fish 2007: 6) several factors conspired to help the films provoke nostalgia for different types of viewer. For French audiences, Pagnol's national standing, the fact that the novels to be adapted had been bestsellers two decades earlier, and, perhaps most importantly, the ubiquity of Pagnol's films on French television, all meant that the new films were already in a dialogue with a national past that was not restricted to the early twentieth-century setting of the story. As Bowles argues, 'already a cultural icon at the time of his death in 1974, since then Pagnol's legacy has continued to expand through regular dissemination of his films on television and home video' (2012b: 391). In short, French audiences had grown up with Pagnol, and these new adaptations offered them a recapitulative experience that combined the new and the deeply familiar. The desire of British second home owners to buy in France may also be interpreted in the context of nostalgia. Buller and Hoggart contend that such buyers were endeavouring to find a replacement for a now-disappeared British countryside – lost to the outward creep of the suburbs, and to the steady modernisation of agricultural practices and the landscapes they engender – by purchasing in rural France (Buller and Hoggart 1994: 13). France-as-Britain had a clear precedent in filmmaking too, again as a means of conjuring an earlier, vanished, species of British countryside. Roman Polanski's 1979 adaptation *Tess* – itself a proto-Heritage picture, produced by Berri, with high production values and a canonical literary source – had eschewed the real Dorset/Wessex setting of Hardy's novel for location shooting in Normandy, Brittany and Pas-de-Calais. Whilst this move also avoided the risk of the director being extradited to the USA from Britain,[3] the effect was to film *Tess* in settings more accurate to the novel's Victorian era than those that actually remained in the UK. As with *Jean de Florette* and *Manon des Sources*, the cinematography of *Tess* was well received. With a conscious evoking of the agricultural landscapes of Courbet and De la Tour (Pulver 2005) the film's diffusely ekphrastic pictorial properties, its painterly compositions that foregrounded the wistful beauty of both its female lead (Nastassja Kinski) and the landscape, were allied to a tragic narrative to evoke the satisfying melancholy that underpins nostalgia.

Nostalgia may be understood as a key component of the heritage film. Focusing on a particularly British context, Andrew Higson defines these as a 'cycle of quality costume dramas' (Higson in 1999: 109) and it is evident that many of the texts that have come to be grouped under this term are decidedly British in terms of their setting, source material, participants and production. A range of screen texts have been bracketed under the 'heritage' term, including: the films of Merchant Ivory;[4] movies as diverse as *A Passage to India* (1984) and *Another Country* (1984); and prestige television productions such as *Brideshead Revisted* (1981) and *The Jewel In the Crown* (1984), many of which have dealt with the waning of British imperial power and associated lifestyles. For Higson, the representation of an English past 'as visually spectacular pastiche, inviting a nostalgic gaze' (ibid. 109) is their principal connecting element, as well as a tendency to 'reverential use of picturesque rural spaces' (Higson, in 2006: 248). Equally, other critics have drawn attention to the 'increasingly pan-European' (Street 1997: 113) phenomenon of the heritage film. Caughie and Rockett describe both *Jean de Florette* and *Babette's Feast* (1987) as examples of 'Heritage cinema in Europe' (1996: 186) while Street discerns 'heritage themes and stylistics' (1997: 113) in Martin Scorsese's adaptation of *The Age of Innocence* (1993). For Ginette Vincendeau heritage cinema is unequivocally a European phenomenon that 'emerged in the 1980s with the success of European period films' (2001: xvii); her list of examples including the French adaptations *Cyrano de Bergerac* (1990), *La Reine Margot* (1994), *Les Destinées sentimentales* (2000) and, of course, *Jean de Florette*.

An analysis of Berri's adaptations of *L'eau des collines* in terms of heritage film also connects usefully to the questions of place, property and ownership that have exercised this chapter. Michael Atkinson characterised many heritage adaptations contemporary with *L'eau des collines* as 'entranced with the leisure of wealth' (1998: 47) and even a cursory survey of heritage films points to the recurrence of desirable properties, fastidious attention to style and dress, characters who enjoy extended periods of recreational travel, and the general absence of work as either a topic or an implied means to fund characters' lifestyles. Rather, these pictorial/material pleasures are typically presented as the 'natural' purview of those who inhabit – and inherit – them, while an existence predicated on accumulated capital, interest and rents is assumed, though rarely pursued as a theme. It is self-evident that the same cannot be said for the Berri adaptations. Even with the success of Ugolin and César at its height, with 'Les Romarins' secured and the carnation enterprise proving lucrative, this is nonetheless an existence in which the elderly César is required to work outside, and where coins are jealously hoarded in a hidden jar. At other times in the films work is presented, at considerable length, as onerous, debilitating and ultimately fatal. Yet the films' pictorial qualities also manage to out-gun this dimension of the narrative by presenting the physical context of the tragic story, the landscape of Provence, in a fashion that rendered it extremely desirable to viewers, helping to turn some of them into visitors. If *Jean de Florette* and *Manon des Sources* did not offer property fantasies on the scale of *Brideshead Revisited* or *Pride and Prejudice*'s Pemberley, they certainly suggested – when allied to the depressed value of houses in the French country – more attainable dreams of Provençal holidays and second homes where one could enjoy the sunshine and vistas associated with the films, but without the unpleasant complications of their plots. This was not a phenomenon without a precedent; the 1972 film *Deliverance*, filmed in Rabun County, Georgia, was in almost every respect a very different film to *Jean de Florette* and *Manon des Sources* but also combined outdoor scenic pleasures with the theme of an unwelcoming response to visitors from a tight-knit rural community. A narrative of city-dwelling adventurers coming to the Chattooga river seeking whitewater adventure but encountering sexual violence and a fight for their lives would not seem likely to prompt a 20-million-dollar-a-year rafting industry with annual visitor numbers climbing from a pre-film figure in the hundreds to a modern day total in the tens of thousands. Yet *Deliverance* is widely credited with the effect (Welles 2012).

Conclusion

Connell describes how both literary and film tourism 'emphasise the interconnections between people, plot and place' (2012: 1011). The longer-term outcomes of the adaptations of *L'eau des collines* and of Peter Mayle's Provence stories, and of the audience responses they brought about, indicate how plots are not always subject to the control of their authors, how people and places can face unexpected change. Just as César and Ugolin discover that water cannot be turned off and on without incurring dreadful and unexpected consequences, so the interest in and popularity of Provence that was generated by these texts proved to have unplanned and undesirable results. Twenty years after the release of the films the owners of the real property used as 'Les Romarins' were still experiencing unwanted attention in the form of trespassers seeking out the house of Jean de Florette (Falconer 2005), film tourists pursuing that specific physical connection with a cherished screen location. In the case of Peter Mayle, an excess of sightseers inspired by *A Year in Provence* led the author to relocate to The Hamptons in the USA in the mid-1990s (Steinbach 1996), the very time his work was at the peak of its popularity.

'They're capricious, these springs!' (Pagnol 1988: 330)

Notes

1. Actually, wading in would probably be done with a fuller consciousness of the famous scene in *La Dolce Vita* (1960).
2. Stefania Campo (2009), *I segreti della tavola di Montalbano: Le ricette di Andrea Camilleri*.

3. Polanski was, at the time, wanted in the USA following a conviction for sex with an underage girl.
4. Though, of course, James Ivory and Ruth Prawer Jhabvala were non-English members of that team.

REFERENCES

Atkinson, M. (1998), 'Michael Winterbottom: Cinema as Heart Attack', *Film Comment*. Jan/Feb 1998.

Bazin, A. (1995), 'The case of Marcel Pagnol' (Trans. Alain Piette and Bert Cardullo, Ed. Bert Cardullo), *Literature Film Quarterly*, 23: 3, 204–8.

Bowles, B. (2012a), *Marcel Pagnol*, Manchester: Manchester University Press.

Bowles, B. (2012b), 'Performing national consensus: populism in the work of Marcel Pagnol, 1929–38', *French History*, 26: 3, 367–94.

Buller, H. and Hoggart, K. (1994), *International Counterurbanization: British Migrants in Rural France*, Aldershot: Ashgate.

Butler, R. (1990), 'The influence of the media in shaping international tourist patterns.' *Tourism Recreation Research*, 15: 46–53.

Campo, S. (2009), *I segreti della tavola di Montalbano: Le ricette di Andrea Camilleri*. Torino: Edizioni Il leone verde. (Kindle book)

Caughie, J. and Rockett, K. (1996), *The Companion to British and Irish Cinema*, London: BFI Publishing.

Chaney, E. (1998), *Elizabeth David: A Biography*, London: Macmillan.

Connell, J. (2012), 'Film Tourism – Evolution, progress and prospects', *Tourism Management*, 33: 1007–29.

Cunningham, D. (2008), 'It's all there, it's no dream': *Vertigo* and the redemptive pleasures of the cinephilic pilgrimage', *Screen*, 49: 2, 123–41.

David, E. (1950) *A Book of Mediterranean Food*, 2nd revised edn, London: John Lehmann.

De Bernieres, L. (1998), *Captain Corelli's Mandolin*, London: Vintage.

Debord, G. (1983 [1967]), *Society of the Spectacle*, Detroit: Black and Red.

De Maistre, X. (2004), *A Journey around My Room*, London: Hesperus.

Falconer, K. (2005), 'The landscape of *Manon des Sources*', *The Times*, 8 August 2005.

Fernandez-Young, A. and Young, R. (2008), 'Measuring the effects of film and television on tourism to screen locations: a theoretical and empirical perspective', *Journal of Travel & Tourism Marketing*, 24: 2–3, 195–212.

Fish, R. (ed.) (2007), *Cinematic Countrysides*, Manchester: Manchester University Press.

Forbes, J. (2001), '*Germinal*: Keeping it in the family', in G. Vincendeau (ed.), *Film/Literature/Heritage: A Sight and Sound Reader*, London: BFI Publishing.

Frodon, Jean-Michel and Loiseau, Jean-Claude (1987), *Jean de Florette: La Folle aventure du film*, Paris: Herscher.

Hall, C. M. and Muller, D. (eds) (2004), *Tourism, Mobility and Second Homes: Between Elite Landscapes and Common Ground*, Clevedon: Channel View Publications.

Higson, A. (1999), 'Re-presenting the national past: nostalgia and pastiche in the heritage film', in L. Friedman (ed.), *British Cinema and Thatcherism*, London: UCL Press.

Higson, A. (2006), 'Rural spaces and British cinema', in C. Fowler and G. Helfield (eds), *Representing the Rural: Space, Place and Identity in Films about the Land*, Detroit: Wayne State University Press.

Hunter, I. Q. (2013), 'A Psychogeography of British Trash Cinema: New maps of the Field in England', Conference paper given at the University of Lincoln, 28 May 2015.

Hunter, I. Q. (2016), *Cult Film as a Guide to Life*, London: Bloomsbury.

Jewell, B. and McKinnon, S. (2008), 'Movie Tourism – a new form of cultural landscape?' *Journal of Travel & Tourism Marketing*, 24: 2–3, 153–62.

Mayle, P. (1989), *A Year in Provence*, London: Vintage.

Ostria, V. (1986), 'Claude Berri sur les traces de Pagnol: Le tournage de *Jean de Florette*', *Cahiers du Cinéma*, 380. February.

Phillips, M. (2007), '*The Lord of the Rings* and transformations in socio-spatial identity in Aotearoa/New Zealand', in R. Fish (ed.), *Cinematic Countrysides*, Manchester: Manchester University Press.

Pagnol, M. (1988), *The Water of the Hills (Jean de Florette & Manon of the Springs)*, London: Picador.

Pagnol, M. (1991), *My Father's Glory & My Mother's Castle*, London: Picador.

Pianaro, R. (2010), *Brunetti's Cookbook*, New York: Atlantic Monthly Press.

Pulver, A. (2005), 'Girl Interrupted: Roman Polanski's *Tess*', *The Guardian*, 26 March 2005.

Scott, W. ([1810] 2012), *The Lady of the Lake*, <https://www.gutenberg.org/files/3011/3011-h/3011-h.htm> (accessed 20 February 2018).

Seel, P. (1993), 'Hoax en-Provence: "Provence is not for sale and neither are we": a native gives his view of the second British invasion', *The Guardian*, 26 February.

Steinbach, A. (1996), 'Adieu, Provence Profile: author Peter Mayle is no longer at home with his celebrity in the little French village he made so famous', *Baltimore Sun*, 25 June.

Street, S. (1997), *British National Cinema*, London: Routledge.

Tonner, D. (1992), 'A week in Provence; Homes', *The Times*, 19 August 1992.

Vincendeau, G. (ed.) (2001), *Film/Literature/Heritage: A Sight and Sound Reader*, London: BFI Publishing.

Welles, C. (2012), *40 Years Later, Deliverance Causes Mixed Feelings in Georgia*, <www.marketplace.org> (accessed 25 March 2018).

2. 'A TOURIST IN YOUR OWN YOUTH': SPATIALISED NOSTALGIA IN *T2: TRAINSPOTTING*

Douglas McNaughton

Ostensibly adapted from the novel *Porno* (2002), Danny Boyle's *T2 Trainspotting* (2017) was released 21 years after the 1996 cult classic original. Reviewers drew particular attention to the sequel aspect of the film: for Mark Kermode, the film is about 'remembering the glory days of yore' (Kermode 2017a). For Catherine Shoard, audience response to the film is symptomatic of a general nostalgic retreat from reality: 'The reason for all that heady anticipation was not because we couldn't wait to see what the characters are doing now. It's because we can't get enough of the past' (Shoard 2017).

This chapter argues that *T2 Trainspotting* is a film suffused with nostalgia, for the lost youth of the protagonists, and for the original film. Actors, settings and set-pieces from the original are recreated, restaged and replayed. The film engages with nostalgia and memory in various ways, including recreations of iconography and dramatic spaces, the embodied nostalgia of ageing actors, and the replaying or simulation of archive materials to mimic and comment on the processes of memory. The sequel's debt to the original film also raises complex questions about adaptation and intertextuality against the increasingly global distribution of media texts. In its nostalgia for the previous film, *T2* is not simply an adaptation of the novel *Porno*, but more complexly is an adaptation of the original *Trainspotting* film.

This chapter first sketches the social and historical context for 'the *Trainspotting* cultural moment' (Paget 1999) and the first film's cult status. It then outlines some aspects of adaptation theory and its application to *Trainspotting*, and discusses sequels and the compulsion to repeat with regard to *T2*. The chapter then focuses on spatialised nostalgia, the semiotics of space and *T2*'s revisiting of key dramatic sites from the first film. It then discusses the 'embodied nostalgia' of ageing actors and the experiential gap between actors and audience. This leads to a discussion of the sequel's shift from the first film's depiction of the crisis of (Scottish) masculinity, to the flawed and absent fathers of the second film. Failed masculinity thus becomes a focus for nostalgia around lost families, and families that never were, in the second film. The chapter then discusses reflexive nostalgia, and the way *T2* flaunts its nostalgic tendencies and mechanisms. The chapter closes with a meditation on the author's personal response to *T2* in the context of theories of postmodern culture.

The *Trainspotting* Cultural Moment

Adapted from Irvine Welsh's 1993 cult novel, the movie *Trainspotting* was released in 1996. Duncan Petrie (2000) situates it within a stylish, confident 1990s New Scottish Cinema. In this cultural moment, the previous proletarian, masculine and urban associations epitomised by Clydesideism in film have been replaced by representation of new social and cultural identities as a result of post-industrialism (Petrie 2004). Like the book, the 1996 film follows a group of heroin addicts in Scotland's capital city Edinburgh in the late 1980s. Mark Renton (Ewan McGregor) gets involved in a drug deal along with his friends Simon 'Sick Boy' Williamson (Jonny Lee Miller), Spud (Ewen Bremner), and the psychotically violent Francis Begbie (Robert Carlyle). At the end of the film, Renton double-crosses the group and steals the money. Unable to return to Edinburgh, he is last seen crossing Waterloo Bridge in London, going into self-imposed exile.

Trainspotting was the most successful independent release of 1996 in the US (Smith 2002: 9–10). Derek Paget describes 'the *Trainspotting* cultural moment' (1999: 129) and ascribes its success to the fact that 'The novel and its adaptations gave voice to a generation, and allowed them to speak out in a variety of media' (1999: 129). The film and its paratexts became a global cult phenomenon (Lash and Lury 2007). Irvine Welsh wrote a sequel, *Porno* (2002), set ten years after the events of the original novel. The characters reunite to shoot a porn film in Simon's Leith pub; Renton again betrays his friends for money and flees the country. This decade-later sequel was not to happen as a film. As *Trainspotting* and *T2 Trainspotting* scriptwriter John Hodge explains:

> Conversations about making a follow-up to *Trainspotting* had occurred sporadically over the years, and I had even written a draft in the early 2000s, after the publication of *Porno*, but the script was no good and the time was not right, and after that I felt it was buried forever. (2017a: vii–viii)

As the twentieth anniversary of the first film approached however, momentum built for a sequel. According to Hodge, director Danny Boyle 'insisted we must now go to Edinburgh and there, inspired by our surroundings, we would thrash this out once and for all' (Hodge 2017a: viii). Hodge remained uninspired until he accompanied Boyle to Edinburgh's Cameo cinema. The wall was covered with pictures of actors and directors who had visited the cinema, and Boyle points out a photo of himself and Hodge:

> *There*, he said, *there* we are. And sure enough, there was the image of the two of us, from eighteen years earlier, on the opening night of *Trainspotting*, when we had introduced the film at the Cameo. Eighteen years younger ... And I think it was that moment in the Cameo, really, that sense of *coming back*, that unlocked the script for me. (Hodge 2017a: viii, original emphasis)

This is clearly a spatially induced nostalgic response on the writer's part. Nostalgia is etymologically derived from the Greek *nostos* (return home) and *algia* (longing) (Niemeyer 2014: 7). Nostalgia can also be seen as the desire to be young again; however, 'even if the idea of yearning for youth seems logical, it does not explain why sick people were healed upon coming home' (8). The desire to return home, and the longing for lost youth, seem to be connected here. Pam Cook's definition of nostalgia in film is useful: 'These debates are themselves suffused with nostalgia, which can be defined as a state of longing for something that is known to be irretrievable, but is sought anyway' (2005: 3). Nostalgia, memory and history are intertwined in her definition, in which authenticity is key to the recovery of history.

While the plot of *T2 Trainspotting* concerns Renton's diegetic homecoming, the film is also about rewarding audience expectations through nostalgia. As an adaptation, it references the original film in a variety of ways. Key to this is the reconstruction of iconography and spaces. The combination of place and memory did appear to unlock Hodge's creativity, but in a dialectical process, this sense of being inspired by place and nostalgia for events that took place there suffuses the film. As a consequence, *T2 Trainspotting* is much less an adaptation of *Porno* than it is an adaptation of the original *Trainspotting* film, as this chapter explores.

'So What You Been Up To for 20 Years?': Adaptation and Nostalgia

T2 Trainspotting revisits the characters twenty years after the events of the first film. Having built a life in Amsterdam, Mark Renton returns to Edinburgh following a cardiac scare on a gym treadmill. He finds Simon involved in various blackmail schemes with Simon's Bulgarian girlfriend Veronika. They receive a £100,000 EU grant to redevelop Simon's run-down Leith pub, but plan to turn it into a brothel. Begbie escapes from prison and vows revenge on Renton for double-crossing them in the original. Begbie pursues Renton through the half-refurbished pub, but is knocked out and delivered to the police. Spud writes up the first film's events as a novel, and is enlisted by Veronika to swindle Renton and Simon out of the EU grant. In the closing sequence, Renton returns to his childhood bedroom and dances to Iggy Pop's *Lust for Life*, which opened the original film, and the trainspotting-patterned walls of his bedroom seem to turn into a tunnel, racing by.

Analysing the adaptations and intertexts of *Trainspotting* in 1999, Derek Paget draws on Brian McFarlane's 'relative transferability' between texts in different media to overcome the 'fidelity debate' (Paget 1999: 131). Drawing on Roland Barthes and Seymour Chatman and their ideas of 'cardinal/catalyser' and 'kernel/satellite' respectively, McFarlane argues that 'cardinal/kernel' functions must be transferred between adaptations for 'a certain basic recognition of similarity' (131). Drawing on McFarlane, Paget rejects fidelity criticism favouring literary 'originals' by focusing on intertextuality:

> the well-read audience recognizes, acknowledges and even enjoys the transference between media of cardinal/kernel functions; they then compare and contrast (and further engage with) differences in catalyser/satellite enunciation. These readerly exercises are simultaneous during viewing, and constitute part of the pleasure of seeing something already 'known' transformed into something 'similar-but-different'. (Paget 1999: 132)

These processes are at work in *T2 Trainspotting* on a variety of levels, taking in the cast of characters, the double-cross plot, settings, soundtrack and many other elements. John Hodge comments: '*Porno* (2002) offered certain key pillars for the narrative – Begbie in jail, Simon running a pub but dreaming of vice, Renton in exile, Spud much as ever' (Hodge 2017a: vii). *T2 Trainspotting* takes only a few cardinal/kernel elements from its supposed locus, *Porno*, and the film seems much more concerned with revisiting the first film than the sequel novel. The 'showing through' (Paget 1999: 132) of *Trainspotting* into *T2* is a major pleasure of the film. In this sense, it is fidelity to the first film that may be the prime source of pleasure for audiences – as will be demonstrated, *T2* is significantly 'similar-but-different' to *Trainspotting*.

Sequels and the Compulsion to Repeat

As a sequel, *T2 Trainspotting* draws on various intertexts of which *Porno* is only one. Carolyn Jess-Cooke defines the sequel as:

> a framework within which formulations of repetition, difference, history, nostalgia, memory and audience interactivity produce a series of dialogues and relationships between a textual predecessor and its continuation, between audience and text, and between history and remembrance. (Jess-Cooke 2009: vi)

Jess-Cook's 'profit principle' paraphrases Freud's 1920 essay 'Beyond the Pleasure Principle'. Freud argued that the compulsion to repeat was a consequence of repressed trauma, and the loops and repetitions within the two *Trainspotting* films mirror the cyclic repetitions of addiction. Jess-Cooke argues that 'Sequels necessarily address fans of the original, and are usually highly self-conscious of audience expectations' (10), and the cult following for *Trainspotting* may help to explain its 'memorialisation' (9) in *T2*. Jess-Cooke argues that 'the sequel is essentially a response to a previous work, a rereading and rewriting of an "original" that additionally calls upon an audience to reread and rewrite their memories of a previous text' (2009: 12–13).

There is already a repetitive quality to the first film. Murray Smith notes the narrative loops and repetitions within the original *Trainspotting*, highlighting the film's 'playfulness around time and space' (2002: 56). In *Trainspotting*, the opening Princes Street chase is repeated later in the movie, but is darker in the second telling, where Renton gets caught rather than escaping (60–1). Smith discusses the 'propulsive pacing and malleable time and space of *Trainspotting*' (52), including its use of the freeze frame. Channelling Proust, Smith calls these freeze-frames 'Renton's tea-dipped madeleine' (81–2). The freeze-frames engage with memory and nostalgia, providing 'the elegiac countercurrent which runs against the tide of Renton's jaundiced view of the past' (82). Moreover, the end credits use stills of the characters, 'perhaps functioning to create a kind of nostalgia *for the film*' (82). So while the first film has youthful exuberant verve, 'great stylistic panache' (86), in its complex narrative structure and energetic stylistic tricks it too is at heart a nostalgic film, a nostalgia more fully developed in the loops and repetitions of the sequel.

For example, Renton's double-cross of the gang with the collusion of Spud is not unlike that of Veronika in the second movie, except she returns home to Bulgaria instead of fleeing to exile. In another causal loop, Veronika gets the idea of swindling the EU money out of Renton and Simon from reading Spud's manuscript (which is also Welsh's novel) recounting the events of the first film. As Boyle comments on the DVD commentary, when Begbie returns to prison at the end of *T2* 'the circle begins again'. Boyle also references Proust, arguing that 'time loops, it isn't just a straight line . . . There is a kind of loop of time of Spud writing this book which takes you back to the first film' (2017). As well as narrative repetition, many of the 'time loops' referencing the first film take the form of recreating its iconography and dramatic spaces.

Spatialised Nostalgia: Recreated Iconography and Revisited Spaces

The repetitive quality of film sequels might be understood by considering television's seriality. Anthony Giddens discusses the need for ontological security in an increasingly unmanageable world (in Garner 2013: 204–5). Popular culture provides continuity and reassurance, particularly given the serial quality of television soaps. Much serial television functions through forms of repetition and difference that can manifest themselves as self-referentiality or self-cannibalism. As Ross Garner argues: 'recognising allusions within a text may also cue affective response in audience members, such as stimulating nostalgic feelings' (Garner 2013: 194–5). This argument uses the 'citationism' of intertextuality (Garner 2013: 197). Garner builds on this to propose the term *intradiegetic allusion*: 'explicit reference to a series' past within a continuous narrative structure . . . should be specified as an "intradiegetic allusion" since it is a direct reference to that text's past within its present, instead of an outward reference to another text' (198). The seriality of film sequels allows this 'intradiegetic allusion', as can be seen in *T2 Trainspotting*. For example, Renton running on the treadmill at the start of *T2* recalls the iconic chase scene that opened the first film. Where the original scene was backed by 'Lust for Life', in this sequence, youthful vigour is replaced by the stasis of middle age. Renton is literally running on the spot, so rather than displaying the 'propulsive pacing' (Smith 2002) seen in the original, the treadmill surface is a physical loop keeping him expending energy merely to stay still.

Spud's relapse into addiction in *T2* is explained as a consequence of the clocks changing and Spud missing various deadlines including work, benefits and childcare appointments. But in another loop, this sequence recalls a scene from the original. Jonny Murray explains that:

> Spud's set-piece job interview on speed from the original . . . is refurbished in the new film as an older man regaling an addicts' support group with the tragicomic tale of how failure to know about British Summer Time ruined his life. His moral? The clocks move relentlessly forward whether we know it or not. (Murray 2017)

A montage of clocks rams the point home and functions as a reminder of time passing – not only intradiegetically for the characters, but extradiegetically for the audience.

Later, the characters visit a 1980s club night – another spatialised form of nostalgia – where Renton encounters Begbie in a toilet cubicle, recalling the scene in the original where he dives into the bowl of 'the worst toilet in Scotland'. The toilet scene is lifted from *Porno* but developed here as Begbie pursues Renton through a multi-storey car park, which leads to another recreation of the first film. Countering the stasis of the treadmill's loop in *T2*'s opening, returning to Edinburgh in search of his past revitalises Renton. Echoing the opening chase in *Trainspotting*, which as discussed was itself repeated within the film, the scene where Renton escapes in the second, and slides off a car bonnet, is nostalgic both for the character's youth and for the first film. Director Danny Boyle comments:

> Ewan was saying that one of the things he remembers . . . feeling as a character, you know, this is scary and dangerous but at least it's fun and the adrenalin is back again, you know they get this, what's missing in their lives . . . because a lot of the film they do spend time like, trying to relive the recklessness, the effortless bravado of the past, when it's easy. (Boyle 2017)

Shooting the scene, McGregor was inspired 'to do a muscle memory of the first film here' (ibid.) and recreated the same smile of triumph, which Boyle's camera frames in the same way as the first film.

The Corrour train platform sequence in *T2* repeats the scene from *Trainspotting* where the characters go to the country, recreating the framing of the train pulling away to reveal the characters lined up on the platform – and it is revisiting this site that Renton references Simon's dead baby from the first film, signifying more loss and regret. It is also here that the word 'nostalgia' is used for the only time in the film, evoking a specifically spatialised form of remembrance:

> Simon: Nostalgia. That's why you're here, Mark. A tourist in your own youth. Just because you had a near-death experience and now you're feeling all fuzzy and warm. An innocent stroll down the byways of your own memory. (Boyle 2017)

On the DVD commentary, screenwriter John Hodge (2017b) recalls that the producers wanted to set this scene in a cemetery to save money. Boyle however insisted that the scene be shot at Corrour, commenting on the effect that returning to the apparently unchanged location had on him. This has something of

Burke's sublime about it (O'Keeffe 2009), with majesty nature contrasting the transience of human life: 'to the mountain . . . our twenty years is a fly flitting past them'. In addition, this location offered the scene the pathetic fallacy: 'you get this gift on the day, which is that it was a misty day, so the melancholy that builds into the scene, is expressed in the landscape as well' (Boyle 2017).

When Renton visits his father, his parents' flat is recreated and shot from the same angle, but his mother has died in the interim and is represented by a shadow silhouette projected behind her empty chair. The shadowy presence-in-absence of Renton's late mother is a reminder of change and loss specifically evoked by place. Similarly, Renton's bedroom is recreated, and in the first scene set there, he goes to play 'Lust for Life' on his record player, but flicks the stylus up at the first beat. *T2 Trainspotting* is thus both proffering but denying, promising but withholding the youthful verve of the original film's opening chase. Only in the closing scene, back in his bedroom, does Renton let the song play. And the final image, cut together with a clip of his younger self, shows Renton dancing on the spot, again a kind of loop, recalling both the original film, and the opening treadmill scene of this one. Referencing the 'vertiginous' (Petrie 2000: 196) detox sequence from *Trainspotting*, the room becomes an endless tunnel, looping around him into infinity, and suggesting that everyone is doomed to repeat the same mistakes.

The semiotics of the spaces used as film locations reward further examination. Given the film's themes of decay and disappointment, the fact that Simon's flat is beside a scrapyard is no coincidence. The ironically named Port Sunlight pub is in the middle of a post-industrial wasteland – a ruined site, emblematic of Scotland's industrial history and vanished secure working-class masculine identities of the past. It is an equivalent of the *disabitato*, used in many post-war Italian films to depict 'the overgrown edges of the city' or *terrain vague* (Mariani and Barron 2011: 309). *Terrain vague* offers a nostalgia for a mythical past, balanced against a longing for a positive future (310). Here, the waste ground on which the pub sits signifies the decline of Leith's prosperous industrial past, against the growth of service economies in Scotland. Boyle remarks on the marginal nature of this building, both geographically and socially: 'We wanted a building that felt like it was right at the end of the world, certainly of the post-industrial world, literally falling off the cliff of the post-industrial world so it looked hopeless' (Boyle 2017).

Whilst the pub's situation is marginal, it is also a liminal site, offering the potential for change or rebirth. It is therefore fitting that the reunion and final confrontation between the four key characters happens in this liminal space. The bare rafters of the pub's upper floor, the skeleton framework of the partially built walls, and the grid created by the brothel room's mirrored tiles create cages around the characters, visually suggesting not only that Renton is trapped by Begbie but that both are trapped by their past. As Begbie smashes the mirrored room around him, Renton climbs through a hole in the roof into the attic, and in another example of 'muscle memory', McGregor mimics his escape from the toilet bowl (Boyle 2017), again referencing the iconography of the first film. Renton in the mirrored room in *T2* mirrors the shot of Renton's passport in the shiny metal locker in the first film. A similar shot of Spud finding the stolen money in the locker in the first film is echoed when Spud leafs through displays of mirrored tiles in *T2*. This shot foreshadows *T2*'s climax, as Begbie's pursuit of Renton turns the pub into a mirrored cage where Renton has to confront his life choices. The sight of McGregor's visibly aged face intercut with clips from the first film raises the nostalgic force of ageing actors, playing characters who have aged in parallel across the same length of time.

Embodied Nostalgia and Experiential Response

This chapter has already discussed how popular culture provides continuity within the audience's life cycle. In this instance, the reuse of the actors inspires senses of nostalgia and loss in both audiences' and actors' reactions to the ageing characters, forcing them to renegotiate the construction of identity. Ross Garner discusses the 'embodied nostalgia' of returning actors and the affective impact it has on audiences – particularly in television soaps, where story time runs parallel with real time, and characters' ageing is indexed to the audience's ageing. The actors' physical presence is important to this:

> the return of an actor provides just as much stimulus to nostalgic sentiment as does their returning character. An actor reprising his or her role also emphasises the passing of (extra-)diegetic time, as the ageing body of the performer . . . affects nostalgic responses by recognisably, but differentially, embodying the character. (2013: 201)

As well as *T2*'s reconstructions of narrative sites such as Renton's bedroom, there are reconstructions of key scenes using younger doubles of the actors. For example, when they visit Corrour and remember Tommy's death from AIDS, a Tommy body double is seen walking in the distance. Simon and Renton recalling their first heroin use is illustrated with shots of young body doubles running exuberantly down Edinburgh's Leith Walk. The characters seem to see their younger selves, highlighting the film's theme of regret for past choices and creating slippages between past and present. This was the cause of some disquiet for the actors, who found it difficult to articulate the experience:

> there was a, young kids who were cast as us for some flashback moments . . . and they were in our original costumes which had been in storage for twenty years . . . it was like almost like seeing us again and it was an odd, it was odd to confront yourself in that way. (McGregor in Sloan 2017)

For reviewer Mark Kermode, the physical ageing of both actors and audiences was key to the film's effect:

> it seemed to be a film that was aimed at somebody who had been there the first time round and had subsequently aged and . . . it felt like it was speaking to me. It is a film about ageing, it is a film about regret . . . because for a start you're revisiting characters who the first time you saw them were skinny and sinewy and . . . living on that kind of adrenal rush and now twenty years later they're not. (Kermode 2017b)

Kermode argues that *T2* is fundamentally predicated on the film's and the viewer's relationship to the original: 'I have no idea what that film would feel like if you don't have that baggage . . . my feeling is it's a film that's best appreciated if you saw *Trainspotting* 20 years ago, and all those things, memory and all the rest of it, all come together in the experience of watching *T2*' (Kermode 2017b).

Kermode suggests that nostalgia is therefore intrinsic to the viewing experience. *T2 only* functions in relation to the first film and it *only* functions properly if there is a passage of two decades between viewing original and sequel, an experiential gap giving the required distance in which to experience the embodied nostalgia of the ageing actors, mapped onto the parallel ageing and ontological (in)security of the viewer: 'the primary concern of the film is about memory and regret and ageing and masculinity in crisis and it makes particular sense that the memory of that film is twenty years ago for me' (Kermode 2017b). The experiential gap was clearly experienced by the production team and actors as well. Danny Boyle comments 'We did try to make the film ten years ago and . . . this is a much more personal film in a way, it's much more about us all really and our ages rather than the other one which is about, just another story' (2017). Hodge concurs: 'this is I think, the characters' chance to grow old and we all grow old too so that's what it's about' (2017b). The original film is thus much more significant as an intertext than *Porno*, which is 'just another story'.

'World Changes . . . Even if We Don't': Failed Fathers and Masculinity

As suggested by the post-industrial settings discussed above, a key theme of both films is the crisis of (Scottish) masculinity, and this is developed in *T2* through the figure of the failed or absent father, a figure that gives the sequel much of its sense of regret. As Duncan Petrie (2004) explains, 'the political impact of Thatcherism and the New Right ushered in a new era of multiple social deprivation and with it increased strains on the domestic family unit'

(163). A key discourse in representations of Scotland involves the 'hard man' and his quest for identity in a post-industrial world. As Sillars and MacDonald explain:

> In the Scottish context, male angst, male dislocation, unstable masculine identities incapable of emerging into maturity have acted as rich metaphors for the dilemma of the stateless nation, haunted by identities and a secure 'place' in the world. (2007: 187)

The figure of the orphan thus has a significant political resonance in Scottish culture, but more pertinently 'the absence of fathers is perhaps an even more frequently recurring figure, this paternal lack a key source of the sense of dysfunction that permeates the representation of the Scottish working-class family, wreaking its ill-effects on the well-being of the child in the process' (Petrie 2004: 182). In this sense, *Trainspotting* and *T2* resemble films such as *Boyz N the Hood* (Singleton 1991) and *La Haine* (Kassovitz 1995). Like *La Haine*, *Trainspotting* presents an 'infantile macho world' (Vincendeau 2005: 63) within a geographically and socially marginalised subculture of generational unemployment and deprivation in which fathers are mostly absent or 'pitiable wrecks' (Vincendeau 2002: 316), adrift in a world in which labour is increasingly feminised. Like the *banlieue* films it resembles, *Trainspotting* tends to sideline women, 'their identity residing in their relation to the males' (2002: 315), and *T2* erases many of the female characters from *Porno* in favour of revisiting Diane (Kelly Macdonald) from the first film in order to evoke Renton's regret at paths not taken.

The title of the original film comes from a short section in the *Trainspotting* novel, 'Trainspotting at Leith Central Station', inexplicably not included in the first film. In the novel, the characters visit desolate, derelict Leith Central railway station where an 'auld drunkard' asks if they are trainspotting. Begbie is disturbed by the drunkard; it transpires that the 'auld wino' is his father (Welsh 2004: 308). The scene is realised on screen in *T2* as Begbie reads out Spud's recounting of the incident, through a combination of archive footage and Robert Carlyle playing Begbie's father. The failure of masculinity, specifically failed or absent fathers, suffuses *T2*. Spud's addiction leads him to attempt suicide as a penance, telling his partner: 'Fergus [Spud's son] needs things to be simpler; I know how embarrassed he is about me. I could not be the man that you both need.' Renton lies about having two children, then admits that they do not exist; he is married but getting a divorce. He declares, 'I'm 46 and I'm fucked. I've got no home.' Simon lost his baby to cot death in the first film; grotesque visions of the baby haunt Renton while he is going through heroin detox. Renton tells Simon that she died 'because her father, someone who was supposed to watch over and protect her, was too busy filling his veins with heroin instead of checking to see if she was breathing properly'. In *T2*, Simon claims to have a son he never sees. After escaping from prison, Begbie tries to induct his teenage son into a life of crime, and is appalled at the boy's reluctance to join this macho world – his son attends catering college and prefers a career in the service industries. Rationalising his disappointment after his son refuses to physically fight him, Begbie declares that the boy cannot be his. In addition, Begbie is impotent and takes Viagra; an encounter with a much younger woman in a club (who calls him 'daddy-o') leads to his pursuit of Renton through the car park. Only after asserting his masculinity through violence does the Viagra take effect.

Another signifier of the 'infantile macho' world is Simon and Renton's enjoyment of outdated popular culture. Veronika is reluctant to visit Simon's flat, claiming it is too messy. Simon asks, 'It's not a mess is it?'; Renton replies tactfully, 'No. It's just masculine.' This is a homosocial space in which the characters consume popular culture, with piles of DVDs round the walls recalling the VHS cassettes of the first film. But it is also a deeply nostalgic space. The popular culture referenced in *Trainspotting* was already out of date in 1996: Iggy Pop's *Lust for Life* was released in 1977; Simon's idol Sean Connery played James Bond in 1962–7 and 1983; Archie Gemmell's goal against Holland was in 1978. The obsession with the past suggests fear of the future, as reflected in Renton and Simon's raid on an Orange Lodge, in which they steal cash cards and discover that the pin numbers are all 1690, the date of the Battle of the Boyne. Renton's voiceover asks: 'And faced with an uncertain future, is it any surprise that they find comfort in the past, searching for relevance in the twenty-first century while looking back to the seventeenth?' Following the Orange Lodge scene, Renton, Simon and Veronika return to Simon's flat to celebrate. Backed by John Barry's *007 Theme* (1963) they reference moments from the original *Trainspotting*; Simon produces his air rifle, they watch classic football goals on YouTube, they debate the events of 1974, and the sequence climaxes with the men sliding through rain in football tops in a clear visual reference to a shot from *Trainspotting*'s title sequence. They are still discussing the same outdated popular culture they were discussing twenty years earlier – Connery's Bond, 1970s pop music, forty-year-old football victories. As Veronika comments: 'You live in the past. Everyone here lives in the past. Where I come from the past is something to forget but here it's all you talk about. That and the weather. So boring.'

Robert Munro, in *The Conversation*, relates the film's backward-looking characters, nostalgic for a 'simpler' time, to contemporary discourses of Donald Trump and Brexit balanced against a globalised economy and the nimbler, forward-looking Veronika character from the EU:

> T2 ... seems to wonder what has become of the enthusiasm of its characters, and us ... As our quartet end the film either where they started, or worse off, Veronika, the Bulgarian sex worker being exploited by Sick Boy, takes off with the hundred grand. She returns home to a notably sunnier future, and a reunion with her family. While we wallow in the past, incapable of accepting a post-national present, somewhere out there people are still choosing life after all. (Munro 2017)

Like the alienated protagonists of *La Haine* (Vincendeau 2005), though to different ends, Mark and Simon are obsessed with popular culture of the past. Middle-aged Scottish men are positioned here as backward-looking and conservative; the young European woman is forward-looking and progressive, perhaps functioning metonymically for Scotland's position relative to the EU in a time of national upheaval.

The Time Is Out of Joint: Reflexive Nostalgia

In the scene above, *T2* is aware of its nostalgia. Pam Cook argues for a reconciliation between history and nostalgia, arguing that 'where history suppresses the element of disavowal or fantasy in its re-presentation of the past, nostalgia foregrounds those elements, and in effect lays bare the processes at the heart of remembrance' (Cook 2005: 4). Audiences can be aware of the performative element of such activities, consciously enjoying the playful or affective qualities of nostalgic representation:

> the nostalgic memory film ... has the potential to reflect upon its own mechanisms, and to encourage reflection in audiences. The more self-reflexive nostalgic films can employ cinematic strategies to actively comment on issues of memory, history and identity. (Cook 2005: 5)

This reflexivity is expressed in various different ways in *T2*, with its reconstructions of the original being the most obvious, alongside reuse of clips. For example, as Begbie reads out Spud's story it is illustrated by clips from *Trainspotting*, and past and present blend. In another reused clip, Spud leaves a comical boxing session and seems to see his younger self run down Calton Road. The final scene features a reused clip of Renton taking drugs, intercut with the older McGregor mimicking his pose from twenty years earlier.

The reused clips, and reconstructions of younger versions of the characters, mean that the present in *T2* is haunted by its possible futures/alternative presents in an embodied nostalgia of place. The first film used a form of magic realism to transform the iconography of British social realism into surreal sites thematically expressing escape from poverty through drug use or crime. *Trainspotting* explores 'the redemption of material impoverishment through aesthetic transformation' (Smith 2002: 33) as its narrative spaces are transformed subjectively through drug use. *T2 Trainspotting* however uses the manipulation of space and time to materialise its theme of nostalgia for lost youth. The slippage between the two films creates a Foucauldian *espace autre* (Freeman 1999), simultaneously now and then, the same spatial site but composed out of several temporal layers, crossing the striations of past and present and constructing a sometimes bewildering liminal space. This hauntological quality gives these scenes their air of regret and nostalgia, not just for the lost youth of the protagonists, but for audiences' memories of the first film, and the passing of time between their initial viewing and now.

The combination of old and new footage uses remembrance and memorialisation to transform these fragments of Edinburgh into hauntological sites. Jacques Derrida, in *Specters of Marx*, discusses hauntology as a way of thinking about historical and ontological disjunction. He quotes from *Hamlet*, saying that hauntology is a way of thinking about ways in which 'time is out of joint'. It prioritises not what is present, but what is absent, and ghosts of the past, or of lost futures that can haunt the present – drawing on Marx's comment that Europe is 'haunted' by Communism. Mark Fisher (2012) builds on Derrida to argue that hauntology has a specific connection to modernity and the 'global village'. Places can push back against modernity, occupying both past and present:

> Haunting can be seen as intrinsically resistant to the contraction and homogenization of time and space. It happens when a place is stained by time, or when a particular place becomes the site for an encounter with broken time. (2012: 19)

Derridean hauntology also draws on the French *ontologie* to highlight that hauntology denotes a fundamentally bewildering, alienating condition. The collision of past and present is clearly incomprehensible to the hapless Spud, who seems to see his younger self running away from him: 'time is out of joint'. This image comments on the way in which returning to the same site can inspire memories of situated events, as with Hodge's Cameo anecdote – and is, of course, a visual metaphor for the fact that Spud's youth has literally run away, returning to the theme of memory, nostalgia and regret that permeates the film. For Fisher, hauntology is about 'the failure of the future', something with which the protagonists of *T2* are constantly grappling.

Another way in which the film engages with issues of memory, nostalgia and regret is through the use of what Laura Marks calls 'analog nostalgia' (Schrey 2014: 27) in the form of brief simulated '8mm' clips of small boys (presumably, Simon and Mark as children). Schrey argues that 'analog nostalgia' evokes the seventeenth century's 'artificial ruins' (28), offering the promise of indexicality and thus authenticity. However, Sapio (2014) argues that the aesthetic of home movies results in the creation of a *meta-family*. Digitally produced vintage effects both reflect and create nostalgic fantasies of family. Significantly, Sapio argues that most home movies are created by fathers. Thus, the invisible father suggested here is a-presence-in-absence that nonetheless acts as a structuring paradigm for the image. Nostalgia for family, families that never were, for Simon's dead baby and absent son, for Renton's non-existent children and particularly for fathers that might have been, suffuses *T2 Trainspotting*.

'Choose Life . . . Choose Watching History Repeat Itself'

Another example of 'reflexive nostalgia' involves the reworking of the first film's iconic 'Choose Life' monologue. Part of the 'Trainspotting cultural moment' involved its circulation through paratexts through 'transformation and dispersion from short story to novel, to film, to poster, to film soundtrack, marketing tie-in products and stage performance' (Lash and Lury 2007: 21). With *Trainspotting*, for some consumers, 'the poster eclipsed the film' (23) and circulated in culture through a range of reinterpretations. The 'Choose Life' monologue, distributed in the form of innumerable branded paratexts such as posters (Suskind 2017), is reworked for *T2* when Veronika and Renton meet for a drink in Harvey Nichols and she asks Renton 'What's Choose Life?'. The original monologue, ironically riffing on an anti-drugs public health campaign, is a cynical commentary on hegemonic consumer society and the constraints of 'respectable' life in late capitalist Western society: 'Choose life. Choose a job. Choose a career. Choose a family. Choose a fucking big television set.' In *T2*, the monologue is reworked as:

> Choose life. Choose Facebook, Twitter, Instagram and hope that someone, somewhere cares. Choose looking up old flames, wishing you'd done it all differently. And choose watching history repeat itself. (Boyle 2017)

This cynical commentary on social media-saturated contemporary life draws attention to how fast society has changed in twenty years – many of these terms would be incomprehensible to the characters in the original film. But this is not just an updated list satirising consumer society in the 21st century; it contains one of the keys to the film, not just its narrative construction, but one of its ongoing thematic concerns. The phrase 'choose watching history repeat itself' is central to *both* films in their obsession with loops, repetition and flashbacks. For screenwriter John Hodge, this scene offers a meta-commentary on the *Trainspotting* phenomenon itself:

> What she's saying to him is 'What's *Trainspotting*?' . . . it's the shock of . . . realising he's with someone who's so young that Choose Life means nothing to them or *Trainspotting* means nothing to them and . . . provoked, he responds by being himself again. (2017b)

Danny Boyle relates the reworking of the Choose Life monologue to Renton's rediscovery of his identity, as the 'mocking litany of modern choices' becomes angry and leads to 'the more confessional side' whereby Renton offers 'an analysis of himself' (Boyle 2017). This scene and its engagement with the first film provokes Renton's confrontation with his own ageing and rediscovery of self as a result of his return to Edinburgh. The film is thus suffused with what Svetlana Boym calls reflective nostalgia, which 'dwells in algia, in longing and loss, the imperfect process of remembrance . . . reflective nostalgia lingers on ruins, the patina of time and history, in the dreams of another place and another time' (2001: 41) and the 'nostalgic rendezvous with oneself' (50).

Individualised Nostalgia and the *Punctum*

And finally, to consider the personal, phenomenological aspects of nostalgia. I lived in Edinburgh for over twenty years. I watched *T2 Trainspotting* during its theatrical release in my new home town of Brighton. Watching the film was intensely nostalgic.

Fredric Jameson criticises pastiche in postmodern culture more generally, which is prone to 'cannibalising the museum and wear[ing] the masks of extinct mannerisms' (cited in Garner 2013). Cannibalisation is representative of a contemporary nostalgic pastiche culture. Jameson is critical of this simulated nostalgia because he sees it as a waning of affect, a reification or evacuation of human autonomy from the cultural artefacts produced under capitalism. So postmodern cultural objects are 'depthless' when compared to past equivalents (Garner 2013: 199). Similarly, Fred Davis argues that nostalgia produced by film and television does not have the same individuality of association as do more private forms of memory. 'Davis suggests that the nostalgia constructed through popular cultural forms is a reified, waning version of the feeling since it is linked to industrial production, rather than subjective recollection' (Garner 2013: 199). Garner argues that the embodied presence of actors helps to 'restore the experience of temporality . . . the existential or experiential feeling of time itself' to the postmodern experience, providing 'an alternative to the "reified" form of nostalgia that has been perceived as characteristic of po-mo media texts' (2013: 209). This experiential authenticity may offer a resistance to the impact of the postmodern (209).

There is a critical distinction then between industrial, commodified nostalgia and more subjective, authentically affective forms connected to media consumers' life experiences. Significantly for the purposes of this chapter, some of the moments that were nostalgic for me were not those constructed as nostalgic by the film. For example, in the opening sequence, when Renton returns to Edinburgh, the new tram (a system introduced into Edinburgh in 2014, the year I left the city) passes through Edinburgh city centre in a montage of brief shots. One of those very brief shots shows West Maitland Street, opposite Haymarket Station, where I lived when I first moved to Edinburgh. That shot means nothing to someone who hasn't been there, but it took my breath away on first viewing.

This response can be theorised by using Roland Barthes' idea of the *punctum*. Barthes (1993) argues that there are two ways of understanding images. The *studium* is detached and objective; the *punctum* is more personal and potentially painful. Barthes likens this to a sting, or a wound. The *punctum* is a specific detail with meaning for a particular viewer. Barthes uses a photograph of his mother to demonstrate this. The picture of the mother is not reproduced in his book as it would only interest the reader's *studium*; only for Barthes himself does it have *punctum*, the wound, personal meaning. Barthes argues that this phenomenon is intrinsic to photography, insisting that cinema 'is not a *specter*' (89, original emphasis). But images like *T2*'s shot of West Maitland Street, for me, contain the *punctum*, thereby problematising Barthes' contention that cinema cannot be a spectre in the way that he means. The Edinburgh constructed in *T2 Trainspotting* is a haunted landscape, haunted by the original film and the gap between the two, and by my own parallel memories of my life in that gap.

Conclusion

Nostalgia in *T2 Trainspotting* thus functions on multiple levels. First, within the diegesis, the nostalgia of the characters for their own youth. Second, as a reified media product, nostalgia through Garner's 'intradiegetic allusions' and the construction of 'hauntological landscapes' through the incorporation of clips and reconstructions of scenes and sites from the first film. Third, through the 'embodied nostalgia' of the ageing actors, as an index of the parallel time passing for both characters and audiences. And fourth, on an individual level, the 'punctum' of Edinburgh on screen in 1996 and 2017, gives this audience member a very personal connection to the film, thereby challenging critics of the postmodern such as Jameson and Davis, by demonstrating the capacity of reified media texts to stimulate individualised, subjective and therefore arguably authentic nostalgic responses. My connection to Edinburgh means there *is* an *individual* private nostalgia as well as the generalised nostalgia other *Trainspotting* fans may feel, thus complicating the arguments of critics of the postmodern. There is both a reified nostalgia at work – though the value or otherwise of that is still open for debate – *plus* a 'subjective recollection', which adds another layer of nostalgic meaning for the individual viewer.

In its nostalgia for and obsessive replaying of the first film, *T2 Trainspotting* is an adaptation not of the novel *Porno* but an intertext of the meta-narrative of the original *Trainspotting*. As such, it draws on a variety of intertexts in order to construct a film designed to appeal to an audience familiar with the original and engage in what Paget calls 'readerly exercises' of recognising intertextual connections as part of the pleasure of viewing. As a highly critical *Variety* review noted, 'the characters spend way too much time lounging around recalling the old days, because that's really a way of recalling the first movie' (Gleiberman 2017). As comments by Kermode and others show, recognising that time has passed for the characters in tandem with that of the audience contributes another layer of significance to this readerly exercise. In playing out the theme of middle-aged disappointment, nostalgia for lost youth and the limitations of free will, its 'compulsion to repeat' the images and tropes of the first film lead it to construct the city of Edinburgh as a liminal space. This space is not just nostalgic, but hauntological – haunted by vanished pasts and lost futures. As Simon says, when Renton offers him his share of money from the first film: 'What am I supposed to do with that? Buy a fucking time machine? Live my life all over again?' This is exactly what the characters want; and this film sequel works as a time machine to do just that.

References

Barthes, R. (1993), *Camera Lucida: Reflections on Photography*, translated by R. Howard, London: Vintage.

Boyle, D. (2017), *T2 Trainspotting* [DVD]. Sony.

Boym, S. (2001), *The Future of Nostalgia*, New York: Basic Books.

Cook, P. (2005), *Screening the Past: Memory and Nostalgia in Cinema*, Abingdon: Routledge.

Fisher, M. (2012), 'What is Hauntology?' *Film Quarterly*, 66: 1, 16–24.

Freeman, N. (1999), 'See Europe with ITC: stock footage and the construction of geographical identity', in D. Cartmell, I. Q. Hunter, H. Kaye and I. Whelehan (eds), *Alien Identities: Exploring Difference in Film and Fiction*, London: Pluto, pp. 49–65.

Garner, Ross (2013), 'Remembering Sarah Jane: intradiegetic allusions, embodied presence/absence and nostalgia', in D. Mellor, M. Hills and B. Earl (eds), *New Dimensions of Doctor Who: Adventures in Space, Time and Television*, London: I. B. Tauris, pp. 192–215.

Gleiberman, O. (2017), 'How Danny Boyle blew the sequel to *Trainspotting*', *Variety*, <https://variety.com/2017/film/columns/how-danny-boyle-blew-t2-trainspotting-1202026532/> (accessed 12 November 2018).

Hodge, J. (2017a) *T2 Trainspotting: Screenplay*, London: Faber & Faber.

Hodge, J. (2017b) DVD Commentary. *T2 Trainspotting* [DVD], Sony.

Jess-Cooke, C. (2009), *Film Sequels: Theory and Practice from Hollywood to Bollywood*, Edinburgh: Edinburgh University Press.

Kermode, Mark (2017a), 'T2 Trainspotting review – still in a class A of their own', *The Guardian*, 18 January <https://www.theguardian.com/film/2017/jan/29/t2-trainspotting-danny-boyle-sequel-review> (accessed 21 April 2017).

Kermode, M. (2017b), 'Trainspotting review', BBC5 Live, <https://www.youtube.com/watch?v=oi8a3c1a6gc> (accessed 21 April 2017).

Lash, S. and Lury, C. (2007), *Global Culture Industry: The Mediation of Things*, London: Polity.

Mariani, M. and Barron. P. (2011), 'Cinematic space in Rome's *Disabitato*: between Metropolis and Terrain Vague in the films of Fellini, Antonioni, and Pasolini', *Modernism/Modernity*, 18: 2, 309–33.

Munro, R. (2017), 'Trainspotting's obsession with the past says a lot about today', *The Conversation*, <http://theconversation.com/t2-trainspottings-obsession-with-the-past-says-a-lot-about-today-72117> (accessed 20 April 2017).

Murray, J. (2017), 'Trainspotting sequel is more about losing life than choosing it', *The Conversation*,<https://theconversation.com/trainspotting-sequel-is-more-about-losing-life-than-choosing-it-71962>(accessed 20 April 2017).

Niemeyer, K. (2014), 'Introduction: media and nostalgia', in K. Niemeyer (ed.), *Media and Nostalgia: Yearning for the Past, Present and Future*, Basingstoke: Palgrave Macmillan, pp. 1–23.

O'Keeffe, D. (2009), *Major Conservative and Libertarian Thinkers: Edmund Burke*, New York: Continuum International Publishing.

Paget, D. (1999), 'Speaking out: the transformations of *Trainspotting*', in D. Cartmell and I. Whelehan (eds), *Adaptations: From Text to Screen, Screen to Text*, pp. 128–40.

Petrie, D. (2000), *Screening Scotland*, London: BFI.

Petrie, D. (2004), *Contemporary Scottish Fictions: Film, Television and the Novel*, Edinburgh: Edinburgh University Press.

Sapio, G. (2014), 'Homesick for aged home movies: why do we shoot contemporary family videos in old-fashioned ways?' in K. Niemeyer (ed.), *Media and Nostalgia: Yearning for the Past, Present and Future*, Basingstoke: Palgrave Macmillan, pp. 39–50.

Schrey, D. (2014), 'Analogue nostalgia and the aesthetics of digital remediation', in K. Niemeyer (ed.), *Media and Nostalgia: Yearning for the Past, Present and Future*, Basingstoke: Palgrave Macmillan, pp. 27–38.

Shoard, Catherine (2017), 'Choose life? Trainspotting's realism hit a nerve, but we want escapism now', The Guardian, 19 January, <https://www.theguardian.com/commentisfree/2017/jan/19/choose-life-trainspotting-2-escapism> (accessed 21 April 2017).

Sillars, J. and MacDonald, M. (2008), 'Gender, spaces, changes: emergent identities in a Scotland in transition', in N. Blain and D. Hutchison (eds), *The Media in Scotland*, Edinburgh: Edinburgh University Press, pp. 183–98.

Sloan, J. (2017), 'T2: Ewan McGregor and Jonny Lee Miller on gear changes and nostalgia', *On Demand Entertainment*, <https://www.youtube.com/watch?v=bLl0ZX7n6g0> (accessed 21 April 2017).

Smith, M. (2002), *Trainspotting*, London: Palgrave Macmillan/BFI.

Suskind, A. (2017), 'The story behind the groundbreaking "Trainspotting" poster', *Vice*, <https://www.vice.com/en_uk/article/ypkxn5/the-story-behind-the-groundbreaking-trainspotting-poster> (accessed 18 November 2018).

Vincendeau, G. (2002), 'Designs on the *Banlieue*: Mathieu Kassovitz's *La Haine* (1995)', in S. Hayward and G. Vincendeau (eds), *French Film: Texts and Contexts*, 2nd edn, London: Routledge, pp. 310–27.

Vincendeau, G. (2005), *La Haine*, London: I. B Tauris.

Welsh, I. (2004), *Trainspotting*, London: Vintage.

3. '200 MILES OUTSIDE LONDON': THE TOURIST GAZE OF *FAR FROM THE MADDING CROWD*

Shelley Anne Galpin

The British film industry provides well-known benefits for national tourism, with its ample opportunities to exhibit the nation at its best (Creative England 2015). 'Period' or 'costume' dramas are a particularly prominent example of this, exploiting Britain's history by the display of attractive historical buildings and apparently timeless landscapes. These dramas utilise a clearly nationalistic approach in the idealised aesthetic choices, as well as in the use of celebrated British literature or the lives of famous British figures as the sources for many period films. However, despite the apparently nationalist stance of the material, recent years have seen a number of foreign directors taking the helm of period films with a British setting. One of the major benefits of this trend, at least from a marketing point of view, is that it presents the opportunity to package the films as fresh, original takes on what are often highly familiar subjects. With the Scandinavian film and television industries proving highly influential over the last decade or more, Andrew Pulver (2015) notes the 'current fad for bringing in Scandi directors to freshen up British period pieces', citing *The Imitation Game* (Morten Tyldum, UK/US, 2014) and *Tinker Tailor Soldier Spy* (Tomas Alfredson, France/UK/Germany, 2011) as examples. To this we could add Lone Scherfig's work on *An Education* (UK/US, 2009) and *Their Finest* (UK/Sweden, 2017). If we were to spread the net further afield we might also include US director Cary Fukunaga's work on *Jane Eyre* (UK/US, 2011) and Jane Campion, of New Zealand and Australian heritage, with her Keats biopic *Bright Star* (UK/Australia/France, 2009), as further examples of foreign directors who have brought their vision to bear on quintessentially British subjects.

Thomas Vinterberg's adaptation of Hardy's *Far from the Madding Crowd* (UK/US, 2015) would also seem to follow this pattern, with the Danish Dogme 95 co-founder appearing on the surface to be an unusual choice for an adaptation of British canonical literature. Many commentators, most notably Andrew Higson (2011), have described the ways in which representations of Britain, or England, in film have an ideological role in constructing the way we view ourselves, or are viewed, as a nation. The fashion for non-British directors tackling filmic representations of British cultural products or icons raises the question of the impact these outsider perspectives have on the ways in which British nationhood is portrayed through these films. However, whilst it is tempting, as well as commercially convenient, to imagine that non-British directors bring a vision that is somehow fundamentally different to the way that the material would be treated by a director who has grown up surrounded by British culture, I would suggest that this view is rather too simplistic. In this chapter, I will consider *Far from the Madding Crowd*'s evident appeal to the 'tourist gaze' and the ways in which it conforms to the characteristics of a conventional British period drama and adapts techniques from Hardy's own writing. Following on from this, I will explore the ways in which the choice of a director such as Vinterberg, who is well-known for producing more modern, and often controversial, material, raises expectations that are difficult to meet fully when undertaking a new adaptation of familiar material.

SIGNPOSTING THE 'TOURIST GAZE'

Far from the Madding Crowd opens with the caption 'Dorset, England 1870, 200 miles outside London'. Whilst the locating of films, particularly period films, within a specific geographical and temporal location is not an unusual practice, the 'signpost' indicating the distance of the action from London is more anomalous. Given that the action of the film does not take place in London at any point, nor are any references made to London during the film, it is a little strange that it should open by so pointedly informing the audience of the distance from this particular city. Whilst this could, of course, be read as a reference to the title, with London representing the 'madding crowd', residents of southwest England may take issue with the filmmakers for failing to identify another metropolitan area closer to Dorset than London, at the aforementioned '200 miles'. Given the likely transnational audience for the film (in addition to the employment of non-British creative talent it also received both US and UK funding), it is probable that the signposting is due in part to the desire for the film to appeal to the 'armchair tourist' (Barton 2016: 165) and the need to identify the setting of the film in relation to well-known English locations. The desire to appeal to the tourist gaze would also explain the objections of some critics to the film on the grounds of its visually pleasing aesthetic, with Mark Kermode (2015) complaining that the film 'could have done with a little more mud' and John Walsh (2015) that it was 'all chocolate-boxy pastoral cuteness'. Indeed, Robbie Collin (2015a) went so far as to describe the film as a 'mini-break on film' and suggested that the name of Dorset had been retained, instead of Hardy's fictional 'Wessex' in order to appeal to those audience members who might be inspired to visit the region following a viewing of the film.

Discussing the concept of the 'tourist gaze', Urry and Larsen (2011) identify this gaze as:

> constructed in relationship to its opposite, to non-tourist forms of social experience and consciousness . . . The gaze . . . presupposes a system of social activities and signs which locate the particular tourist practices, not in terms of some intrinsic characteristics, but through the contrasts implied with non-tourist social practices, particularly those based within home and paid work. (3)

Further to this, in considering attitudes towards the land Newland (2016) also notes that 'the working countryside is often not seen to be a "landscape" (especially by those that work it)' (7), adding to the differentiation between visual displays that are intended for consumption by an outsider gaze and the everyday environment of rural workers suggested by Urry and Larsen. This distancing of the tourist gaze from that of inhabitants and communities for whom the subject of the gaze represents their living and working space is particularly significant when it comes to analysing the treatment of the land in an adaptation of Hardy's work. I would suggest that Hardy's own writing does not conform to this oppositional treatment of landscape as either a practical space or an object of admiration; he frequently incorporates descriptions of small details or broader images of the landscape alongside development of the narrative action. It is therefore consistent with Hardy's storytelling that the natural environment should be displayed both prominently and with a degree of reverence within the film.

The distinction between the tourist gaze and the gaze of the rural worker is also broken down in Hardy's work, such as in this example from *Far from the Madding Crowd*:

> Being a man not without a frequent consciousness that there was some beauty in this life he led, [Gabriel] stood still after looking at the sky as a useful instrument, and regarded it in an appreciative spirit, as a work of

art superlatively beautiful. For a moment he seemed impressed with the speaking loneliness of the scene, or rather with the complete abstraction from all its compass of the sights and sounds of man. (12)

In this extract we see Gabriel's gaze shifting between what could be described as a 'workers' gaze', which has been 'looking at the sky as a useful instrument', to something that clearly resembles the tourist gaze, regarding his surroundings 'in an appreciative spirit, as a work of art'. The narrative statement that Gabriel is 'not without a frequent consciousness that there was some beauty in this life he led' also demonstrates that the distinction between the gaze of the tourist and the gaze of the worker or inhabitant has been blurred here.

This pattern is quite typical of Hardy's writing. As nature is so ubiquitous within his novels, characters are frequently defined by their relationship with the land. For Hardy's characters, the landscape is both their work and their leisure, and therefore it is frequently represented as both a place of toil and the subject of admiration. As readers of Hardy's novels, our expectations of characters are very often informed by their relationship with the land. Thus, characters such as *The Return of the Native*'s Diggory Venn, *The Woodlanders*' Giles Winterbourne and the eponymous Tess of the D'Urbervilles are marked as good and pure (explicitly, if controversially so, in the case of Tess) through their presentation as being 'of the land'. On the other hand, characters such as Eustacia Vye in *The Return of the Native*, Fitzpiers and Mrs Charmont in *The Woodlanders* and, in differing ways, both the seemingly perfect Angel Clare and the rakish Alec D'Urberville in *Tess of the D'Urbervilles*, are constructed as threats to the pure, natural characters through the invasion of a landscape to which they do not belong.

We also see these oppositions at work in Hardy's *Far from the Madding Crowd*, in which Gabriel Oak is presented as having a deep understanding of the landscapes that he inhabits whereas Sergeant Troy, associated with the cultural institution of the army, is clearly marked as an outsider. As both of these men, along with the character of Mr Boldwood, represent the different romantic opportunities offered to Bathsheba, these contrasts are particularly significant in signalling to the reader which suitor is the most appropriate choice for the novel's heroine. This adaptation builds on these binary oppositions. From the outset, Gabriel (Matthias Schoenaerts) is depicted in functional work clothes, the fabrics largely consisting of muted colours. He is frequently shown working with his flock of sheep or tackling other farm work. Indeed, his capability at coping with the demands of running a farm are emphasised throughout; he rescues Bathsheba's (Carey Mulligan) farm from certain disaster no less than three times during the course of the narrative. In contrast, Troy is depicted first in his scarlet sergeant's uniform, which appears out of place once he moves from the town where he is first introduced to the more rural backdrop of the farmland. Following his marriage to Bathsheba he adopts a rather dandyish style, dressing in well-tailored suits that again appear ill-chosen for his new life as a farmer. This is accompanied by textual evidence of his lack of ability and inclination, such as Bathsheba's emasculating comment that he fails to undertake 'proper farm work', and his persistence in futilely practising his sword exercises in the farmyard. Despite criticisms that have been levelled at the film for prioritising the beauty of the setting, I would suggest that in this respect it echoes Hardy's own techniques. The film's interpretation of the novel's characters clearly maintains the distinction between those who are of the land and those whose presence disrupts the natural course, and Vinterberg utilises the prominent place of the landscape within the *mise en scène* to highlight these character traits. The harmony between Gabriel and the natural world provides important character information, highlighting his suitability to be Bathsheba's partner and therefore increasing the tension of the narrative as she fails to acknowledge this to herself.

Hardy the 'Cinematic Novelist' and the Difficulties of Adaptation

As the previous section highlights, this film can be seen to exercise a certain amount of fidelity to the source novel. The issue of an adaptation's perceived faithfulness to the original text is a topic that has been the subject of much critical discussion, with a continued tension between the instinctive tendency to measure the effectiveness of an adaptation by assessing its similarity to its source and the need to acknowledge the properties of different media. As a number of adaptation theorists have noted, filmic adaptations of literary sources can never hope to simply replicate the 'original', and will always become a new entity (Geraghty 2008; Wood 1999). This line of argument has become a familiar feature of critical explorations of film and television adaptations. However, in a somewhat refreshing departure from this, when discussing the 2007 film *Atonement* (Joe Wright, UK/France/US), Griggs (2012) highlights the desire of the director to maintain a closeness to the structure and tone of the novel. This is despite the fact that the novel is itself highly self-reflexive in its literariness, and therefore a difficult source to successfully transfer to film. Griggs notes Wright's instinct that:

> the book works, so we tried to be faithful to it. [We] kind of had faith that the film would work too if we stuck to the truth of the novel . . . We kept the book by our side throughout the whole process. (Wright, quoted in Griggs 2012: 346)

This statement is very similar to comments made by the makers of *Far from the Madding Crowd*:

> We all felt this desire to be very loyal to Hardy . . . obviously we had to do artistic choices but we did look at this novel as the Bible. The actors were carrying the script under one arm and the novel under the other, and so was I. (Vinterberg 2015)

Whereas recent scholarship on adaptation has tended to emphasise the futility of a film attempting to accurately depict a literary source, these quotations demonstrate that, in some cases at least, filmmakers do unashamedly wish to create an adaptation that can be considered faithful to some degree. Here Vinterberg acknowledges the need to exercise what is often called 'artistic licence', and Wright's adaptation of *Atonement* makes some key alterations, most notably at the very end of the film, in order to adapt the narrative to the medium of film. However, in both cases, the filmmakers are seeking for ways to communicate the narrative in ways that capture not only the key plot points, but also the narrative technique of the novelist. In *Atonement* this is achieved by film's adherence to the fragmented structure of the novel, complete with the late revelation of the narrative twist. In *Far from the Madding Crowd*, as I have identified above, this is achieved through the visual emphasis on the natural world, and the ways in which this is used to enhance characterisation.

That an adaptation of a Hardy novel is visually striking is no great surprise, with many critics commenting on the highly evocative nature of his prose style. David Lodge (cited in Wright 2005) described him as a 'cinematic novelist . . . who imagines and presents his material in primarily visual terms, and whose visualisations correspond in some significant respect to the visual effects characteristic of film' (9). The almost filmic way in which Hardy presents his narratives has been widely recognised, a particularly notable trait given that almost all his novels were written before the advent of moving films. Somewhat paradoxically, Lodge and others have suggested this as making Hardy's novels more problematic to adapt for the screen due to the perceived difficulty of doing justice to his detailed visual imagery (Wright 2005). Scholarship on Hardy adaptations has often considered the relationship between Hardy's written style and the on-screen depiction of his works and, in a similar vein to the criticisms noted above by Kermode and Walsh, previous adaptations of Hardy's novels have been accused of failing to capture the myriad representations of nature, both human and environmental, that inhabit Hardy's novels.

Hardy's novels were famously controversial in their day, with his later works *Tess of the D'Urbervilles* and *Jude the Obscure* both attracting censure for his challenging of the accepted norms of sexual morality (Kramer

1999; Boumelha 1985; Schoenfeld 2005). However, film adaptations of Hardy's works have been accused of losing the more challenging representational features in favour of a somewhat sanitised depiction of Wessex life. Discussing the visual elements of Hardy's novels, and their adaptations, Webster (2005) argues:

> whereas Hardy's use of painting led to innovations in his narrative technique and can be seen as a parallel to the development of his increasingly profound exploration of social themes, in cinematic versions the opposite is more often the case – they tend more towards the picturesque and the production of stereotypical images with a 'Hardyesque' feel to them. These film versions generally present a safe, familiar version of Hardy's fiction accentuating the pastoral or striving for an authenticity which is validated by a sense of the painterly. (21)

Similarly, Niemeyer (2003) suggests that 'a familiar Hardy is also a safe Hardy: when the full scope of his vision is hemmed in, Hardy offers little that challenges or questions our dominant ways of thinking' (56). Thus, previous adaptations of Hardy novels have been criticised for tending towards a reductive idealisation that fails to adhere to the full range of representations and complexity found within Hardy's writing. As I will demonstrate, this adaptation of *Far from the Madding Crowd* can also be considered to follow this pattern. The critical objections to the appeals to the tourist gaze, discussed above, highlight the attractiveness of the film's visual style and demonstrate that this film also tends towards the 'production of stereotypical images with a "Hardyesque" feel to them' and 'accentuates the pastoral' in its depiction of Dorset.

Towards the beginning of the film, and following the introduction of Bathsheba and Gabriel, there is a dramatic scene in which Gabriel loses his flock of sheep, and with them his farm and livelihood. This loss happens in shocking style, with Gabriel's inexperienced sheep dog herding the flock over a steep cliff edge. The shots of falling sheep in Vinterberg's film are undoubtedly alarming, and the tragedy of the moment is initially well conveyed. However, these images are followed by a shot of Oak which strikes a notably different tone; depicted in silhouette he dramatically shoots his sheepdog before dropping to his knees and beating the ground in anguish. The sunrise that he is depicted against is so spectacular though, that its beauty distracts from the emotional significance of the moment. Whilst this is clearly a point of crisis, the use of silhouette and the visual emphasis on the beautiful skyscape lends the depiction a sense of the poetic, rather than placing emphasis on the catastrophic consequences of this event for the character. This continues when Oak goes down to the beach to survey his dead sheep, with the sheep portrayed in long shot, appearing as little more than fluffy lumps on the perfect sandy beach. The entire seascape is bathed in a calming yellow morning light, and the beauty of the scene again undermines our appreciation of the tragedy of the moment. Gabriel is once more depicted in long shot, from behind, meaning that as viewers we are not encouraged to empathise with him in this moment of crisis. Rather, we are invited to marvel at the beautiful scenery within which his moment of crisis is occurring.

When we compare this with Hardy's original version of this scene, the tendencies noted by Webster and Niemeyer are certainly in evidence. Whilst Oak's first view of his dead sheep in the novel is described as 'a heap of two hundred mangled carcases' (1874: 32), the image of the dead sheep in the film is a great deal more sanitised. Hardy's description continues by stating:

> By the outer margin of the pit was an oval pond, and over it hung the attenuated skeleton of a chrome-yellow moon, which had only a few days to last – the morning star dogging her on the right hand. The pool glittered like a dead man's eye, and as the world awoke a breeze blew, shaking and elongating the reflection of the moon without breaking it, and turning the image of the star to a phosphoric streak upon the water. (Ibid.: 33)

This description presents a rather sinister version of nature, in which there is a malevolence that the beautiful sunrise and seascape of Vinterberg's film do not capture. The linguistic allusions to sickness and death in descriptions such as 'the attenuated skeleton of a chrome-yellow moon' and the 'dead man's eye', as well as references to change and decay in the reference to the fading moon and the distorted images of the moon and star in the pool, present the

Figure 3.1 Gabriel surveys his dead flock in *Far from the Madding Crowd* (Fox Searchlight/BBC Films/TSG Entertainment/DNA Films & 20th Century Fox Home Entertainment)

landscape in this moment as a site of destruction. To characterise nature in this way is typical of Hardy's writing in general, in which the natural world can be both beautiful and terrible, and in which characters are often subject to random acts of fate that can improve or destroy their lives without warning. This conceptualisation of nature creates an entirely different tone when compared to the scene as portrayed in the film, which presents a more benign characterisation of nature through the warmth of the calm, sandy beach, and implies rejuvenation in the beautiful and hopeful image of the sunrise.

From this moment alone, it is evident that Vinterberg's vision for *Far from the Madding Crowd* is apparently not going to differ substantially from the other Hardy adaptations referenced by Webster and Niemeyer, at least in the relationship between narrative action and visual spectacle. As in previous Hardy adaptations, pleasing visual display wins out over a more varied and complex depiction of the diegesis. Given the previous output of the director this may be considered surprising, with films such as *Festen* (Denmark/Sweden, 1998), possibly his most celebrated work, famously not shirking away from the unpalatable subject of abuse within families, and shot it in such a way as to heighten the realism of the characters and situations. Even a film with a less realistic approach such as *It's All About Love* (Italy/France/Canada/Spain/US/Japan/Denmark/Germany/Netherlands, 2003) features disturbing images, including that of dead bodies repeatedly shunting into the bottom of an escalator as unheeding commuters step over them. However, despite Vinterberg's previous willingness to engage with taboo and disturbing subject matter and imagery, *Far from the Madding Crowd* continues in a similar vein, with the Dorset scenery being displayed to magnificent, if largely unchallenging, effect throughout the film.

Charlotte Bruus Christensen, the cinematographer of *Far from the Madding Crowd*, has noted that the portrayal of the landscapes within the film played a dominant role in her conversations with Vinterberg about the novel, and that they both wanted to 'treat [the landscape] as a character' (Christensen, quoted in Dehn 2015). This approach is also not unfamiliar when interpreting Hardy's work, with landscapes frequently described as being as central as the characters to his novels. The opening of Hardy's novel *The Return of the Native* is perhaps the most notable example of this: the entire opening chapter, 'A Face on which Time makes but little Impression', consists of an extended description of the novel's setting, Egdon Heath (1999: 9–12). The use of the word 'face' to describe the landscape is especially significant here, with Christensen observing that 'Hardy depicted landscape with the same degree of intimacy and attention to detail as he did the human face' (Oppenheimer 2015: 26). Whilst Christensen herself has acknowledged that 'you can't get the landscape exactly as Hardy describes it', she goes on to say that she hopes they 'captured it in a magical way' (quoted in Dehn 2015), emphasising that the somewhat idealised treatment of the landscapes was a creative choice made in response to the impossibility of accurately reproducing the natural world as Hardy describes it.

As I have shown, this adaptation does not adhere precisely to the image of Wessex created by Hardy, with the use of the natural world being narrower and more idealised than that found in the novels. However, as the report of Christensen's and Vinterberg's discussions around the treatment of the landscapes demonstrates, the visual style of the film was developed by considering both the practical considerations of transforming words to images and approaches taken by Hardy in his writing. In this adaptation, Vinterberg and Christensen have chosen to celebrate the beauty of the landscapes in which the narrative is set, using the striking nature of this visual choice to develop the characterisation of the central figures in the film. However, despite the emphasis placed by both Vinterberg and Christensen on the 'artistic choices' that contributed to the narrative and aesthetic style of the film, it is somewhat naïve to consider the film as an artistic product alone. As noted earlier in the discussion of the film's appeal to the tourist gaze, films also operate as cultural representations, with period films in particular contributing to the image of a time and place in the minds of the audience. In addition to this they are also a commercial product, with the associated need to attract audiences. It is to these broader issues that I now turn.

'A Thomas Hardy Film, Not a Thomas Vinterberg Film'

As noted in the introduction, Vinterberg, who co-founded the Dogme movement with Lars von Trier, would seem to be an unusual choice to direct an adaptation of a Thomas Hardy novel. For a director who had previously signed up to a manifesto that forbids 'genre movies', 'temporal and geographical alienation' and the introduction of props or non-diegetic music, a British period drama appears to be quite a departure (von Trier and Vinterberg, 'The Vow of Chastity', as reproduced in Hjort and Bondebjerg 2001: 9). Even when we take into consideration the fact that directors following the Dogme guidelines frequently break at least some of the 'rules' laid down in the manifesto, a look at Vinterberg's back catalogue still identifies *Far from the Madding Crowd* as something of an anomaly. After the huge success of Vinterberg's first Dogme film, *Festen*, he went on to make several films that received a mixed critical reception, including both Danish language and English language films. Vinterberg's previous English language films demonstrate experimentation with different genre elements, including the sci-fi fairy tale *It's All About Love* and *Dear Wendy* (Italy/US/Netherlands/Spain/Denmark/France/Germany/UK, 2005), scripted by Lars von Trier, which puts an anti-firearm twist on the modern Western, both of which yielded mixed reviews. He began to attract more critical acclaim in 2010 with a return to more low-key, character-driven narratives, first in the Danish film *Submarino* (Denmark/Sweden, 2010), and then a few years later with the hugely successful *The Hunt* (Denmark/Sweden, 2013). It was the latter film in particular that re-established Vinterberg's place as a director of note on the world stage.

Whether his films have been successful or not, however, it is notable that Vinterberg tends to exercise a greater degree of creative control over his projects than he did over *Far from the Madding Crowd*. Instead, he was hired by Andrew Macdonald and Allon Reich of DNA Films, a British production company, and worked with a script written by the novelist and screenwriter David Nicholls. This is a distinction that Vinterberg himself noted, commenting in an interview that he 'felt the relief of not having written it myself; of knowing I was doing a Thomas Hardy film, not a Thomas Vinterberg film' (Vinterberg, quoted in Pulver 2015). It is particularly significant that Vinterberg is tackling the idea of authorship head-on in this statement, suggesting that whilst he has operated as an 'auteur' on many of his films, he recognises that this is not the case on *Far from the Madding Crowd*. Perhaps unexpectedly, he presents the lessening of individual control as a positive, stating:

> It's always been me-me-me-me all the way through my career. But in a studio movie like this, there's a script, some executives – all very smart people – and as the director, you are not the king, you are a member of the board. I enjoyed that. I thought: let's do this, as a commune, as a collective. (Ibid.)

The fact that Vinterberg acknowledges the distinction between his role on *Far from the Madding Crowd* and his role in earlier works goes some way to explain the rather anomalous position of the film within his filmography. However, for all Vinterberg's playing down of his creative input into the film, he cannot fail to be aware, as, no doubt, were the producers, that the attaching of his name to a project inevitably raises certain expectations. Indeed, promotional material for the film suggests that the choice of Vinterberg was directly informed by the need to make the adaptation 'feel different' (Macdonald, quoted in 'Promotional Featurette', Vinterberg 2015).

Finding a new angle on the source material was particularly central to the development of this film as Hardy's novel has been adapted previously, in an adaptation that remains so iconic that it is frequently referred to, albeit inaccurately, as the 'original' *Far from the Madding Crowd* (John Schlesinger, UK, 1967 – note the title of John Walsh's review as just one example of this line of thinking). In a clear attempt to emphasise the 'difference' of this new adaptation, the promotional material for the film emphasised Vinterberg's position as an outsider bringing a new perspective. Both Michael Sheen and Carey Mulligan, for instance, allude to Vinterberg's status as a foreign director in promotional interviews, arguing that 'the fact that he comes from another culture in film and country brings something fresh to this movie' (Sheen, quoted in Thompson 2015), and 'it's ... a really great thing to have a foreign director come in and tell a quintessentially British story' (Mulligan, quoted in 'Promotional Featurette', Vinterberg 2015).

This approach appears to have been successful, with Vinterberg's foreignness being widely commented on in reviews. Many critics apparently tried hard to look for signs of Vinterberg's personal stylistic qualities within the film. In *Sight & Sound*, Thirza Wakefield (2015) commented on 'Vinterberg's otherness' as a means of 'open[ing] his eyes to the distinctive Dorset setting' of the source novel. Similarly, David Sexton (2015) suggests that Vinterberg 'finds in Hardy a bitter fatality that seems thoroughly Nordic'. Writing in *The Sunday Telegraph*, Robbie Collin (2015b) also argues for the aptness of the choice of director, stating that 'it makes perfect sense that Thomas Vinterberg, the frosty Dane who brought us *Festen* and *The Hunt*, would eventually turn his hand to Thomas Hardy. His handsome adaptation ... gets the book's windblown soulfulness just about exactly right'. However, Collin (2015a) also notes that the film may not quite live up to expectations in this respect, arguing that 'Vinterberg has come back with something far more conventional: the film is less of a soul-gnawing, nordically inflected tragedy than a superior Sunday-evening costume drama'.

Whilst the tendency to ascribe something original to the visionary potential of foreign directors works well as a marketing tool, these critical responses point us towards one of the major problems with tackling well-known material. I have alluded above to the desire of the filmmakers to remain 'loyal' to the novel, whilst also needing to make their own 'artistic choices'. The potential conflicts here are particularly acute when canonical literature is adapted by directors known for a unique style. When filming familiar stories directors have to make a choice between prioritising their own vision and allowing the culturally accepted image of the material to dominate their individual creative input, an issue I have explored previously in relation to adaptations of Brontë novels (Galpin 2014). As Cobb identifies, the heritage film is often considered to fall into the category of 'art cinema' despite a frequent lack of emphasis on the 'artists' who created the film:

> The important point to note about the circulation of heritage films as a kind of art cinema is that they do so without the expectation of individual expression that constructs art film auteurism, while often making up for that lack by trading on the cultural and artistic prestige of a literary source. (Cobb 2012: 114)

The decision to hire Vinterberg, a director known for exercising his personal vision, to direct an adaptation that aimed for some level of fidelity to this famous work of literature, exposes the tension implicit in Cobb's argument. The associations of the director's previous output, specifically low-key depictions of modern day characters in realistic settings, are effectively in competition with the rather different expectations raised by the status of the film as a Hardy adaptation. As a British period drama adapting a canonical novel, this film was more likely to be commercially successful if it met the expectations of audiences who are very familiar with the conventions of the literary adaptation. It is therefore no surprise that Robbie Collin (2015a) compares the film to a 'superior Sunday-evening costume drama', as the audiences for the Sunday evening costume drama are highly likely to be the same audiences to whom a new adaptation of a Thomas Hardy novel will appeal.

I noted above that the idealised treatment of the landscape can be read as appealing to the tourist gaze, and as an attempt to show fidelity to the techniques used by Hardy. In addition to this, it can also be read as situating the film within a recognisable genre. Referencing Smith's work on 'mood cues', Cardwell notes:

> On almost every occasion ... classic-novel adaptations begin with generic long-take long shots of generic content (carriages, large houses, countryside) accompanied by elegant classical music. These shot sequences establish a mood that is then reinforced, developed and heightened through the use of other generic shots and scenes throughout the adaptation. (2002: 146)

Given this definition, it is not surprising that Collin felt inclined to compare *Far from the Madding Crowd* to the generic Sunday-evening classic novel adaptation. After a brief scene in which we are introduced to the character of Bathsheba through her voiceover and a dimly lit scene in which only her profile is visible, the film opens out into a montage sequence of sunlit shots of the Dorset countryside (see Figure 3.2 for one example of this). This is accompanied by Craig Armstrong's sweeping score, very much the 'elegant classical music' of Cardwell's description. This opening is constructed mainly of shots of Bathsheba and Gabriel interacting with each other and with the landscape and does therefore serve to introduce the central characters and situate them within the film's location. However, the extended nature of the sequence, and the inclusion of shots that are detached from any character point of view and serve merely to highlight the beauty of the location, indicate that this serves as something more than a basic introduction to the people and places of the film. The sequence introduces a reverence for the landscape that is

Figure 3.2 Early shots of the landscape setting the mood for the film to come in *Far from the Madding Crowd* (Fox Searchlight/ BBC Films/TSG Entertainment/DNA Films & 20th Century Fox Home Entertainment)

maintained by the interspersing of both long shots and close-ups of natural subjects throughout the film. The film's adherence to the genre characteristics of the classic novel adaptation are therefore indicated from the outset, suggesting its unambiguous attempt to attract audiences who would be well-schooled in how to read and respond to these mood cues.

As a feature film, the appeal of this particular adaptation is also expected to stretch well beyond the boundaries of the British Sunday teatime audience to appeal to audiences in different parts of the globe. I have already indicated the transnational nature of the creative team behind the film, with the Danish Vinterberg directing alongside the British producers and writer. We can also add to this the Danish cinematographer and the Belgian leading man Matthias Schoenaerts, who stars alongside the well-known British actors Carey Mulligan and Michael Sheen, who plays Mr Boldwood. The finance from both the UK and the US also indicates that an appeal to audiences on both sides of the Atlantic was expected, in addition to the appeal to the European continent that the attaching of notable names from European countries would be likely to attract. Considering the ways in which national identities are both maintained and propagated through filmic depictions, Elsaesser (2015) notes the tendency for 'self-exoticism, or auto-ethnography, which is the perpetual temptation of . . . co-produced, multi-platform "national cinema as world cinema", where films and directors represent themselves to the (big) Other as they imagine the other imagines them' (18). Through the criticisms of Vinterberg's *Far from the Madding Crowd* it is possible to see this tendency at work, with an idealised, or 'self-exoticised' vision of rural England being presented to the global audience.

In considering the English relationship with the landscape Cardwell quotes Adam Nicolson, who points out, 'we know as we look at them [panoramic landscapes] they are not true to the real state of the country, that they are the most obvious of selective fictions', but 'everything the English continue to think about England is poured into these pictures like a bucket. They seem to be overbrimming with the English national consciousness, which is not consciousness of a flag, or a language or even really a race, but of a landscape' (Nicolson, quoted in Cardwell 2002: 138).

The reverential approach to the landscape that I have identified as being established from the outset of the film can be read as part of the 'self-exoticisation' identified by Elsaesser, and this quotation from Nicolson highlights the extent to which the English landscape can be used as a synecdoche for England, and English culture as a whole. That this glorification of the English countryside occurs here despite the presence of so-called 'outsider' perspectives, in the shape of Vinterberg and the other non-British creative talent who worked on the film, indicates the power of the enduring image of rural Englishness, and its importance in both establishing the tone of the film, and creating a market for it both domestically and abroad. The commercial need to meet domestic and global audience expectations, 'the (big) Other' of Elsaesser's statement, through familiar depictions of the environment within which the narrative takes place, supersedes any alternative perspective that the non-British creative talent might bring to the film.

CONCLUSION

Despite the expectations raised by the hiring of Vinterberg as the director of this adaptation, it is clear that the treatment of landscapes owes a great deal to the idealised image of England that tourist boards like to export. The 'fresh' approach that is expected of foreign directors, not to mention the other creative talent who work on films, is a useful marketing tool for rebranding familiar material. However, in practice this 'freshness' is often in opposition to the ingrained expectations of what a film of a particular genre, with deep national associations predating the attaching of creative talent to its production, will look like. These expectations work to enforce the notion that familiarity brings with it less commercial risk than more radical departures from the norm. Those critics who looked for this adaptation to present a radical reimagining of the source material were disappointed. Despite Vinterberg's past as a director of films that are innovative and challenging in both their narrative choices and their visual style, when working with an adaptation of canonical material the demands of the genre conventions and the expected aesthetic style are in evidence.

Far from the Madding Crowd is arguably a rather conventional British period drama, complete with emphasis on the romantic aspects of the narrative and idealised depictions of the landscape, despite the film's focus on the land as a working entity. However, as I have suggested, this conventionality should not prevent us from recognising the ways in which Vinterberg and the other creative talent on the film have used these genre elements to construct their own interpretation of the novel. The film negotiates the need to adhere to genre conventions whilst also demonstrating an interpretative approach to Hardy's novel that employs Hardyesque techniques of utilising the landscape as both a key aid to characterisation and as a character in itself.

Finally, however, it is worth noting the strength of perceived nationality when matched against the appeal of international collaboration. Hardy's narratives have been shown to have universality in their treatment of human experiences of love and loss, with Michael Winterbottom transplanting *The Mayor of Casterbridge* to a frontier town in the American West (*The Claim*, UK/France/Canada, 2000) and *Tess of the D'Urbervilles* to modern-day India (*Trishna*, UK, 2011). Despite this, as the initial caption suggests, the film is firmly rooted in its geographical and national location. Although *Far from the Madding Crowd* draws creative personnel from around Europe, the evidence of this is difficult to discern in the finished product. Writing in these times of uncertainty around international collaborations, most notably for the UK with the dominance of the Brexit referendum in the current political climate, it is not difficult to draw parallels between this political separatism and the practice of constructing familiar and distinct national identities through film products. Whilst the film could have reflected the collaboration between different national styles, most notably the British producers and writer(s) and the Danish director and cinematographer, as some critics noted, it contains little evidence of Scandinavian traditions. We can therefore conclude that, despite financial and creative co-productions being a familiar feature of the modern film industry, the evidence of international collaboration is more difficult to locate within the filmic output that results. Instead, we see the self-perpetuating nature of national identity at play, with the possibility to adapt the source material into something more universal and global being eclipsed by the desire to represent the nation in a way that is coherent and attractive but, most importantly, familiar.

References

Barton, R. (2016), 'The ironic gaze: roots tourism and irish heritage cinema', in P. Cooke and R. Stone (eds) *Screening European Heritage: Creating and Consuming History on Film*, London: Palgrave, pp. 163–79.

Boumelha, P. (1985), *Thomas Hardy and Women: Sexual Ideology and Narrative Form*, Madison: University of Wisconsin Press.

Cardwell, S. (2002), *Adaptation Revisited: Television and the Classic Novel*, Manchester: Manchester University Press.

Cobb, Shelley (2012), 'Film authorship and adaptation', in D. Cartmell (ed.), *A Companion to Literature, Film and Adaptation*, Chichester: Blackwell, pp. 105–21.

Collin, R. (2015a), 'Far from the Madding Crowd review: a mini-break on film', *The Telegraph*, 30 April, <www.telegraph.co.uk/film/far-from-the-madding-crowd-2015/review/> (accessed on 4 December 2017).

Collin, R. (2015b), 'Love in a Cold Climate', *The Sunday Telegraph*, 3 May.

Creative England (2015), 'Quantifying film and television tourism in England', 4 March, <www.creativeengland.co.uk/film-and-tv/film-tourism-research> (accessed 4 October 2018).

Dehn, G. (2015), 'Far from the Madding Crowd: How Wessex was Won', *The Telegraph*, 30 April, <www.telegraph.co.uk/film/far-from-the-madding-crowd-2015/carey-mulligan-behind-the-scenes/> (accessed 11 December 2017).

Elsaesser, T. (2015), 'European cinema in the twenty-first century: enlarging the context?' in M. Harrod, L. Mariana and A. Timoshkina (eds), *The Europeanness of European Cinema: Identity, Meaning, Globalization*, London: I. B. Tauris, pp. 17–32.

Galpin, S. A. (2014), 'Auteurs and authenticity: adapting the Brontës in the twenty-first century', *Journal of British Cinema and Television*, 11: 1, 86–100.

Geraghty, C. (2008), *Now a Major Motion Picture: Film Adaptations of Literature and Drama*, Lanham: Rowman & Littlefield.

Griggs, Y. (2012), 'Writing for the movies: writing and screening *Atonement* (2007)', in D. Cartmell (ed.), *A Companion to Literature, Film and Adaptation*, Chichester: Blackwell, pp. 345–58.

Hardy, T. (2000 [1874]), *Far from the Madding Crowd*, London: Penguin.

Hardy, T. (1999 [1878]), *The Return of the Native*, London: Penguin.

Higson, A. (2011), *Film England: Culturally English Filmmaking since the 1990s*, London: I. B. Tauris.

Hjort, M. and Bondebjerg, I. (2001), *The Danish Directors*, Bristol: Intellect.

Kermode, M. (2015), 'Far from the Madding Crowd review – solid, but needs more mud', *The Observer*, 3 May, <https://www.theguardian.com/film/2015/may/03/far-from-the-madding-crowd-review-solid-needs-more-mud> (accessed 4 December 2017).

Kramer, D. (1999), 'Hardy and readers: *Jude the Obscure*', in D. Kramer (ed.), *The Cambridge Companion to Thomas Hardy*, Cambridge: Cambridge University Press, pp. 164–82.

Newland, P. (2016), 'Introduction: approaching British rural landscapes on film', in P. Newland (ed.), *British Rural Landscapes on Film*, Manchester: Manchester University Press, pp. 1–23.

Niemeyer, P. J. (2003), *Seeing Hardy: Film and Television Adaptations of the Fiction of Thomas Hardy*, Jefferson: McFarland.

Oppenheimer, J. (2015), 'Pastoral Romance', in *American Cinematographer*, 96: 6, 26–30.

Pulver, A. (2015), 'Far from the Madding Crowd director Thomas Vinterberg: "It's always been me-me-me-me – until now"', *The Guardian*, 28 April, <https://www.theguardian.com/film/2015/apr/28/far-from-the-madding-crowd-thomas-vinterberg-interview> (accessed 1 December 2017).

Schoenfeld, L. B. (2005), *Dysfunctional Families in the Wessex Novels of Thomas Hardy*, Lanham: University Press of America.

Sexton, D. (2015), 'Far from the Madding Crowd review: a revelation of how affecting Carey Mulligan can be', *Evening Standard*, 1 May, <https://www.standard.co.uk/goingout/film/far-from-the-madding-crowd-review-a-revelation-of-how-affecting-carey-mulligan-can-be-10217851.html> (accessed 4 December 2017).

Thompson, B. (2015), '"Lightness and life to Far from the Madding Crowd: there is so much going on", actor Michael Sheen says', *Ottawa Citizen*, 11 May.

Urry, J. and Larsen, J. (2011), *The Tourist Gaze 3.0*, London: Sage.

Vinterberg, T. (2015), 'Promotional Featurette: Thomas Vinterberg' [Bluray], 20th Century Fox.

Wakefield, T. (2015), 'Film of the week: Far from the Madding Crowd', *Sight & Sound*, May <www.bfi.org.uk/news-opinion/sight-sound-magazine/reviews-recommendations/film-week-far-madding-crowd> (accessed 4 December 2017).

Walsh, J. (2015), 'John Walsh on Thomas Vinterberg's Far from the Madding Crowd: I'm shocked someone thinks that such a classic film needs a remake', *The Independent*, 22 May, <www.independent.co.uk/arts-entertainment/films/features/john-walsh-on-thomas-vinterbergs-far-from-the-madding-crowd-im-shocked-someone-thinks-such-a-classic-10267538.html> (accessed 4 December 2017).

Webster, R. (2005), 'From painting to cinema: visual elements in Hardy's fiction', in T. R. Wright (ed.), *Thomas Hardy on Screen*, Cambridge: Cambridge University Press, pp. 20–36.

Wood, R. (1999), *The Wings of the Dove: Henry James in the 1990s*, London: BFI.

Wright, T. (2005), 'Hardy as a cinematic novelist: three aspects of narrative technique', in T. R. Wright (ed.), *Thomas Hardy on Screen*, Cambridge: Cambridge University Press, pp. 8–19.

PART II

RADICAL CONTINGENCIES: NEGLECTED FIGURES AND TEXTS

4. REFRAMING PERFORMANCE: THE BRITISH NEW WAVE ON STAGE AND SCREEN

Victoria Lowe

This chapter examines the adaptation of two stage plays to the screen during the 'British New Wave' period of the late 1950s and early 1960s. It locates these adaptations in relation to a specific national context, namely the symbiotic relationship between stage and screen in England. This began in the first decade of cinema when adaptations of theatre plays were seen as a means of raising the cultural status of film. The nearness of production centres and the exchange of personnel then helped to create a climate in which the exchange of practices and ideas was facilitated (Brown 1986). However this shared history is contentious as British cinema has been criticised for its overdependence on theatrical or literary source material and therefore the influence of the theatre has often been seen to be detrimental (Elsaesser 1972: Armes 1978). Criticism was particularly directed at stage-to-screen adaptations because of their shared identity as performance media. The 'theatrical' was understood to be in implicit opposition to the 'cinematic'.

> In film criticism, the term theatrical is nearly always a term of abuse. The need of film theorists to slough off the associations with the theatre has been an essential aspect of some versions of cinema's history. (Lacey 2003: 159)

This chapter, on the other hand understands the stage-to-screen adaptation in more productive terms, arguing that the hybridity of these textual products had a specifically national dimension in the way they integrated theatrical and cinematic elements. As David Forrest argues, the theatrical antecedents of the British New Wave films distinguished them from other national cinematic movements of the time:

> The New Wave aspired to retain and reform the indigenous cultural elements which define the British cinema (a realist aesthetic and theatrical style) confirming the art cinema textual product of the New Wave as uniquely British. (Forrest 2013: 78)

There is much to be gained from thinking about these films as stage adaptations and this challenges histories of the period, which can neglect the adaptive status of these films. The period in question has been looked at in detail by theatre scholars and by film scholars but has generated debates specific to these disciplines rather than cross-disciplinary investigations (Higson 1984: Hill 1986: Rebellato 1999). Studies have also tended not to distinguish between the literary and the dramatic sources of the New Wave (notable exceptions being Lacey 1995 and Palmer and Bray 2013). This has meant that aspects of the performance text, such as use of space, acting, design and sound have been neglected. Furthermore, 'theatre' is treated as a homogeneous entity, when in fact there were many different types of theatre in the period under consideration, from the writer-led output of the Royal Court to the non-hierarchical performance practices that marked Joan Littlewood's Theatre Workshop. This chapter will therefore investigate questions of performance in two film adaptations: *The Entertainer* (1960) and *The Kitchen* (1961). I argue that particular aesthetic challenges to the status quo were asserted that crossed both stage and screen mediums and offered new representational practices in design, sound and acting styles across both forms. Tony Richardson, a director who worked in both theatre and cinema, argued in 1959 that practitioners needed to challenge established norms across all cultural forms:

> It is absolutely vital to get into British films the same sort of impact and sense of life that what you can loosely call the Angry Young Man cult has had in the theatre and literary worlds. It is a desperate need. (Richardson, quoted in Welsh and Tibbetts 1999: 64)

In comparison to the French New Wave directors, who sought to distance themselves from the adaptation, the British New Wave actively sought to draw upon the energy generated by developments in other media. To a certain extent, this was determined by a specific industrial context. Film adaptations of stage plays were trying to work commercially within a restricted local market, using established properties to draw up on the theatrical movement's articulation of revolution versus stasis. By adapting these plays, the producers sought to identify new, younger audiences for the films and thus began to challenge the imposition of censorship rules that regulated both the theatre and cinema of the time.[1] Thus as Robert Shail argues, 'literary' sources gave a base 'from which to build inroads into the more conservative film industry' (2012: 42).

The parameters of what is called the 'New Wave' in the theatre are usually demarcated by the first production of *Look Back in Anger* at the Royal Court in 1956, though this narrative of radicalism challenging conformity has been challenged by scholars such as Rebellato (1999) and Shellard (2000). The British New Wave movement on film is thought to start a little later with *Room at the Top* (1959) and consist of just nine films, though again the notion of a canon has been called into question by scholars such as Taylor (2006) and Hutchings (2001).[2] It is possible to see play (as opposed to novel) adaptations as a grouping in themselves because of how film adaptations sought to absorb or depart from the aesthetics and practices embedded in the theatre productions. For instance, as Lacey (1996) points out, when poetic realism gained more currency as a style in films it then made its way back into the theatre as a new visual aesthetic via designers such as Jocelyn Herbert, who then bought those ideas back into cinema in her designs for films in the late 1960s such as *Isadora* (1968) and *If . . .* (1968). Acting styles also crossed between the two mediums, with many actors emerging from the theatre to challenge the look and sound of film in Britain in the late 1950s and early 1960s by broadening the range of types of characters and accents. This was partly due to changes in the funding of actors' training, which introduced grants for the poorest students and therefore enfranchised a much broader social mix of regional and working-class acting talent. For instance, Penelope Houston wrote approvingly of the 'freshness' that actors such as Alan Bates and Joan Plowright brought to the film adaptation of *The Entertainer*:

> They share the same qualities of likeableness and seriousness, energy and a kind of unstressed and unshowy honesty. This kind of purposeful acting is something encouragingly new on the British screen and the cinema cannot be allowed to imagine it can continue to do without it. (Houston 1960: 2)

Directors and writers also moved between stage and screen at the time. Tony Richardson, at the same time as directing *Look Back in Anger* at the Royal Court, was part of the Free Cinema movement that preceded the New Wave. The roots of this movement were in the film journal *Sequence*, co-founded by the stage and film director Lindsay Anderson in 1947. The journal railed against films 'without vitality', therefore demonstrating concerns shared with those who dismissed the prevailing theatrical culture in the 1950s. Out of this emerged the Free Cinema Group who collectively arranged to present a programme of films at the National Film Theatre in February 1956. Their first manifesto famously asserted:

> As film makers we believe that
> No film can be too personal
> The image speaks. Sound amplifies and comments. Size is irrelevant
> Perfection is not an aim
> An attitude means a style. A style means an attitude. (Anderson quoted in Izod *et al.* 2012: 52)

Whilst Anderson claimed the Free Cinema movement had petered out by 1959, the group forged a number of personal and professional relationships that crossed between stage and screen. Richardson was clear that he thought it was no help to have directing experience in the theatre when it came to films. Yet his idea was that Woodfall, the company he set up to produce films with producer Harry Saltzman and the playwright John Osborne, would be a 'parallel organisation to the English Stage Company – a Trojan horse that would break down the citadel walls of the British film industry – and provide opportunities for fresh, innovative work by new writers, actors and directors' (Murphy 2014: 381).

Both film adaptations examined in this chapter derive from plays first put on at the Royal Court by the English Stage Company, one of a number of institutions that became famously associated with challenging theatrical orthodoxies. From 1956 to 1965, the Court was under the artistic directorship of George Devine, who acted as a sort of mentor to many of the New Wave directors, designers and actors. Devine promoted a system that emphasised creative production as emerging from a close relationship between writer, director and designer. Thus particular staging practices emerged during the rehearsal period that might take a written text in a completely different direction in performance. The adaptations had to negotiate translating the dramaturgical space of these theatrical performances into the film medium, often drawing on principles established by the Free Cinema movement, which took filming out of the studio and into the street, yet still dealing with characters in a fiction played by actors rather than using 'real people' as many of the Free Cinema documentaries had done. As Taylor rightly identifies, the implications of utilising the documentary realist tradition of the Free Cinema movement as the aesthetic mode of representation in a range of adaptations has come to dominate scholarly discussion of the British New Wave films, in the sense that 'allegedly, these new British films were unable successfully to contain their use of locations within their narratives' (2006: 15). Thus we have critics such as V. F. Perkins (1962) talking about the films in terms of 'landscape mongering',

Higson (1984) in terms of 'narrative excess' and finally Hill (1986) in terms of 'surplus and noticeability', all of which seem to invalidate the films as the documents of lived experience that these critics are claiming they were intended to be. Whilst not denying these interpretations of the films, reframing the debate in terms of how these films adapt the dramaturgical spaces of the original theatrical source material offers a different understanding of them as reframed performances. So whereas the possibilities of the theatre auditorium are put to work to provide metaphors for the action in the plays (the cramped and claustrophobic single-room setting of the flat in *Look Back in Anger*, the music hall in *The Entertainer*), the films could be seen as using their settings to 'perform', albeit with obviously different effects.

THE ENTERTAINER

The genesis of the play appears to have derived from a meeting between writer John Osborne and actor Lawrence Olivier in 1958. In his autobiography Osborne (1991: 135) recalls that Olivier approached him to write something suitable to star in, although Osborne claims that he had already had the idea to write something about the dying out of music hall as a form. Olivier (1982: 212), on the other hand recalled that he had hated *Look Back in Anger* on first viewing but that a subsequent visit with Arthur Miller persuaded him of its merits as a play. Despite the New Wave playwrights' so-called use of 'kitchen sink' realism, it's clear that *The Entertainer* was a significant departure from any form of naturalism. The structure of the play is nonlinear, with Archie's music hall turns punctuating the action on stage and dislocated in time and space from the rest of the play. Osborne gave indications on the sparseness of the décor in the play text, 'furniture and props are as basic as they would be for a short sketch' (1993b: 1), and this was replicated in the simple set, designed by Alan Tagg in the play's performance at the Royal Court. In Osborne's text, the initial description of the setting also describes a very specific location that is designed to point to a particular social milieu rather than as directions for anything that is achievable within a theatre space:

> The action takes place in a large coastal resort . . . this is a part of the town the holiday makers never see – or if they do, they decide to turn back to the Pleasure Gardens . . . they don't even have to pass it on the way from the central station, for this is a town on its own . . . It is not residential. It is hardly industrial. It is full of dirty blank spaces, high black walls, a gas holder, a tall chimney. (1993: 1)

It therefore operates more as metaphor for Archie's situation – the reality behind the garish façade. Despite this description being more realisable on film, the actual opening of the film shows the tourist part of Morecambe, with the parade, sea front and pier teeming with visitors. Nigel Kneale, who co-adapted the film version with Osborne, claimed that the Morecambe had seen the film as an opportunity to promote the seaside town and so had gone to considerable expense in doing the town up before filming started, somewhat negating the symbolic purpose of Osborne's original setting (Murray 2006: 69). This points to a difference between the function of place on stage and on film. As the conventions of the theatre mark off the playing space from everyday life, it follows that setting can more easily work as a metaphor. This is often a notable feature of Osborne's plays – the characters are often trapped within the three walls of the stage in the same way as they are trapped by life – whether this is Jimmy Porter railing against the establishment in *Look Back in Anger* or the dysfunctional family trapped in their cramped, third-rate digs in *The Entertainer*. The use of a recognisable environment on film means that different interests are involved in the representation and the metaphoric function of the setting can be undermined despite the director's best intentions, as is clear from an article before the film was released:

> We intend says director Richardson to make the atmosphere of an English seaside resort an extra comment on Osborne's characters and situations. (Osborne 1993)

The linking of place with thematic concerns becomes clearer in certain scenes later in the film, particularly when Jean and Archie share a bottle of champagne and some chips whilst sitting on a bit of a deserted scrub ground overlooking a rather dilapidated amusement park, with a rollercoaster prominently visible in the centre of the frame between the two characters. If it were ever in doubt, the rollercoaster recalls the vicissitudes of Archie's life as an entertainer, with scrubland signifying the decay behind the bright façade of the seafront. Taylor therefore argues that 'Richardson's use of the wasteland allowed connections to be made between the characters and the films' spaces' (2006: 52).

Although superficially the play seems a departure from *Look Back in Anger*, in many ways it displays the same preoccupations. Whilst the music hall scenes set it apart from the earlier Osborne play, most of the action in *The Entertainer* takes place in a small, cluttered domestic dwelling, in which another group of people (in this case a dysfunctional family) air their disappointments with each other and the world beyond the living room. It's a play about waiting and reacting and this sense of treading water is brought to a head at the end of the second act, with news of Billy's death at Suez, which precipitates the final decline shown in the third act. The weariness is articulated most cogently by Archie's daughter Jean, who laments:

> Everyone's tired all right. Everybody's tired, everybody's standing about, loitering without any intent whatsoever, waiting to be picked up by whatever they may allow to happen to us next. (1993: 75)

Despite this outburst, overall in the play, Jean is very much a reactive character whose function, returning from London, seems designed to force each of the characters to a point of reckoning. Her relationship with Archie seems to be one of simmering resentment that boils over in the final act, when she accuses him of 'apathy' and 'not bothering' (ibid.: 76).

Reviews were generally positive, with most of the attention going to Olivier for his performance as Archie Rice. Harold Hobson in the *Sunday Times* remarked that, 'Its theatrical effect is enormous', singling out Olivier for particular praise: 'you will not see more magnificent acting than this anywhere in the world' (quoted in Shellard 2000: 84). For many, Olivier's performance came to acquire a symbolic value; that of the abandonment of old forms of theatre and embrace of the new. Olivier's career was in limbo before the play; acclaimed for his Shakespearean work but still representing the theatrical establishment that the New Wave claimed to be rebelling against. However, Lacey points out that there were consequences to the play being dominated by Olivier's performance, in that, whilst the music hall sections were a key metaphor for the collapse of Britain as a world power, they also served 'as a context for the playing out of the primary emotional despair' (1995: 105). Olivier's barnstorming performance therefore accentuated this emotional identification with Archie, an effect that complicated the play's attitude to conservatism and change, as it thus appeared to lament British loss of imperialist power rather than critique it (Rebellato 1999: 42). It appears then that a celluloid preserving of Olivier's performance was at least one of the reasons for Woodfall's decision to adapt the play in 1960 (see Taylor 2006). Initially James Cagney was in the running for the lead role, with adaptor Nigel Kneale objecting strongly to Olivier playing Archie on film because he thought he would be too theatrical for the film medium. Indeed in his biography, Kneale recalled that Olivier objected to the first draft of his screenplay as he felt that he had cut all his best lines (Murray 2006: 76). The film therefore not only depicts scenes and locations that are only mentioned in the play, but more crucially involves a different protagonist. Whilst Jean, in the play, is one of a chorus of characters who circulate around Archie, in the film she is given much greater prominence. Such a move seems designed to appeal to a more youthful audience, but was also introduced in order to balance out the over-dominance of Archie, in terms of character and Olivier's performance. It presents a more identifiable and sympathetic protagonist – one more in tune with the demands of classical film narrative, whose experience structures the film and gives a point of identification for a younger audience.

The difference is notable right from the very start, as we are shown images of a seaside town full of people walking down the streets, with trams in the background, from the point of view of someone walking about it, as if we are seeing these pictures from a particular perspective. In the montage of shots, this viewpoint is revealed to be Jean (Joan Plowright), and the camera settles on a close-up of her face, as she is seen to be looking and thinking, before cutting to a playbill announcing the appearance of 'Archie Rice – star of radio and television'. Jean then turns to listen to a passer-by comment on whether they have ever heard Archie on the radio. Thus a key theme of the film, the infiltration of mass culture on traditional working-class culture, is introduced, but (crucially and unlike the play) through the perspective of Jean. Introducing Jean at this point also revives what was becoming a key New Wave film trope, that of the environment seen from the perspective of the returning outsider, the one who leaves, but never feels quite at home in either place. This scene is followed by an extended flashback sequence (not in the play) that shows Jean's existence in London and sets up the context for her visit back up north. We see her at work in her art studio, supervising a class of young people and then as she dismisses the class, in order to meet her fiancé, a shot in the mirror of her studio shows both Jean and the young people now dancing in the classroom, implicitly showing her connection with but distance from this group of people.

The subsequent conversation between Jean and her fiancé Graham sets out Jean's dilemma: whether to stay with her job, working with under-privileged young people, or to go off with Graham to South Africa. As Lacey notes, a female character's decision was still predicated on her relationship to marriage and motherhood, but it is notable that their clearly articulated position at the beginning of the film changes the perspective towards its key themes to a certain extent (Lacey 1995: 185). This is borne out by the rest of the film in which she carries on being the perspective through which the action is seen and we are made aware of her watchful presence right through to the end, when she stays with Archie for his final performance. This introduces a different resonance to the adaptation in which we are watching Archie's decline through her eyes; the view of the younger generation on the one that preceded it. Therefore it is less of a lament for the loss of Britain's imperial power than an indictment of an old, turgid Britain, one that sends its youth to fight in a useless war and has nothing to offer a vibrant new generation. This is reinforced by Plowright's luminous performance, with Richardson concentrating the camera frame on her watchful eyes, seeing and understanding the demise of her father as somehow necessary to the renewal offered by the next generation.

It is perhaps for this reason that the film seems more subdued than the play, as the playwright Arnold Wesker identified in a review on the film's release, with a plea for the film to be understood on its own terms:

> *The Entertainer* is a film about a third rate society and a third rate comedian who is touched by the political scene he prefers to ignore; and in so far as Archie Rice can boast of no moral standards, it is about the decay of the British personality. Its theme could have been handled flippantly – imagine the Boulting Brothers; it could have been handled viciously – imagine Kazan; instead it is handled with a sadness that is loving. (Wesker 1960: 2)

Wesker here is defending the film adaptation, with an appeal to how different it was in tone from previous British or American films, as reviews were not universally positive. Many were marked by a consideration of how well or ineffectively the film adapted the play, showing that these films were often seen within in a perspective of their relationship to the stage. For instance, Penelope Houston in *Sight & Sound*:

> The Morecambe locations are conspicuously well used and the combination of an emotional and an ironic comment in a scene such as the memorial service parade is something purely of the cinema. Yet the writers – Osborne himself – have not faced the main difficulty. The claustrophobic tautness is not just a stage technique but the means by which the play clinches its emotional grip. Let it relax and we are left with a series of isolated impressions rather than a dramatic entity. (Houston 1960: 2)

Houston's review therefore seems to articulate the uncertain status of the film in its combination of what are understood to be opposing theatrical and cinematic elements. Changes in setting, the opening out of the characters in terms of motivations and the balance between them all add up to a particular textual identity that reveals the mixing of theatrical and cinematic dramaturgies. A similar effect, though achieved through different means, can be understood in relation to the second case study, *The Kitchen*.

THE KITCHEN

Arnold Wesker's *The Kitchen* was first performed at the Royal Court in 1959 with John Dexter directing and Jocelyn Herbert as designer. It was adapted as a film in 1961 by Sydney Cole, directed by James Hill. Although it shares other New Wave films' theatrical antecedents, it hasn't been co-opted into the canon of British New Wave films. This is perhaps because there was no Woodfall contribution, either in production or direction, and because on the whole it replicates the interior setting of the play, eschewing the comprehensive 'opening out' demonstrated by other play adaptations. But it seems more likely that Wesker's original play, which moves away from the domestic sphere and observes a collective at work, with the setting clearly functioning symbolically as a comment on wider society, was resistant to the New Wave film trope of the disaffected protagonist, reacting to or railing against changes in post-war British society. Wesker's play was also clearly more experimental in form than the Osborne/Richardson collaborations. Stephen Lacey has described how in rehearsal, the staging of the play moved away from naturalism towards a more Brechtian presentation (1996: 241). It was also more explicitly political: *The Kitchen* showed how workers are alienated by their labour and exploited by the workings of capitalism, using this as an allegory for wider society.

In the play text, Wesker describes how each of the characters relates to the others in the hierarchy that structures the kitchen environment, and by telling us which food they are preparing he gives a sense of how their individual contribution is necessary for the whole system to function. This focus on the collective is noted by Wesker in the introduction when he states:

> Each person has his own particular job. We glance in upon him, highlighting as it were the individual. But though we may watch just one or a group of people, the rest of the kitchen staff does not. They work on. (1976: 9)

The first production of the play was a one-off performance on a Sunday night in September 1959 as part of the Royal Court's experimental season. It then opened at the Belgrade in Coventry in June 1961, before opening at the Court itself on 28 June 1961. The cast were pretty much unknown although Rita Tushingham, fresh from her appearance in the New Wave film *A Taste of Honey* (1960), had the small part as Hettie, again demonstrating the porous boundaries between stage and screen at the time.

A key and often overlooked element of the production was its radically new approach to design and use of sound. Its designer Jocelyn Herbert was part of a group at the Royal Court (among them directors Lindsay Anderson and *The Kitchen*'s director John Dexter) who, influenced by Brecht and directions in European theatre, were moving away from the constraints of naturalistic design and pushing towards a more abstract presentation of the setting. Herbert has written how the motivating impulse for her design was initially the 'movement' that she thought was the most important aspect of the play: her set had to allow for the section where the speed and rhythm of the meal service built to an almost unbearable frenzy. Thus the placing of the stoves was key and 'other elements just had to take their positions around them (Courtney 1993: 37). For the first Sunday performance, they used trestle tables for the stoves and put black material on them. She wanted to show a contrast with the sweets and salad tables so a last-minute addition was covering them with white sheets. The importance of sound to the production was clear as she recalls that the serving points made from orange boxes were covered in tin so they made the right clashing noises during the frenzied service. Sound was also highlighted by the growing hiss of the ovens as they are turned on at the beginning of the performance, and was coordinated with the lights getting brighter one by one. Key to the whole production was the revelation of the building of the theatre itself. Herbert remembers how:

> [they] used the bare stage for the first time with the back wall and all the pipes showing. It was a real breakthrough and I think it was also the first time we put the lighting rig above the set and allowed everything to seen. (Herbert in Courtney 1993: 38)

Overall John Dexter recalls how, '*The Kitchen* pointed me in the direction –not of minimalism that's the wrong word – but of provoking the audience to think for themselves and to use their imagination' (Dexter, in Courtney 1993: 38).

The film, as is common with most of the adaptations of plays, came a couple of years after the performance at the Royal Court. It was produced by the cinematographers' trade union ACTT and financed almost entirely by the National Film Finance Corporation. This public subsidy arguably endowed it with the ability to be more experimental. It also gave Wesker complete control of the script and the final say in any changes, though the adaptation is officially attributed to Sidney Cole. In terms of the push towards the more anti-naturalistic presentation developed by Herbert and Dexter, the film gives us a more 'realistic' setting in the shape of an identifiably working kitchen. We see the workers preparing, eating and serving 'real food'. In fact, a montage about twenty-five minutes into the film clearly communicates who is responsible for which task in the kitchen and shows close-ups of fish being gutted and vegetables being chopped in preparation for the service. On the other hand, by keeping the majority of the action in the kitchen and resisting the temptation to follow the characters outside for the most part (there are a couple of sequences where Peter follows Monique out into the night at the beginning and then we see the lovers drift round London streets during the break), the film echoes the play's demarcation of the kitchen as a symbolic, dramatic space where all the action is played out. An interview on set with writer and producer reports:

> They both agreed that an essential ingredient of the play, the feeling of claustrophobia and isolation which wears down the characters, would be lost if the action was spread out beyond the confines of the kitchen itself. (Russell Taylor 1961: 5)

Therefore, unlike *The Entertainer*, maintaining the temporal and spatial aspects of the world articulated in the theatrical production offered opportunities for the spectator to 'engage with each image's inherent multiplicity of meanings' rather than have their perspective on the action directed by the camera (Bazin quoted in Keil 2006: 83).

The film adaptation, again unlike *The Entertainer*, also resisted creating a clearly defined protagonist and maintained the emphasis on the collective, like the play. Although the affair between Monique and Peter is given more prominence in the film, it still resists the single-protagonist driven narrative of the classical film, to encompass all the inhabitants of the kitchen. Specifically, cinematic techniques such as the close-up are used, but in a different way to the cinematic realism utilised in the rest of the film and thus could be understood as mimicking the anti-naturalistic presentation of the play. The film begins with a sequence that is only described in the play: the fight between Peter and Gaston, the Cypriot cook. There are no titles before this sequence and the first shot of the film is of a close-up of a man's face, held in momentarily static, painful physical exertion before it reveals the context for the action, the fight between two men. The fight itself then is played out within the dramatic space, without the 'shot: reverse shot' by which cinematic space is usually constructed. The sound is also key here, as there is very little dialogue and the non-diegetic music is percussive and abstract in its scoring of the images, echoing the expressionistic use of sound in the original performance. There is no attempt to obey the rules of classical Hollywood narrative, using long shots to establish where the characters are or moving from a broader to more specific location. The opening of *The Kitchen* thus positions its audience in a similar way to that of the theatre audience, as an observer of the action, rather than suturing them into the narrative.

At the end there is also a device used that deploys the potentialities of the medium for theatrical effect. In the play, the written stage directions describe how the owner of the Kitchen, Marango, is left facing his staff:

> who stand around, almost accusingly, looking at him. And he asks again, 'What is there more? What is there more?' We have seen that there must be something more and so the lights must slowly fade. (1976: 71)

The slow fade of the lights here is designed to give the audience space to think about the implications of what they have just witnessed. In the film, after Peter has taken an axe to the gas pipes and the ovens close down, we are left with the characters surrounding him and Marango delivers his final speech, to both Peter and the workers at large, asking rhetorically, as in the play, 'What is there more?' The frame used here is a wide one so that we get a clear sense of linking the characters and their behaviour to their environment.

There is no sense that the film ends with Peter as the key protagonist. Slowly, the figures fade out one by one from the kitchen setting and then Marango, as the only figure left, is finally faded out too, leaving the bare, empty space of the kitchen as the final image before the film ends. This is a literal representation of Peter's speech during the play's quiet 'interlude', where the characters become philosophical about their situation. As the new Irish recruit, Kevin, lays down, exhausted by the madness of the service, Peter reflects on their situation:

> Like this place, this house – this too, it'll always be here. That's a thought for you Irishman. This – this madhouse it's always here. When you go, when I go, when Dimitri goes – this kitchen stays. It'll go on when we die, think about that. (Wesker 1976: 35)

The film's ending uses this cinematic technique to echo the dramaturgical rendition of space in the play and therefore moves towards a more poetic expression of the characters' predicament, reinforcing the play's political message of how workers are alienated from their labour and environment.

New Wave films often adapted their sources to accentuate aspects that would appeal to younger audiences and *The Kitchen* is similar to others in this respect. As in *Look Back in Anger*, the film's soundtrack leans heavily towards modern jazz. A sequence in the middle of the film conveys the chaos of service through rapid cutting and close-ups, and is underpinned by its score, which seems like an improvised jazz set with soaring saxophone solos and high-pitched trumpets. Sound is clearly as important here as it is in the play, with a clear sense of structuring the narrative from the use of percussion to score the opening sequence, through the buildup of jazz in the first section, followed by the quiet interlude, in which the diegetic strumming of the guitar emphasises the reflective mood. It's also perhaps worth noting that the film doesn't draw up on star performers, unlike *The Entertainer* and *Look Back in Anger*, with many of the actors (e.g. James Bolam) making the transition from the stage production to the film. This underlines the emphasis on the collective and mitigates against the possibility of a 'star' performance undermining a sense of the ensemble.

Reviews for the film were mixed, although, like those of the *The Entertainer*, many were notable in basing their evaluations, whether positive or negative, on an understanding of the film's status as an adaptation. Jonathan Miller in the *New Statesman* complained that 'the pattern of the drama is hidden under a heap of competent but boring cinematic trivia' (1961: 1), whilst the anonymous reviewer in *The Guardian* argued that 'the job of adaptation has been done skillfully and with a very proper emphasis on the text rather than on cinematic decoration' (Anon 1961: 9). Most notable in all the reviews was a sense that the film was striving for something different from other films of the time:

> If it fails, as I think it does, it is because it asks to be judged on a level to which most British films never aspire . . . for once the screen adaptation preserves the radical tone of the original . . . but these qualities are mainly expressed through dialogue. (Sulik 1961: 11)

This view was echoed by a long piece by David Robinson:

> In theory, *The Kitchen* is exactly the sort of British film we have been looking for for years. The play has not been adulterated; it is boldly presented with its full original text in its single claustrophobic setting of a big restaurant kitchen . . . So what is wrong? Something pretty vital has been mislaid from stage to screen . . . I think that the difference is that while the play succeeded in being at once documentary and intensely dramatic, the film hesitates somewhere between. *The Kitchen* is probably one of the most honest sincere and thoughtful British films since the war and so its failure is all the sadder. (1961: 5)

The film of *The Kitchen* provides an interesting counterbalance to its contemporaries. Its adoption of a more stylised realism than in other films associated with the New Wave sets it somewhat apart from other film adaptations and perhaps made it ultimately doomed not to succeed commercially, or to be co-opted into the canon of the British New Wave. Indeed, it was screened outside the West End at the International Film Theatre in Notting Hill in what was described in one review as 'a cinema devoted to continental and minority films' (Sulik 1961). This then demands a question about how it can be understood as an 'indigenous' cultural product, particularly when its place of exhibition puts it alongside films from a European art-house sensibility. On one level this is a problem with defining the limits of the national within particular parameters that will always be exceeded (Hjort and Mackenzie 2000: 5). As David Forrest has astutely observed, 'New Wave films were consistently marked by a balance of European stylistic subversion with a firm commitment to national cinematic and cultural tropes' (2013: 77). These cultural 'tropes' then involved a utilisation of representational means outside classical film-making strategies, engendered by the adaptation process from stage to screen. Therefore, the mixture of cinematic and theatrical codes, even potentially the breaking down of the distinctions between them, can be understood as distinctive cultural poetics.

CONCLUSION

If we acknowledge that the aesthetic relationship between theatre and cinema is not fixed but historically and culturally contingent, we can see how film's links to theatre in the UK were utilised at different times and with different effects to construct a distinctive cultural identity for its output. This reimagines the relationship between theatre and cinema as one of facilitating a 'cross-media poetics' rather than undermining the essential identity of each individual dramatic form. Recovering the history of adaptations between stage and screen then, as Gledhill argues, brings into view 'the particular significance of this relationship for British culture (highlighting) the nature of the media as cultural spaces open to each other's products and practices' (Gledhill 2003: 178). Whilst Lacey (2003) is right to argue that a rejection of theatricality and embrace of 'realism' was one of the features that characterised the New Wave adaptation, there was also an attempt within both theatre and film to move away from realism and naturalism. Therefore, the film of *The Entertainer* attempted to use its real-life settings in ways that functioned symbolically, in the same way as the theatre play, but avoided being dominated by Olivier's performance by making Jean the key protagonist. Whereas film adaptations, such as *The Kitchen*, repurposed the theatricality that was deemed to have had such a deadening influence on the development of British cinema, and deployed it as a dynamic tool with which to expose the discontents of cinematic realism.

NOTES

1. For a more detailed discussion of how censorship affected the transition of stage plays to the screen, see Aldgate (1995).
2. According to Zahry-Levo (2010: 232) those films are: *Room at the Top* (1959), *Look Back in Anger* (1959), *The Entertainer* (1960), *Saturday Night and Sunday Morning* (1961), *A Taste of Honey* (1961), *A Kind of Loving* (1962), *The Loneliness of the Long Distance Runner* (1962), *This Sporting Life* (1963) and *Billy Liar* (1963).

REFERENCES

Aldgate, A. (1995), *Censorship and the Permissive Society: British Cinema and Theatre 1955–65*, London: Clarendon Press.
Anon (1961), *The Guardian*, 15 July.
Armes, R. (1978), *A Critical History of the British Cinema*, Oxford: Oxford University Press.
Brown, G. (1986), '"Sister of the stage": British film and British theatre', in C. Barr (ed.), *All Our Yesterdays: 90 Years of British Cinema*, London: British Film Institute, pp. 143–67.

Courtney, C. (1993), *Jocelyn Herbert: A Theatre Workbook*, London: Art Books International.
Elsaesser, T. (1972). 'Between style and ideology', *Monogram*, 3, 2–10.
Forrest, D. (2013). *Social Realism: Art, Nationhood and Politics*, Newcastle upon Tyne: Cambridge Scholars Publishing.
Gledhill, C. (2003), *Reframing British Cinema 1918–1928: Between Restraint and Passion*, London: British Film Institute.
Higson, A. (1984) 'Space, place, spectacle', *Screen*, 25, 2–21.
Hill, J. (1986), *Sex, Class and Realism: British Cinema 1956–1963*, London: British Film Institute.
Hjort, M. and MacKenzie, S. (2000), *Cinema and Nation*, Oxford: Routledge.
Houston, P. (1960), *Sight & Sound*, 29: 4.
Hutchings, P. (2001), 'Beyond the New Wave: Realism in British Cinema, 1959–63', in R. Murphy (ed.), *The British Cinema Book*, London: BFI, pp. 146–52.
Izod, J., Magee, K., Hannan, K. and Gourdin-Sangouard, I. (2012), *Lindsay Anderson: Cinema Authorship*, Manchester: Manchester University Press.
Keil, C. (2006), '"All the frame's a stage": (Anti-) theatricality and cinematic modernism', in A. Ackerman and M. Puchner (eds), *Against Theatre. Creative Destructions on the Modernist Stage*, Basingstoke: Palgrave Macmillan, pp. 76–91.
Lacey, S. (1995), *British Realist Theatre: The New Wave in its Contexts*, London: Routledge.
Lacey, S. (1996), 'Naturalism, poetic realism, spectacle: Wesker's "The Kitchen" in performance', *New Theatre Quarterly*, Cambridge University Press, 12: 47, 237–48.
Lacey, S. (2003), 'Too theatrical by half: film versions of *The Admirable Crichton* and *Look Back in Anger*', in I. Mackillop and N. Sinyard (eds), *British Cinema in the 1950s*, Manchester: Manchester University Press.
Miller, J. (1961), 'Review' [*The Kitchen*], *New Statesman*, 21 July.
Murphy, R. (2014), 'New morning: optimism and resilience in Tony Richardson's *A Taste of Honey* and *The Loneliness of the Long Distance Runner*', *Journal of British Cinema and Television*, 11: 2–3, 378–96.
Murray, A. (2006), *Into the Unknown: The Fantastic Life of Nigel Kneale*, London: Headpress.
Olivier, L. (1982), *Confessions of an Actor: The Autobiography*, London: Weidenfeld & Nicolson.
Osborne, J. (1991), *Almost a Gentleman: An Autobiography 1955–1966*, London: Faber & Faber.
Osborne, J. (1993), *Look Back in Anger* in *Plays: One*, London: Faber & Faber.
Palmer, R. B. and Bray, W. R. (eds) (2013), *Modern British Drama on Screen*, Cambridge: Cambridge University Press.
Perkins, V. F. (1962), 'The British cinema', *Movie*, 1, 2–7.
Rebellato, D. (1999), *1956 and All That: The Making of Modern British Drama*, London: Routledge.
Robinson, D. (1961), 'Stage screen and kitchen', *Financial Times*, 14 July.
Russell Taylor, J. (1961), 'Two on the set', *Sight & Sound*, 30: 2.
Shail, R. (2012), *Tony Richardson*, Manchester: Manchester University Press.

Shellard, D. (2000), *British Theatre since the War*, Trowbridge: Redwood.

Sulik, B. (1961), 'Review' [*The Kitchen*], *Tribune*, 21 July.

Taylor, B. F. (2006), *The British New Wave: A Certain Tendency*, Manchester: Manchester University Press.

Welsh, J. and Tibbetts, J. (1999), *The Cinema of Tony Richardson*, Albany: State University of New York Press.

Wesker, A (1960), 'Here is a film of pain and feeling', *The Tribune*, 19 August. Wesker, A. (1976), *The Kitchen: A Play in Two Parts with an Interlude*, in *Three Plays: The Kitchen: The Four Seasons: Their Very Own and Golden City*, Harmondsworth: Penguin.

Zhary-Levo, Y. (2010), 'Looking back at the British New Wave', *Journal of British Cinema and Television*, 7, 2: 232–47.

5. WHY WE DO NOT ADAPT JEAN RHYS

Sarah Artt

> Jean Rhys is the patron saint of girls, then women like me, who have always been so mute, cast aside, their subjectivity surrendered in the big novels, world. . . . Rhys who speaks for her mute vagabonds, her former (and present) selves, struggling from the bottom, sinking delirious in bottles of rouge, Pernod and barbituates – always another, please. The kept woman speaks back! (Kate Zambreno, *Heroines*)

Jean Rhys and her unlikeable female protagonists are dangerous and difficult to place; they defy our popular notions of relatable or likeable. It is therefore no surprise that Rhys has rarely been adapted for the screen. As Erica L. Johnson and Patricia Moran note in one of the few recent scholarly books devoted to Rhys, she is associated with global modernisms and cosmopolitanism, 'a philosophy that her characters are seen to both embody and reject' (2015: 6). This is one aspect that makes Rhys a writer whose work deserves to be read, adapted, seen and studied today. Although her work continues to evoke strong responses in readers, scholarly work on Rhys is sporadic. Adaptations can bring the work of neglected authors to the attention of new readers (both casual and scholarly), particularly when, as Jim Collins has noted, 'the literary adaptation exists in a dialogic relationship not just to the source novel but to a host of best-selling opera recordings, travel books, shelter magazines, and even cookbooks' (2010: 133). However, existing screen adaptations of Rhys do not lend themselves to this, nor are these adaptations particularly intertextual, in spite of *Wide Sargasso Sea*'s widely noted connection to Charlotte Brontë's *Jane Eyre*. This chapter will explore the failings of two of the existing adaptations: *Quartet* (1981) and *Wide Sargasso Sea* (2006), and suggest that there is now a greater appetite to see Rhys's difficult women on screen.

Elaine Savoury writes that 'both the plot and visual intensity of Rhys's writing lend themselves to the cinematic' (Savoury 2009: 43). Yet there has been a reluctance to adapt Rhys for the screen, in spite of her appeal to readers: 'readers embrace Rhys's strangeness and indeed, she inspires an almost cult-like following' (Johnson and Moran 2015: 8). This aspect of Rhys's limited reception within academia resonates with some of the ongoing debates surrounding fidelity criticism and the affective turn in film theory. Where notions of fidelity to a source have been rightly dismissed for their limited approach, which tends to privilege one medium over another, David Evan Richard notes: 'the stigma of fidelity has encouraged adaptation studies to be quick to dismiss the senses and emotional responses as if they were diametrically opposed to critical objectivity' (2018: 146). Richard's remarks are pertinent here, in considering Johnson and Moran's acknowledgement of readers' emotional responses to Rhys. This kind of affect can be a problem for the scholar attempting to achieve critical distance, but Richard's approach opens up other avenues for exploration. Attempting to find a way to acknowledge Rhys's affect poses a challenge to scholars and to adapters of her work. The stigma of emotional response has potentially limited the amount of scholarly engagement with Rhys's work, as well as its adaptation to the screen. What is required here is an approach to adaptation that is both personal, and critically rigorous.

In the wake of the critical success of adaptations that depict female protagonists struggling with the intensely personal ordeals of poverty, social precarity and powerlessness, ranging from the harrowing *The Handmaid's Tale* (Hulu 2017–) to the darkly comic *Fleabag* (BBC 2016–19) on television, and to films such as *Lady Macbeth* (Oldroyd 2016) with its grim, cold female protagonist, it feels as if Rhys's time has finally come. There is now a greater appetite for seeing what might once have been termed 'difficult women' on screen. In an age that is characterised by fractures in the debates around nation and gender, Rhys's narratives navigate vital ambivalences that intersect deeply with the personal, particularly with regard to origins, femininity and nationality; discourses that are much needed in the current political and cultural landscape.

Difficult, Unlikeable Women

Rhys's work is not just difficult in the sense that her protagonists are messy, uncooperative, vain and abject. The difficulty with Rhys is twofold, as Rishona Zimring identifies: 'None of the novels, and this has been one of their challenges to feminist readers, allows a triumphant genesis of female agency and transformation ... Nevertheless, they do allow for a dissonant feminine voice to emerge' (Zimring 2000: 226). It is this dissonant voice, and the lack of triumph experienced by her protagonists, that are so badly in need of revisiting by way of screen adaptation. Her women are sometimes monstrous, but not in the sense that Hélène Cixous suggests. This is not the joyful monstrousness of making trouble advocated in 'The Laugh of the Medusa', nor is it Pussy Riot's revolutionary dissidence. What is troubling about Rhys's protagonists is their sense of oppression, exhaustion and even the ways in which they may revel in their sense of incorrectness. Rhys's women are frequently monsters of loneliness and desperation; at times, their passivity is almost incomprehensible. And yet Johnson and Moran clearly acknowledge a feeling that resonates with my own experience of reading Rhys: '[u]niquely affective, her work evokes powerful feelings, gripping moods, emotions that are difficult to sort out, classify, account for' (Johnson and Moran 2015: 8). Rhys affords us the opportunity to engage with our difficult-to-sort-out thoughts and feelings. Writers such as Maggie Nelson, Kate Zambreno and So Mayer have begun to explore this terrain in their critical work, using the personal as a way into deeper critical engagement; Mayer writes about Jane Campion's *In the Cut*:

> And so New York was where I came to journey into death and to return, following the footsteps of a cinematic Orpheus: Franny, the protagonist of Jane Campion's *In the Cut*, adapted from Susanna Moore's controversial 1997 novel. Franny is a professor of creative writing and a writer, as I am; perhaps that's why I was so attracted to her path. (Mayer 2017)

This combination of the personal and of affect that Mayer employs in their essay is helpful in acknowledging the role of adaptation, and in terms of how I am locating Rhys's work and its introduction to new readers by way of adaptation within a long history of feminist literary archaeology. Rhys's affective power, and Mayer's personal connection to Campion's adaptation work, are important here, as this approach suggests something beyond the joy and tears typically attached to mainstream screen adaptations aimed at female-identified audiences. With Rhys, we do encounter to an extent what Rachel Carroll identifies as 'the desire to revisit and relive a prior cultural experience – as do all remakes and adaptations' (2009: 42) but in a way that permits us to reflect on matters of the personal as they relate to precarity and national identity.

In Rhys's first novel *Quartet* (1928) we meet one of her meekest protagonists, Marya Zelli. British by birth, and Polish by marriage, she is adrift in Paris in the late 1920s. An ex-chorus girl she is now married to Stephan Zelli, a Pole who works as a small-time art and antiques dealer. He promises her happiness and they lead a nomadic existence around Europe as Stephan buys and sells a variety of objects. One day, Marya comes back to their long-term hotel in Paris to find Stephan has been arrested. He is eventually charged with fraud and imprisoned, after which he will be expelled from France. With no money of her own, and Stephan unable to provide for her, Marya is taken up by a wealthy English expatriate couple Lois and H. J. Heidler, who invite her to live with them. HJ begins an affair with Marya, with Lois's knowledge. Marya is uncomfortable and conflicted about this arrangement and eventually breaks with the Heidlers. When Stephan is released from prison, Marya confronts him, and he knocks her unconscious when she threatens to phone the police. Stephan leaves her behind in Paris and the ending makes it unclear whether Marya is still alive. As Armstrong notes, Marya does not quite have the wherewithal of some of Rhys's later protagonists.

Without money, and without the knowledge of how to transform her beauty into anything more than subsistence, Marya's relationship to Paris changes from an that of English insider who has lived in the city for four years to, essentially, that of a foreigner without recourse to the city's authority, unable even to 'understand French' (Armstrong 2013: 181–2).

Marya is miserable and afraid, but, unlike the downbeat chorus girls of Rhys's later novel *Voyage in the Dark* (1934), she is unwilling to openly exchange her erotic performance for money or other forms of security. Marya's passivity and her lack of pragmatism are part of what make her so easy for the Heidlers to exploit. Elaine Savoury remarks on the conundrum of Marya's characterisation:

> Confronted with first person narrative, many ordinary readers want to feel some attraction to the vice that interprets the story. But Marya is more remote than passionate, emotionally and morally confused and often careless. The reader needs to appreciate the novel's style rather than looking to like the main character. (Savoury 2009: 31)

This acknowledgement of setting aside or expanding the notion of likeability in relation to female characters is part of Rhys's affective pull with readers, 'a demimonde of the girl that Jean Rhys writes so well' (Zambreno 2012: 151), and is an idea only just now gaining ground with regard to screen adaptations. Just as there have been plenty of unlikeable male protagonists that fascinate readers and viewers, there is also scope for this with regard to women, and there is now evidence of a viable audience for these characters. In addition to the earlier examples listed, we might also consider the critical success of authors such as Ottessa Moshfegh (*My Year of Rest and Relaxation*) and Tara Isabella Burton (*Social Creature*: 'I've Seen the Future, Baby; It Is Murder'), whose works also deal with difficult, unlikeable female protagonists. Moshfegh's protagonist in particular, in her quest to stay unconscious for as long as possible, is perhaps the current age's version of Rhysian passivity, taking 'trazodone, and Ambien and Nembutal until I fell asleep again' (Moshfegh 2018: 1). One night, Marya is told 'You're a victim. There's no endurance in your face' (Rhys 1977: 58), and later she experiences 'sleep . . . like falling into a black hole' (58) and later still, she experiments with taking veronal in order to sleep for as long as possible. Marya might be considered unlikeable because of her passivity, and yet these characterisations address the ongoing problem frequently articulated by female creative practitioners: the pressure to create narratives that feature overtly heroic women. Neither Marya nor the unnamed protagonist of *My Year of Rest and Relaxation* could be described as heroic, but they are fascinating. Their lack of resilience in the face of tragedy and upheaval, and their inability to deal effectively with the whims of fortune, are particularly refreshing to audiences accustomed to the contradictory demands of a postfeminist culture. These protagonists do not fight against the system and as readers and viewers we are forced to confront the consequences of their passivity.

In Rhys's last novel, *Wide Sargasso Sea* (1966), we encounter a more spirited protagonist who is nonetheless crushed by patriarchy. A postcolonial prequel to Charlotte Brontë's *Jane Eyre*, the story concerns Antoinette Cosway, a young Creole woman who grows up in Jamaica in the 1830s and 1840s where she experiences a traumatic childhood of genteel poverty on a decaying plantation. Once her mother remarries, Antoinette is sent to a convent school in Spanish Town. Her stepfather makes Antoinette an heiress, so at seventeen a marriage is arranged for her with the younger son of an aristocratic English family (the Rochester figure). They marry and honeymoon in the Windward Islands at a small house Antoinette loves from childhood, where they become immersed in a sensual isolation. The husband struggles with what he sees as the strange, unfamiliar landscape, and his tense relationship with the black servants, particularly the powerful Christophine, Antoinette's childhood nurse, who oversees the household of their honeymoon house at Granbois. During the early weeks of their marriage, the husband also begins to question Antoinette's peculiar, fascinating beauty. He hears rumours about Antoinette's past: that her mother was mentally ill, and that Antoinette had mixed race lovers before her marriage. He begins to doubt Antoinette's sincerity, and to be suspicious of her allure. Antoinette becomes increasingly unhappy and begs Christophine for a love potion: 'But Christophine, if he, my husband, could come to me one night. Once more, I would make him love me' (Rhys 1993: 93). After Christophine fails to dissuade Antoinette, she reluctantly produces the potion. A final night of unruly passion makes Antoinette's husband fear she has tried to poison him and he insists they return to England, where he imprisons Antoinette in the attic of his house. The story begins and ends with a disoriented Antoinette wandering the house at night, before setting the fire that blinds Mr Rochester in *Jane Eyre*. While Antoinette is in many ways far less compliant than Marya, she too may be perceived as unlikeable for the way she clings to the importance of love and romance, and her desperation to preserve her marriage.

Multilingual Nomads

In addition to the unlikeability of Rhys's protagonists, they also tend to be both nomadic and multilingual, and their liminal status is frequently a source of anxiety. This anxiety is expressed by the protagonists themselves, and by those around them. For the protagonists, this anxiety is deeply personal, exacerbated by economic precarity and it transforms their cosmopolitan multilinguality into the kind of uncertainty that marks them easily as outsiders. Antoinette expresses this in heartbreakingly stark terms: 'I often wonder who I am and where is my country and where do I belong and why was I ever born at all' (Rhys 1966: 85). Here, Rhys exposes how Antoinette's uncertain status creates anxiety for her and for those around her, as she is taunted with racial epithets. This uncertainty extends to Antoinette's positioning in terms of race, class and language, and is directly related to her husband's growing hatred and resentment: 'Creole of pure English descent she may be, but they are not English or European either' (Rhys 1966: 56). The husband makes this observation as they make the journey to their honeymoon location at Granbois, indicating that the seeds of mistrust are already there, and his inability to place Antoinette into a clear and consistent category registers as a problem for him.

Nearly all of Rhys's writing depicts characters who are multilingual, and though mostly written in English, her work frequently contains French phrases or in the case of *Wide Sargasso Sea* there are words in patois, or clear acknowledgements of linguistic gaps, such as this one: 'The two women stood in the doorway of the hut gesticulating, talking not English but the debased French patois they use in this island' (Rhys 1966: 56–7). The fact that there are, as yet, almost no scholarly editions of her work (there is a Norton Critical Edition of *Wide Sargasso Sea*) complicates matters in terms of accessibility for a monolingual anglophone audience. Elaine Savoury has suggested that particularly in Rhys's European novels there is a sense that 'monolingual expectations were not going to be indulged by Rhys' (Savoury 2009: 32). This presents a certain challenge to the reader, and to the implied adaptor of Rhys's work. In terms of the adaptations discussed here, both are relatively conservative on this score. Where *Quartet* offers some French dialogue with subtitles, the adaptation of *Wide Sargasso Sea* offers no patois dialogue at all. This flattening out of the complexity of Rhys's work has distinct consequences when it comes to the question of nationality and identity. Both adaptations privilege English as the dominant language, and present accented speech as a sign of the female protagonist's naiveté, rather than sophistication. This sense of 'Englishes', or of additional languages spoken imperfectly, is something Rhys's work brings to the fore, calling attention to the sophisticated mobility of her characters. But when the work is adapted to the screen, these are used as markers of vulnerability, and can potentially reinforce perceptions that individuals with imperfect English, or who do not speak in Received Pronunciation, are inherently suspicious.

With their uncertain nationalities and multilingualism, we could easily say that Marya and Antoinette are citizens of the world, a once-celebratory phrase that has since taken on more problematic undertones, ever since former UK Prime Minister Theresa May, in her Conservative Party Conference address in 2016, declared us 'citizens of nowhere'. Marya and Antoinette are vulnerable in the sense that they don't quite belong and they have no stable nationality in an era where marriage meant the wife acquiring her husband's nationality. Neither character has the money or the skills that will allow her to achieve economic stability on her own terms. They are trapped by uncertainty and convention, but also by apparatus. Both Marya and Antoinette are denied any sense of belonging that might have been attached to their national identities because, for the state and specifically for the English men they encounter, they have become suspect with regard to their status. In both adaptations, Marya and Antoinette speak accomplished, but accented English, marking them out as definitively not English, in contrast to the English men who exploit them. Avtar Brah notes, 'According to racialised imagination, the former colonial Natives and their descendants settled in Britain are not British precisely because they are not seen as being native to Britain' (2003: 623). Marya, having removed herself from Britain as a geographical location, and through her marriage to a Polish national, is seen by the Heidlers as having destabilised herself; she is not British, and therefore exploitable. Antoinette is also seen as destabilised precisely because neither her 'Englishness' nor her 'Europeanness' are deemed sufficient by her husband. In these scenarios, it is men who control and judge women's national identity, through language, marriage, sex and money.

This limbo-like state experienced by both Marya and Antoinette becomes linked to their unlikeable status and their vulnerability. Marya and Antoinette show us that to be indeterminately placed within nations and within languages is to be held hostage to the whims of others. This is one of the things that makes Rhys's work so painful and so necessary to our present moment. Her work deserves skilful, nuanced adaptation because it deals directly with the personal consequences of too rigid notions of national identity, and how that might impact on an individual's mobility and economic precarity.

This precarity is further contextualised in *Quartet*: 'Marya, you must understand, had not been suddenly and ruthlessly transplanted from solid comfort to the hazards of Monmartre. Nothing like that. Truth to say, she was used to a lack of solidity and of fixed backgrounds' (Rhys 1928: 14). Marya grows accustomed to an itinerant life as a chorus girl until she meets Stephan, who offers her greater stability. When he ends up in prison, he tells her one of the reasons he was convicted was that 'my lawyer didn't know his métier. Instead of defending me, he told the court I spoke six languages. A stupid affair at Brussels was referred to. This did me in quite' (Rhys 1928: 38). The implication is that Stephan's status as a nomadic European figure with many languages at his disposal is seen as particularly suspicious. His sophisticated, seemingly cosmopolitan status helps to criminalise him further. As Christina Brizolakis has noted:

> in placing estrangement at the centre of her work, she [Rhys] does so less from the perspective of the expatriate who pulverises and refashions metropolitan aesthetic codes than from that of the ethnic, or ethnicized stranger – the subaltern rather than the elite cosmopolitan – who is denied a passport within metropolitan culture. (Britzolakis 2007: 458)

What for many would be considered a marker of cosmopolitan facility – multilingualism – is here used to deny Stephan his liberty, and to then expel him from France at the end of his sentence. In Rhys, potentially cosmopolitan figures become subaltern when they run foul of the state, or come into contact with exploitative expatriates. Rhys's work is precise in pinpointing subtle forms of prejudice that are now very familiar, particularly when it comes to the insidious discourses that continue to characterise matters of immigration in the UK.

Elaine Savoury, writing specifically about the use of language in *Quartet*, notes that Rhys is adept at gesturing towards multilingualism as a fact of existence for her characters, and we see this continued in *Wide Sargasso Sea*:

> the text foregrounds multilingual, that is, transnational life, so the reader must think about which language is being spoken at a given time. Stephan is Polish, speaks English, and adopts an American accent when nervous, which is an interesting sign that he has had reason to conceal his national identity. Marya and Stephan mainly use French with each other. But the emotional trauma of visiting him in prison makes Marya unable to speak it. The text emphasises languages and accents (French, English, American). . . Rhys includes writers and others who speak French, made perfectly understandable in the context of the narrative without the necessity of translation. They particularly would have alerted the reader in the late 1920s to the fact that this is not entirely familiar space and that the British reader's own likely monolingual expectations were not going to be indulged by Rhys. (Savoury 2009: 32)

This perhaps more than anything else is the challenge presented when adapting Rhys, or indeed attempting to render her of interest to new (monolingual) audiences. In order to adapt any of her work, we are forced to acknowledge this linguistic tension: the fact that her characters are nomadic (and not always willingly so), multilingual, cosmopolitan and unhappy. In addition, Savoury suggests that for some readers, her texts may be perceived as a hostile space for the monolingual, whereas for the multilingual these texts feel very different; indeed, they feel familiar in the way they capture a sense of being sometimes out of place, and on the back foot, of being forever asked about one's accent, or origins. Rhys's texts also capture the multivalent pleasures of wrestling with one's additional language(s) and how this might impact on a personal sense of identity in a variety of ways.

To take a more recent example of a novel that also makes use of multiple languages and accents, consider Chimanda Ngozi Adichi's *Purple Hibiscus* (2003): there are many instances of code switching between English and Igbo. Not all the phrases are translated, and yet the book has been incredibly popular and widely read. But the reader is left to her own devices as to how to make sense of these words and phrases. The popularity and accessibility of Adichie's work suggests that it is indeed possible to live with the idea that not everything is intended to be legible to the monolingual English speaker; that one can live with and appreciate these uncertainties. This too is Rhysian affect, like Adichie, the linguistic landscape Rhys evokes may leave the reader with difficult-to-sort-through feelings.

On *Quartet* (1981)

The film adaptation of *Quartet* was made by the Merchant Ivory team in 1981 (before their successful run at E. M. Forster), and stars Isabelle Adjani as Marya and Anthony Higgins as Stephan, while the Heidlers are played by Maggie Smith and Alan Bates. One interesting and not insignificant change we encounter in the film adaptation, is that 'Marya Zelli, aged 28 years, British by birth, Polish by marriage' (Rhys 1928: 29) shifts to being rumoured to be a Creole from Martinique, and then Polish by marriage. She is also played by biracial French actor, Isabelle Adjani. In the novel, Marya is identified by her national origins as British and Polish, and by the fact that she speaks French and English; but with no further remarks about her race or ethnicity we are left to presume her whiteness. The film's additional marking out of Marya as 'exotic' (as she is termed by one of the Heidlers' friends) in terms of her linguistic and national origins aligns her more closely with both Rhys herself and with Antoinette, the white Creole heiress of *Wide Sargasso Sea*. Aligning the female author with her characters is a common tactic, not only in terms of the biographical criticism that surrounds Rhys (see Britzolakis 2007 and

Port 2010, for example), but also in terms of the way living women writers are often expected to align with the values of their female protagonists. Rhys certainly did occupy some of the same categories as her female protagonists (she also worked as a chorus girl, and was born in Dominica; and virtually every short author biography that prefaces her work mentions these facts), and the first film adaptation of her work offers up additional alterations for Marya that attempt to consolidate this alignment further.

In the film, Marya is played as a damaged innocent who does not seem to know quite what is happening to her. This renders her conventionally sympathetic but fails to acknowledge the messier circumstances in which her affair with HJ begins. In the novel, the circumstances of HJ's declaration of erotic obsession are quite astonishing:

> Your [bedroom] door is open because I come up every night and open it. Then I look at you and go away again. One does meaningless things like that when one is tortured by desire . . . I've been watching you; I watched you tonight and now I know that somebody else will get you if I don't. You're that sort. (Rhys 1977: 57)

In response to this Marya feels 'a despair and a kind of hard rage' (Rhys 1977: 57). While the film includes HJ's speech as part of the dialogue, it is delivered in a loud nightclub, just after Marya has ingested what appears to be amyl nitrate. Marya's POV spins, and she's taken to the bar by her American friend Cairn. This spurs HJ's jealousy, and he possessively hurries the dizzy Marya away to a mirrored hallway where he delivers the above observations. Marya's reaction in the film seems more annoyance than anything else, though she does tell HJ 'You're abominably rude and stupid. You've no idea how other people feel.' Yet this reaction does not seem to diminish her interest in HJ, and she appears to be simultaneously repelled and seduced by him, an aspect that is very consistent with the tone of the novel. Shortly afterwards, when HJ enters her bedroom and they kiss for the first time, Marya declares 'I'm so scared', and perhaps she is – afraid of HJ, and of what she will do to survive and assuage her own fear, so she attaches herself to the Heidlers because it means temporary protection. Later in the novel, HJ and Lois discuss Marya as being a source of amusement for them, saying, 'she ought to sing for her supper' (Rhys 1928: 67), which is more or less what she does by posing for Lois's paintings, helping Lois with her make-up and serving as HJ's latest mistress. I offer these observations not as an argument for fidelity, but to point out the complexity that surrounds this ultimately very disturbing arrangement. The Merchant Ivory adaptation gestures at these aspects, but were the story to be adapted now, we might find an even greater readiness to explore Marya's abjection, not just through dialogue, but also through performance and framing.

In some ways, the casting of Bates as HJ in contrast to the much younger Adjani helps with our sympathies: he is far older, he is not conventionally handsome, and we are unclear about Marya's attraction to him. The film's isolated moment of voiceover is puzzling in this regard – it is the only moment we are privy to Marya's thoughts – and it takes places while she and Lois are sharing intimacies. Marya thinks: 'it's no use talking to Lois about Stephan or how things were when I met him. Women like Lois, who've always had money just don't know or understand what it's like for someone like me who's never had any.' In Rhys's novel, Marya is more aware of the reality of her situation in her liaison with HJ. She thinks to herself, 'But of course it wasn't a love affair. It was a fight. A ruthless, three-cornered fight' (Rhys 1928: 91). One of their sexual encounters is described as follows: 'she was quivering and abject in his arms, like some unfortunate dog abashing itself before its master' (Rhys 1928: 102). The way Adjani's face and gestures move from vulnerable, to petulant, to guarded as she navigates her interactions with HJ, Lois and Stephan is very subtle, but the question of how to articulate these important but hidden thoughts is certainly a fraught one. It is these moments in Rhys that offer up 'emotions that are difficult to sort out, classify, account for' (Johnson and Moran 2015: 8), and that are so vital to the appeal and the importance of Rhys's narratives in terms of enriching representation of the female experience, precisely because, as Zambreno declares, Rhys 'writes the books about tarts that do not lie' (2012: 150). These moments are personal to Marya, to the reader/viewer, and Adjani's physical performance attempts to capture this, which is perhaps why the moment of voiceover remains such an odd choice in the film. One of the ways in which recent texts have overcome this problem of conveying inner thoughts is through a more deliberate and consistent use of voiceover and fourth-wall breaking narration, as we see in *Fleabag*, though Agnès Varda's *Cléo 5 à 7* also deploys intermittent voiceover to give access to Cléo's thoughts. Direct address and voiceover serve their purpose in those respective screen texts, by providing clear and consistent access to the female protagonist's point of view. Another way of approaching this problem is by creating a more deliberate alignment between the protagonist and the figure of the author, and potentially further championing the idea that it is valid to engage in writing and representation that acknowledge the personal. This technique is similar to what Rachel Carroll has described as the possibility of 'fidelity as a mode of cultural practice [that] can be complex and productive' (2009: 40), and it reinforces the personal as a key aspect of Rhys's autobiographical work. While Marya and Antoinette share aspects of Rhys's origins in both these adaptations, we might also consider the consequences of making them explicitly writerly figures. Were we to witness Marya or Antoinette keeping a journal or a notebook, we might then gain access to these thoughts they feel unable to share. Their outward show of passivity might be maintained, while suggesting a more silent, though still satisfying form of resistance by offering a visual validation of this kind of female experience.

Despite Savoury's plea that we not go looking to like the main character in *Quartet*, this does not absolve the reader or viewer from attempting to sympathise with Marya's predicament. The film tries to create a sympathetic victim out of Marya, but there is no consistent sense of her ambivalence towards the Heidlers. What Rhys offers us is Marya's thinking about her own situation – her feelings of powerlessness, exhaustion and resignation. These may well be aspects that are perceived as unlikeable (as readers and viewers we want her to help herself), but it is all the more important that these feelings be shown and explored. Otherwise, Marya is just another victim to be rescued.

On *Wide Sargasso Sea* (2006)

The 2006 television adaptation of *Wide Sargasso Sea* tells the story over ninety minutes and omits the novel's early sections dealing with Antoinette's childhood. The husband is named Edward and is played by Rafe Spall and Antoinette is played by Rebecca Hall, while Christophine is played by Nina Sosanya. Like the *Quartet* adaptation, the 2006 *Wide Sargasso Sea* deploys a similar strategy in its portrayal of the protagonist as a somewhat whimsical, slightly sheltered innocent. Antoinette is dropped, by a vaguely unscrupulous step-brother who no longer wants to act as her guardian, into the hands of a husband who wants financial independence from his father. Antoinette seems to have no guile at all, particularly as she enthusiastically shares her love of Granbois, the childhood retreat and 'sweet honeymoon house' with her new husband. Later, when their relationship is troubled, Antoinette requests a love charm from Christophine, but this is prompted by unhappy confusion at her husband's sudden change towards her. In Rhys's novel, Antoinette is not just unhappy, but deeply afraid of her husband and in this sense, she is more like Marya. She tells Christophine: 'I do not know why but so afraid. All the time. Help me' (Rhys 1993: 96). This implies a similar kind of fear as that experienced by Marya, a fear of what she will do to survive, to comfort herself, to try and gain some measure of peace with her childhood demons. Even when Christophine gives her the charm, Antoinette reflects 'she did not want to do this. I forced her with my ugly money' (Rhys 1966: 97). This too aligns her with Marya in Rhys's *Quartet*, who can assess her relationship with the Heidlers as a fight rather than a love affair. In the novel, Antoinette is portrayed as confident and knowing in the first days of her honeymoon. On arrival at Granbois, she tells her husband 'This is my place and everything is on our side' (Rhys 1966: 62). In the novel, the phrase 'sweet honeymoon house' (Rhys 1966: 53) is delivered in a mocking tone by Amélie, the black servant girl the husband later seduces. The adaptation replicates this scenario, but only after the phrase is first delivered in a sincere way by

Antoinette. When Amélie (Lorraine Burroughs) delivers the line 'I hope you will be very happy, sir, in your sweet honeymoon house' in the adaptation, it establishes Amélie's flirtatious nature, and faithfully renders her as she's described in the novel by Antoinette's husband: 'sly, spiteful, malignant perhaps, like much else in this place' (Rhys 1966: 55), observations that reinforce the husband's suspicion of difference.

Where *Quartet*'s adaptation adds layers to Marya's identity, setting her further apart from the white, English, upper-class Heidlers, *Wide Sargasso Sea* suggests no ambiguity around Antoinette's race, by casting the white British actor Rebecca Hall. In addition, the authoritative Christophine is played as oddly subdued by Nina Sosanya. The adaptation fails to suggest the constant sense of threat and unease that characterises the narrative, and much like the problems with the Merchant Ivory *Quartet*, this is down to the absence of the female protagonist's point of view. The decisions taken with regard to casting, language and accent mean that Antoinette's subjectivity cannot be fully explored here. Her difference needs to be more fully marked out for us by making effective use of these key processes. Clumsy attempts to convey Edward's discomfort with the landscape and to evoke 'that green menace' (Rhys 1966: 123) are offered with amplified insect sound and quick zoom shots of bamboo. There is little sense of Antoinette's point of view apart from the sequences in England that bookend the story. The shift from the couple's powerful sexual attraction to boredom and disorder is jarring, precisely because Edward's repulsion at the foreign landscape is not sufficiently built up, nor is it connected to Antoinette and Christophine by the imagery on offer.

Nowhere is the adaptation's unhelpful adherence to fidelity to Rhys's text more obvious than in one of the numerous sex scenes. Ecstatic in her discovery of sensual attraction and bodily pleasure, Antoinette questions why she now wants to live, and Edward says it is because he has wished it. Antoinette worries that this could mean Edward will change his mind and that this in turn will directly impact her well-being. The adaptation has Antoinette offer up the following abject line 'say die and I will die' during sex, indicating that Edward is in complete control of her, including her orgasm. In the novel, the same line is followed by the husband's observation: 'I watched her die many times. In my way, not in hers. In sunlight, in shadow, by moonlight, by candlelight. In the long afternoons when the house was empty . . . very soon she was as eager for what's called loving as I was' (Rhys 1966: 77). The adaptation fails to contextualise the couple's erotic attraction as tinged with dissipation and decadence, nor does it suggest that their desire for one another will have an ephemeral quality that will not sustain the relationship. The screen adaptation is at pains to show their initial attraction to one another through scenes of tender, hesitant flirtation, and later their passionate lovemaking at Granbois. But it cannot articulate the gradual dissolution of passion, how they enter into a kind of marital abjection where they are both drawn to and repelled by one another – suddenly Edward is drinking himself into a stupor, and Antoinette is lying in bed all day. This failure to articulate Antoinette's point of view is a problem, but so is the failure to articulate Edward's. The positioning of Antoinette's status as white woman who is neither British, European nor Carribean impacts on the ability to fully convey the narrative's motivations for the unravelling relationship. In addition, the 2006 *Wide Sargasso Sea* fails to portray the painful complexity of the husband's relationship to masculinity and class, just as it fails to offer Antoinette as anything other than a manic pixie dream girl turned mad woman in the attic.

Conclusion

Kate Zambreno in her book *Heroines* (2012), a meditation on the neglected women of modernism, demonstrates that the personal can sit alongside critical rigour. Rhys is frequently referenced in this work that advocates for a radical refocalising of the 'toxic girls' of modernism and surrealism. Zambreno champions Rhys, and notes that like many of her contemporaries she was unnecessarily pathologised, and her work neglected for being too personal: 'Jean Rhys who became an author out of heartbreak and intense emotion, like girls on their LiveJournals or Tumblrs' (2012: 244). This auto-theoretical approach is the ideal method for examining Rhys's work, and it is one that ought to be considered in terms of potential future adaptations, aiming for a more experimental, essayistic approach to adapting Rhys, as well as making space for 'giving voice to the girl who is always a character in the novel' (Zambreno 2012: 150).

We might also consider what space Rhys's work offers for exploring an idea suggested by John Caughie writing about Lynne Ramsay's film *Morvern Callar* (2002) and the way in which the female protagonist's journey from Scotland to Spain offers up 'a space for difference ... not just trying on national identities but imagining not having one' (Caughie 2007: 103). For Rhys's protagonists, being without a clear identity is a problem, but for Caughie, and as I have suggested elsewhere (Artt 2013), the freedom portrayed by films like *Morvern Callar* indicate there are other ways of representing and thinking through nationality and mobility. What we tend to lack is nuance when dealing with these matters. What I'd like to see is an adaptation that accommodates Rhys's multilingual and mixed race characters. I want Antoinette and Marya to be conflicted and uninterested in following rules. Let us heed Zimring's call for a dissonant feminine voice that leaps off the page and onto our screens, and for stories that allow us to sort through our difficult feelings by allowing us to fully witness the anxieties of Antoinette and Marya, and the terrifying uncertainty they experience as a result of the ways they fail to adhere to clear categories regarding language and origins. This is what's missing and that's why we don't adapt Jean Rhys.

References

Adichie. C. N. (2003), *Purple Hibiscus*, London: HarperCollins.
Artt, S. (2013), 'Being inside her silence: silence and performance in Lynne Ramsay's *Morvern Callar*', *Scope: An Online Journal of Film and Television Studies*, February, 25.
Armstrong, D. (2013), 'Reclaiming the left bank', in M. Wilson and K. L. Johnson (eds), *Rhys Matters: New Critical Perspectives*, London: Palgrave Macmillan, pp. 169–85.
Brah, A. (2003), 'Diaspora, border and transnational identities', in R. Lewis and S. Mills (eds), *Feminist Postcolonial Theory*, Edinburgh: Edinburgh University Press, pp. 613–34.
Burton, T. I. (2018). *Social Creature*, London: Bloomsbury.
Britzolakis, C. (2007). '"This way to the exhibition": genealogies of urban spectacle in Jean Rhys's interwar fiction', *Textual Practice*, 21: 3. 457–82.
Carroll, R. (2009). 'Affecting fidelity: adaptation, fidelity and affect in Todd Haynes's *Far From Heaven*', in R. Carroll (ed.), *Adaptation in Contemporary Culture*, London: Continuum, pp. 34–45.
Caughie, J. (2007). '*Morvern Callar*, art cinema and the monstrous archive', *Scottish Studies Review*, Spring, 8: 1, 101–15.
Collins, J. (2010). *Bring on the Books For Everybody: How Literary Culture Became Popular Culture*. Durham, NC: Duke University Press.
Johnson, E. L. and Moran, P. (eds). (2015), *Jean Rhys: 21st Century Critical Responses*, Edinburgh: Edinburgh University Press.
May, T. (2016), Keynote speech to Conservative Party Conference, *The Independent*, October, <https://www.independent.co.uk/news/uk/politics/theresa-may-speech-tory-conference-2016-in-full-transcript-a7346171.html> (accessed 5 September 2018).
Mayer, S. (2017), 'Mourning and Manahatta'. *Verso Books Blog*, <https://www.verso-books.com/blogs/3455-mourning-and-mannahatta> (accessed 28 February 2019).
Moshfegh, O. (2018), *My Year of Rest and Relaxation*, London: Penguin.
Port, C. (2010), '"Money, for the night is coming": Jean Rhys and Gendered economies of ageing', *Women: A Cultural Review*, 12: 2, 204–17.
Quartet. Dir. James Ivory, 1981.
Rhys, J. (1977 [1928]), *Quartet*, London: Penguin.
Rhys, J. (1993 [1966]), *Wide Sargasso Sea*, London: Penguin.
Richard. D. E. (2018), 'Film phenomenology and adaptation: the "fleshly dialogue" of Jane Campion's *In the Cut*', *Adaptation*, 11: 2, 144–58.
Savoury, E. (2009), *Cambridge Introduction to Jean Rhys*, Cambridge: Cambridge Cambridge University Press.
Zambreno, K. (2012), *Heroines*, Semiotexte.
Zimring, R. (2000), 'The make-up of Jean Rhys's fiction', *Novel: A Forum on Fiction*, 33: 2, 212–34.

PART III

RE-ENVISIONING THE NATIONAL IMAGINARY

6. 'TO SEE OURSELS AS ITHERS SEE US': TEXTUAL, INDIVIDUAL AND NATIONAL OTHER-SELVES IN *UNDER THE SKIN*

Robert Munro

In Robert Burns's 'To a Louse' (2001 [1786]), the narrator reflects upon the sight of a louse upon the head of a pompous woman in a church. The host body is unaware of its alien invader, and Burns's narrator cannot help but reflect upon the impropriety of the louse marauding upon its aristocratic body. By the end of the poem the entire congregation of the church titters at the haughty woman with the louse on her head, leading Burns to reflect:

> O wad some Pow'r the giftie gie us
> To see oursels as ithers see us! (2001 [1786]: 133)

Burns's poem is a call for greater self-awareness and objectivity, a desire that we can view our affectations and pretensions from a distance. The congregation has gained this at the expense of the woman with the louse in her hair. They have gained a little greater insight into their selves by their look at an 'other', the haughty woman, whose lack of self-awareness causes their mirth. In this chapter I examine the film *Under the Skin* (Glazer 2013) which performs a meditation on selves, others and other-selves in its depiction of an alien predator in the form of a human female who begins to explore its (her) potential to adopt a human, and female, consciousness with fatal consequences. I will begin by exploring Hegel's work on self-consciousness and his dialectic on self and other which, I argue, is one level to read the film's narrative concern as outlined above.

Introduction

In his definitive work, *The Phenomenology of Spirit* (1807), Hegel advanced the problem of consciousness as outlined by René Descartes, whose famous appropriation 'I think therefore I am' proposed to solve the problem of epistemology by asserting that mind and matter were separate entities. In this sense human consciousness was independent from the materiality of the human body; it arrived from a greater power. As discussed by Pippin (2010), this led to the problem of how these two distinct entities interacted with one another, which was elaborated upon by Immanuel Kant's description of the subject–object relationship. Kant developed a theory of self-consciousness which argued that in order to bridge the subject–object divide, an awareness of the self as a subject was crucial to apprehending a material object that was distinct from the self. Hegel's advancement on Kant's work was to further dissolve the dualistic boundaries that Kant's work arguably still perpetuated. Hegel stated that in order to achieve true self-consciousness, the self had to recognise processes of self-consciousness in others. It is this mutual recognition between self and other that leads to self-consciousness as described in Burns's poem, and in this sense, Hegel proposed that the subject–object was unified, rather than two separate complexly related entities. Hegel articulated a formulation of consciousness that took in the whole of social interaction, and argued that the objects created by subjects, and the consciousness of their creation and cultural and social meanings, evolved and mutated depending on the era of their use. Schalk's (2011) survey of the ways in which Hegel's self/other description of consciousness was adopted by W. E. B. Du Bois shows that a process of double consciousness can often be at work in which the self can be both Self and Other simultaneously. Du Bois wrote of the experience of being black in the United States at the turn of the twentieth century, and how the recognition of being both black *and* American required a double consciousness, which at once saw the self as it would be seen by others, i.e. white American. Schalk extends this to discuss the 'Other-Self', where:

> [it] becomes possible to explore how the self can triangulate via a force which causes the self to identify with or behave as an other so that there then becomes a spectrum of relatedness between self and other, between which lies the other-self. (2011: 200)

In this chapter I discuss *Under the Skin*'s exploration of other-selves in three related ways. First, I explore the process of adaptation made apparent by the discourses surrounding the film's production, exhibition and reception, elaborating upon Hutcheon's (2006: 174) argument that adaptations display the ability 'to be at once both self and Other'. Second, I discuss the narrative trajectory of the film, analysing its relaying of the development of consciousness in its alien protagonist through several key scenes in which the alien-self becomes aware of the human-other to form a conception of itself as an other-self in a particularly traumatic way. This is allied with Du Bois's explanation of double consciousness, as the film explores the alien's recognition of being both human *and* female, which I argue is what results in the traumatic closure of the narrative. Third, I examine how the text explores Scotland's sense of national (self)consciousness, which seems apt for this explanation of the other-self, as a nation that sees itself frequently through an and/or binary of Scottishness and Britishness in the contemporary period, as explored by Connor (2016).

Textual Other-selves, or the Adaptation as Both Self and Other

An alien in the form of an alluring female human, with a plummy English accent, stalks and seduces men in the misty wilds of the Scottish Highlands, seeking to transport them back to her home planet with malicious intent. The film in question is not *Under the Skin*, but *Devil Girl from Mars* (MacDonald 1954), a low-budget, B-movie British science fiction film. Its central plot is repurposed in a very different mode in the film, providing the focus for this chapter: Jonathan Glazer's interpretation of a similar B-movie premise in *Under the Skin*. This adaptation of Michel Faber's novel retains the central premise of that text in its focus on an alien inhabiting a female form who preys upon men, picking them up in her vehicle before they meet a grisly end. I begin by discussing the novel, before examining how the film adaptation can be seen as both other and self, in Hutcheon's (2006) terms, and conclude by discussing how this can be developed to discuss film adaptations as other-selves.

Michel Faber's novel explores the problematic relationship our species has with the planet that has given rise to our existence. It is narrated in a flatness of tone by an alien visitor to the Scottish Highlands, Isserley. Isserley has been sent to earth to work in the harvesting and processing of vodsel meat (voddisin) for her species back on her home planet. In the novel, *homo sapiens* are vodsels, while the aliens self-identify as human beings. *Under the Skin*'s producer James Wilson describes the novel as a 'vegetarian horror story' (FilmNation 2014), and this reading of the text is given further credence by Faber, who states: 'The things that we do now to animals in order to produce a certain quality of meat . . . they're really science fiction things that we do to them' (Hogan 2000). However, this central theme of the novel is not apparent in the film adaptation. While Faber's novel examines the difference between the human and the non-human animal, as I will discuss shortly, Glazer's film shifts the perspective to examine the difference between the human and the non-human alien. Glazer clarifies that this is how he interpreted the novel by saying that the book's driving force 'was to do with eating meat, and it was a satire on corporate greed and crime . . . that wasn't that part that resonated with me at all' (Tobias 2014). While Faber's novel occasionally affords the reader an interior insight into the thoughts of the abducted men, the film adaptation refutes this approach, and without voiceover narration we are not given access to Isserley's thought processes in the film. Therefore, while Faber's novel uses language to conflate the difference between humans and animals by using aliens as an allegorical device, the film instead wonders what it is that makes us human: what is essential about human consciousness that an alien visitor to earth would struggle to apprehend?

Faber's novel drip-feeds the reader information as to who (and what) Isserley is, and why she picks up male hitchhikers by the side of the road. As Dillon's (2011) analysis shows, one of the subtle clues provided by Faber as to the purpose of Isserley's preying is in his use of language and third person narration to convey her perception of our planet and the vodsels who inhabit it. Faber's linguistic reversal, in calling the alien species 'human', and the human species 'vodsel', is one method identified by Dillon (2011: 139) by which Faber performs a 'crucial textual method of destabilising the reassuring divisions that we, the readers, as a species draw between ourselves and the animals we eat, experiment upon, or otherwise do "justified" violence to'. Dillon writes that discourse has been central to the creation of difference between the human and the non-human, and Faber's novel repurposes this discourse:

> While the renaming of human beings as vodsels serves to expose the function of discourse in general in creating, and challenging, species differentiation, the text's rhetorical devices demonstrate how this can occur in one particular way – that is, in and through figurative language. (2011: 141)

Dillon (2011) points to the early parts of the novel, when the reader is led to assume Isserley is human, where her description of the male hitchhikers she picks up is articulated in a language that animalises her prey. For instance, as Dillon (2011) notes, the first description provided to the reader by Isserley reads: 'a hairy youngster . . . ambling along the side of the narrow road' (Faber 2000: 5). This figurative language, used to place the human species within the discursive terrain of the animal, as viewed by an alien species, is repeated throughout the novel. Human beings are 'specimens', and their body parts are frequently equated to those of animals: a vodsel's swollen legs are 'like a giant pair of salmon' (Faber 2000: 108); or, in the more humorously scabrous language Faber often employs, the tip of a vodsel's penis has 'a small hole like the imperfectly closed eye of a dead cat' (2000: 185).

While Dillon (2011) convincingly argues that Isserley begins to feel empathy with her vodsel prey, I would counter that this is perhaps less of a driving force than her ecological empathy with the earth's natural resources. As Dillon (2011) states, Isserley does attempt to rescue the last vodsel she catches, and as her death approaches, she begins to identify herself with a vodsel woman.[1] This very brief and underdeveloped aspect of Faber's novel arguably becomes the structuring theme of Glazer's film, to be discussed shortly. At the end of Faber's novel, Isserley is involved in a car crash while driving a hitchhiker. She cannot, of course, be found by police or ambulance services, so she decides she must activate the car's self-detonating device. In the novel Isserley has some agency over her death, and it is rendered in an elegiac way. She asks a passer-by to move the hitchhiker out of the area before she activates the explosion. Her final thoughts are ones that display not so much her growing sense of empathy for the vodsels, but her appeasement at becoming one with the natural world she so admires:

> The atoms that had been herself would mingle with the oxygen and nitrogen in the air. Instead of ending up buried in the ground, she would become part of the sky: that was the way to look at it. Her invisible remains would combine, over time, with all the wonders under the sun. When it snowed, she would be part of it, falling softly to the earth, rising up again with the snow's evaporation. When it rained, she would be there in the spectral arch that spanned from firth to ground. She would help to wreathe the fields in mists, and yet would always be transparent to the stars. She would live forever. (Faber 2000: 296)

Jonathan Glazer's interviews show that he had no interest in making a faithful adaptation of Faber's novel, stating: 'I was only very briefly faithful to the novel. I was faithful to it for about ten minutes. And then, for the next seven-and-a-half years, I wasn't. For me the novel was just a jumping off point really' (Osenlund 2014). When early versions of the script, first written by Alexander Stuart, then by Milo Addica (who had collaborated with Glazer on *Birth*, 2004) stuck fairly closely to the novel's narrative trajectory, Glazer felt, 'I knew then that I absolutely didn't want to film the book. But I still wanted to make the book a film' (Leigh 2014). Glazer further added, 'The first drafts were much more faithful and illustrative. It was a good adaptation' (quoted in Romney 2014). It was a *good* adaptation, but it wasn't the *true* adaptation that Glazer had in mind, the phrasing that Faber would later use to describe Glazer's film (Tobias 2014). This narrative is further established by the replacement of Milo Addica as scriptwriter with Walter Campbell, who had collaborated previously with Glazer in his advertising career: Campbell had not read Faber's novel, and did not plan to (FilmFour 2014; FilmNation 2014; Tobias 2014). The script at this point had already veered away from Faber's novel towards a two-hander featuring an alien husband and wife, played by Brad Pitt and Scarlett Johansson, who preyed upon the town locals in the Scottish Highlands. With financing for the project proving difficult, even with Pitt's involvement (Leigh 2014; Wiseman 2014), Glazer and Campbell decided to return to their earlier inspiration and tighten their focus on the alien's subjectivity above all else. The relationship between the creative personnel behind the film adaptation and the novel reiterates Hutcheon's (2006) sense of the adaptation as being both self and other. Glazer and Campbell's distillation of the raw narrative material of Faber's novel into something quite distinctly 'other' is notable, and frequently remarked upon in reviews of the film (e.g. Collin 2014). However, we might also describe the text as an other-self, adopting Schalk's (2011) usage of the term. In the processes of adaptation Glazer's film initially remained 'faithful', in the director's terms, to the novel, yet the redrafting of the script, the improvised vérité shooting style, the sound design and score and the finding of the film in the edit – which I'll consider below – might be argued to culminate in the text's description as an other-self; a film adaptation that is still recognisably anchored in the 'self' of Faber's novel, but is divergent enough in its own assertion of self, or to use Fredric Jameson's (2011: 218) terms, 'breathes a different spirit altogether' to become an other-self.

The film adaptation, released in 2013, eschews any foregrounded fidelity right from the beginning. On a black screen the names of production companies give way to only two more credits: 'a film by Jonathan Glazer' and 'Scarlett Johansson'. A small circle of light appears in the darkness and Mica Levi's haunting, discordant score sets the tone. The light bursts through the circle like the light from a movie projector in a darkened cinema. The way that the light spills from a solid circle in the centre (the pupil) in sharp expanding lines creates two more circular spheres around the first (the iris), and we might be looking at an eye. Of course, behind the eye we have a lens, too, reiterating the projector/eye metaphor. This post-credit opening sequence is over three

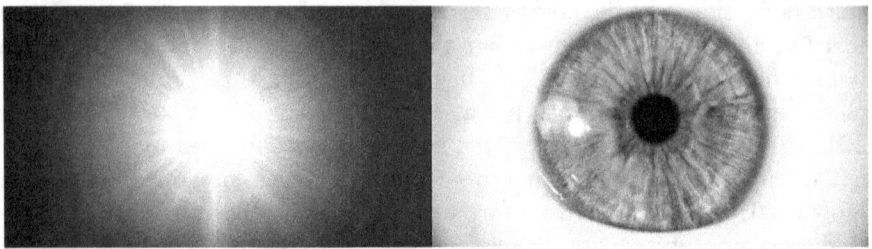

Figure 6.1 Projecting the eye in *Under the Skin* (BFI/Film Four/Creative Scotland/Silver Reel/Sigma Films & StudioCanal)

minutes long and culminates with the confirmation of the image of the eye, as seen above. While it may not be immediately clear to the viewer, this opening is the construction of the alien, from the blackness at the beginning – which Glazer asserts is the only true image of the alien (Romney 2014) – to the appearance of the human eye, or the alien simulacrum through whose gaze the film is filtered. The only sound to accompany Levi's jarring score is Scarlett Johansson's voice, repeating words in an English accent, including 'film'. Glazer recorded Johansson's English accent dialogue lessons and used them to aurally present the alien's own learning of the English language. This opening indicates to the viewer that from the beginning we are witnessing the events in the film through an alien subjectivity. This is clearly at odds with Faber's novel, which drops subtle hints across the opening 150 pages that our protagonist is not what we understand to be human. This indicates the ways in which Glazer must repurpose the figurative language identified by Dillon (2011) in Faber's novel, to find a way to represent the alien's subjectivity cinematically.[2] I would argue that it is also a beginning that declares to the viewer that this film adaptation is distinctly other than the novel it is adapting.

Gendered Other-selves

The alien's journey from dispassionate, femme-fatale temptress to the woman who meets her demise through gendered violence, is marked, as I've argued, by a greater empathy with the human race than is apparent in the novel. Indeed, Glazer's belief that the film is ultimately about having 'faith in mankind' (Tobias 2014) is apparent in the film's departures from the novel. In this section I wish to analyse how *Under the Skin* explores the developing self-consciousness of the alien through a representation of a Hegelian philosophy of the construction of the self. Throughout the narrative of the film we see the alien begin to reflect upon the construction of self in others, most prominently The Deformed Man and the women of Glasgow, to begin to apprehend her own growing self-consciousness, perhaps most clearly seen in a shot in which the alien looks at her naked female body in the mirror. In what follows I analyse several scenes in detail that exemplify how the film probes the development of the other-self in the individual, showing how this also relates to the textual other-self of the adaptation as discussed in the preceding section.

Towards the end of the film's first act, the alien is seeking prey on a secluded beach in the east of Scotland. She begins to seduce a Czech man living in a tent on the beach when a family picnicking is swept to sea attempting to save their dog from drowning. The man, in a swimmer's wetsuit, goes to help, but failing to save the family, he lies exhausted on the beach before the alien bludgeons him over the head with a rock. As she drags her victim across the beach we see in the background a small child wailing uncontrollably. This makes no impression

Figure 6.2 Screaming children in *Under the Skin* (BFI/Film Four/Creative Scotland/Silver Reel/Sigma Films & StudioCanal)

on our alien stalker, who departs the beach with prey intact and the child left screaming. A few shots later, the alien's ally, The Bad Man, returns to the beach to eliminate any traces of the Czech man. The child is still distressed and crying, then struggles to its feet in search of aid. The desertion of the child by both the aliens clearly serves to highlight their lack of empathy. However, the image then cuts to Johansson in her white van as a squeal is heard and her face, for the first time, loses its impassivity. Her facial expression conveys her mind trying to recall the sound and its importance. A look to her right shows another child, strapped into a booster seat in the parallel car, screaming and distressed. This suggests that, in fact, those earlier shots mark the first moment at which something of the human species has penetrated the female alien's consciousness.

When writing of the 'fey elusive women' that recur in Scottish culture, Caughie (1990: 15) discussed the type popularised by Sir Walter Scott's fictions and later personified by William Wallace's wife Murron in *Braveheart*, as noted by Edensor (2002: 148). In this gendered trope, women are pursued by hyper-masculine males in the mist-shrouded, romantically depicted Scottish Highlands. Does *Under the Skin* provide us with the most interesting take on the fey elusive 'woman' yet? This alien, inhabiting a female human form, prowls Glasgow for males to seduce and harvest who will be consumed as an expensive delicacy on her home planet (something not obvious from the film's narrative but made clear in the book). The film ends with a violent reversal of roles, as the alien is hunted down, raped and murdered; indeed, a similar fate that befalls Murron in *Braveheart*, though there is not space here to consider the anti-English rewriting of history which prompts this narrative contrivance in Gibson's film.[3] Osterweil (2014: 45) calls the film 'one of the most important feminist interventions in recent cinematic history'. I have used female pronouns to describe the alien throughout, though a sensible case to avoid this could be made. Faber's novel makes clear that our alien protagonist Isserley is female, and that her alien race also has male members. The issue is more complicated in the film. While Glazer states that the alien goes from 'an "it" to a "she"'

(FilmNation 2014), he also argues that the alien exists on a realm beyond our conscious understanding, and trappings of gender. At the end of the film, after a violent sexual assault, the alien's human skin is removed, revealing a black female form beneath. This would seem to confirm that we can read the alien as a she; however, Glazer argues:

> I don't feel like that *is* the real body ... To me it was the next layer – I don't think you feel like you've seen the alien, you've seen the inside ... The closest you see of the alien in this film, as far as I'm concerned, is an entirely black screen. (Romney 2014)

The point where the film makes this female identification clear is through a series of shots of people, primarily women, going about their daily lives in Glasgow, that are eventually motivated by a shot to show us the peering eye of (we assume) the alien, reiterating the opening of the film. We've seen these shots before in the film: the flatness with which they are presented make us feel

Figure 6.3   From 'an "it" to a "she"' in *Under the Skin* (BFI/Film Four/Creative Scotland/Silver Reel/Sigma Films & StudioCanal)

that they are bewildering and strange. The frying of a fish, the use of a mobile phone on a cigarette break, a *Big Issue* seller on the pavement, a woman in devil horns on a night out: a perplexing montage of what it means to be human (and female) in a big city in the twenty-first century. Where Mica Levi's score is normally discordant and threatening, here it becomes symphonic and uplifting. This sequence was not premeditated, as Glazer and editor Paul Watts discuss in the Bluray extras (Glazer 2014) it came out in the edit, elided from hundreds of hours of material. In this sequence the alien's identification with humanity is beginning to build, as the shots cross-fade incompletely and are layered on top of each other in a golden hue, before Johansson's impassive face forms a centre. The effect is then abruptly removed and all that remains is Johansson's face, momentarily lit by a passing streetlamp before it is plunged into blackness. This sequence signals the moment in which the alien begins the journey from 'an "it" to a "she"', but its last shot foreshadows the film's ending. If we read the sequence as the formation of a female identity, assembled through the montage of women on the Glasgow streets, what of the way it ends – Johansson's impassive face in the blackness of her van, whose passing underneath a street light plunges the image into darkness? If this is Glazer repurposing the brief dalliance with female empathy in Faber's book, as identified earlier, what of the way Glazer intersects Faber's ending?

The alien's journey of discovery, of becoming a woman, sees her abandon her mission abducting Glasgow's men, and she escapes to the west of Scotland where she meets a friendly local man ('The Quiet Man') who takes her in and gives her shelter. As previously mentioned, the alien's burgeoning femininity finds her looking at her naked body in the mirror, wondering what its purpose is and why it enraptures the men whom she has seduced. After an unsuccessful attempt to have sex with The Quiet Man, where it seems to be revealed (as is the case in the novel) that the alien's female form is surface only and does not extend to reproductive genitalia, she escapes in horror. She is met by another man, 'The Logger', who begins to rape her before inadvertently ripping off her skin amidst the violence, revealing the black form beneath. The man departs before returning to set her alight. As with the book's ending, her burnt embers alight from the ground in a plume of smoke to mingle with the chilly rural atmosphere, but this ending is not afforded the quiet satisfaction of the novel as previously discussed. Where the insight into Isserley's subjectivity in Faber's novel repeatedly reiterates her sense of wonder at earth's natural resources, Glazer's film allows for no such reading. If, as Glazer argues, the film is about having faith in humanity then how does such an ending reflect this theme?

Gorfinkel (2016) argues that while the film is literally representative of the ending of Faber's novel, its depiction of 'the transmission between smoke and snow, represent a dialectical transit in two opposing directions . . .'. To this end the alien's existence clearly becomes more precarious the more she self-identifies as human and female, and this ending, while true to the atmosphere of the film (and narrative of the novel), would seem to indicate that it is this very faith in humanity that has led to such a violent demise. Indeed, it is notable that it is the alien's realisation that she does not have female reproductive genitalia that precipitates her flight from 'The Good Man', and her sexual assault and murder. Bolton (2011), reading Lucy Irigaray's work, argues that one way in which women can formulate self-knowledge is to understand the body, female genitalia and sexuality to create a sense of self that is not predetermined by a phallocentric patriarchy. Gorfinkel (2016) also uses Irigaray, specifically applying her work to *Under the Skin* to argue that the film represents the strangeness of the alien as 'clearly forged through gender difference', and argues that the film's resolution reveals the 'irrecoverable gap between non-human and human inner life'. To this extent, then, the film explores the potential development of an other-self between the human and the non-human, yet ultimately forecloses this as a political commentary[4] on gender relations.

NATIONAL OTHER-SELVES

In this final section I wish to focus attention on the question of nation made apparent by the adaptation of *Under the Skin*, to argue that the film highlights the complicated ways in which adaptations remain frequently bound up in the idea of nationhood. Marmysz (2014: 32) calls *Under the Skin* an example of 'the myth of Scotland as nowhere in particular', one of a number of recent films that begin to move towards 'the full obliteration of Scottish distinctiveness'. For Marmysz (2014: 38), *Under the Skin*'s Glasgow setting is irrelevant and unimportant: the Glaswegians only have broad accents to emphasise 'the generally strange, vaguely threatening and exotic nature of the location'. While Marmysz (2014: 39) believes that in *Under the Skin* 'The landscape acts merely as a backdrop against which a universal drama of loneliness and dislocation plays out', I argue that emptying the setting of its importance is problematic for a number of reasons, as it works discursively on multiple narrative and thematic levels that I explore below.

Jonathan Glazer was insistent that the film be made in Scotland, arguing that 'there had to be a kind of wilderness to the film . . . I think it [Scotland] is the least populated part of Western Europe' (Tobias 2014). Furthermore, this idea of Scotland-as-wilderness is a familiar structuring device in cinema: not only in the film that earlier invaded this chapter, *Devil Girl From Mars*, but it is also apparent in Hollywood B-movie film, *The Man From Planet X* (Ulmer 1951), in which an alien invasion is forestalled on a remote Scottish island. The trope abounds in the comedies *I Know Where I'm Going!* (Powell and Presburger 1945), *Whisky Galore!* (Mackendrick 1949) and *Local Hero* (Forsyth 1983). However, as Martin-Jones (2006) argues, it can also be seen in several films depicting the sexual healing of English visitors to post-devolutionary Scotland. Martin-Jones (2005) describes how in the films *Regeneration* (Mackinnon 1997) and *The Last Great Wilderness* (Mackenzie 2002), English visitors are provided with rejuvenation, and the tools with which to rebuild their individual sense of identity through their interactions with the Scottish Highlands. Martin-Jones (2005) reads this as national allegory: Scotland, in this period beginning to come to terms with a sense of differentiation from England and Britain, helping its English visitors to do the same. In this sense the English self is recuperated through its experience of the Scottish other to restore its British other-self. In the aforementioned films we can read a national unity in the restoration of the British other-self in a period of devolutionary disconnect in which political self-determination has been high on the agenda in Scotland, and latterly in England as the Brexit process has highlighted.

Yet how does this relate to *Under the Skin*'s English protagonist? As Connor (2016) notes, in contrast with Marmysz (2014), one cannot read an English woman with a posh accent driving around Scotland (especially Glasgow[5]) in a white van without a consciousness of the national allegory at play. Connor argues that the 'white van is an emblem of New Labour in British politics', before further arguing that the 'White Van Man' became a totem pole of public opinion in the popular press. This stereotypical construct of ordinary, working-class British people was really a representative of a very particular 'ordinary' British public: white, male, middle-aged and English. Connor (2016) reminds us of the uproar caused when the Labour MP Emily Thornberry tweeted a photo of a white van outside a house draped in the St. George's flag of England, with the caption 'Image from #Rochester'. Thornberry was subsequently eviscerated in the popular press for the thinly veiled snobbery of the image, and it highlighted the continued, and one might argue growing, perception of English nationalism as bound up in the image of White Van Man. Connor (2016) writes that 'in a film as allegorically invested as *Under the Skin*, the English/Scottish divide is also emblematic', and further argues that the film's playful use of White Van Man can be read as a political commentary on the divide between the movement in opposite directions between a centre-right reactionary nationalism in England and a centre-left progressive nationalism in Scotland, first incubated through New Labour's approach to devolutionary politics.

The film's use of familiar Scottish iconography is also illuminating in this regard, and its shift from urban Glasgow to rural Scotland is marked by an increasing 'Scottishness'. Faber's novel is set entirely in the Highlands, and never ventures south of Inverness. However, the film's shift of location to Glasgow may, as Marmysz (2014) claims, may de-emphasise any sense of local significance. Yet as the alien begins to identify more with the human race, and particularly its female members, she moves north to what McArthur (1994) has called the 'feminine' spaces of the Scottish Highlands. Hjort (2000) argues that one way in which to discuss the national aspects of film, without falling into the potentially reductive territory of national constructivism, is by analysing how films might 'flag' national themes. Hjort elaborates:

> The presence of a significant number of such elements [language, location, actors] can provide the basis for a given film's national quality, but they cannot, in and of themselves, constitute a theme. Theme implies thematisation, that is, a self-conscious directing of focal awareness towards those meaningful elements that, when interpreted, reveal what a given film is strictly speaking about. A theme of nation will, of course, typically emerge as a result of a 'flagging' of precisely those elements listed above. (2000: 108)

When the alien is listening to the radio for news about the missing family swept off to sea we hear Kaye Adams, a talk show host on BBC Radio Scotland, discuss the fact that next year, 2014, is an important one for Scotland, with the independence referendum on the horizon, as well as the Commonwealth Games and the Ryder Cup. Given that this comes immediately after the invented news bulletin of the missing family from the beach, it shows the efforts that Glazer, and the sound design team, went to in order to make the local specificity apparent.

In the final third of the film, the alien moves from the urban to the rural, and Glazer uses this iconic landscape to augment Faber's novel and turn this iconography on its head. In one of the arresting shots for which Glazer's work is critically revered, a dense fog is whipped across a loch beneath snow-capped mountains by a fierce wind. Moments later, the alien abandons her white transit van (and, adopting Connor's (2016) approach might we say the last vestiges of New Labour Britain?) and is subsumed by the mist. We see Johansson's face lose its passivity, becoming curious as she exits her van to take in the atmosphere. Glazer cuts from a close-up of Johansson's face to an extreme long shot of the alien walking from the mist into the clearer air, along a suitably scenic 'Highland' landscape. From this point on the flagging is more apparent. In a tartan-clad tea room on the banks of a loch, the alien tries, unsuccessfully, to eat chocolate cake. In a shot that seems designed to perpetuate a male gaze, with a close-up of Johansson's lips, she slowly moves the cake into her mouth, before choking to the bemusement of other customers. Gorfinkel (2016) argues that this scene is the alien's first act of self-determination and it is coded through a sexualised stardom, with what she argues are fetishist close-ups of Johansson's mouth and lips.

After meeting The Quiet Man on a bus, he takes her shopping, their purchases including the tartan-packaged loaf of bread *Scottish Plain*, before inviting her to eat with him at home. Here, a short clip of comedian Tommy Cooper performing a skit on television serves a dual purpose. The gibberish language he spouts as a sort of magic spell to make a spoon fly from a glass jar indicates the strange absurdity of the human race to the alien. But, also, it furthers the sense of Scotland as a place lost in time, as is a common trope of cinematic representations of the Highlands. In the living room, a comedian dead for more than thirty years is seen on the television; in the kitchen, the radio plays Deacon Blue's *Real Gone Kid*, a song released by the Scottish band in 1988, while The Good Man washes the dishes and the alien tries to tap out a beat on her fingers. Of course, no visit to the Highlands would be complete without a visit to a castle, but in the reversal of the representative cinematic tropes of Scotland, this is no glamorous trip to a romanticised and heroic past. Like the fog that rolls across the loch, Tantallon Castle – which is actually on Scotland's southeast coast, near North Berwick – is presented as a hostile, claustrophobic and unwelcoming environment. Cinematographer Daniel Landin articulates the film's desire to play with familiar representations of Highland tartanry, stating that the site was chosen because 'it's old and dramatic, but not very pretty' (Stasukevich 2014).

After the failed attempt at intercourse with The Quiet Man, the alien flees to a wooded space, near Drimsynie in Argyll, west of Loch Lomond, and also not in the Highlands. Therefore, while the film's shift away from the urban promises a move from modernity, and surrealism, towards tradition and nature, it is, in fact, nothing of the sort. This is a Highland artifice both in how the film engages with iconic Scottish scenery, and the fact that the scenery is not actually in the Highlands. However, the film's reception indicates that these scenes are read as taking place in the Highlands, with all the connotative power that such representation holds. Reviews in *The Guardian* (Robson 2014), *The Independent* (Aftab 2013), *Sight & Sound* (Wigley 2014), *New York Times* (Holden 2014) and *Variety* (Foundas 2013) all refer to the film's use of the Highlands. But, more than this, most of the film's reviews note the prominence of its Scottish location, with Bradshaw (2014) going further to ask if the alien is: 'the advance party of a colonising power that has conquered England and is coming north? Johansson's alien has clearly hit a Hadrian's Wall of trouble in these misty lands and found that the Scots are not so easy to subdue.'

How notable is it that the alien's last place of shelter is a bothy[6] in the woods, above the bed of which hangs a Lion Rampant flag? The bothy represents the film's 'Highland' fling in microcosm: rural Scotland seen as a place outside of modernity, but its status as safe refuge upended. More than this it might be argued to be a *colonial refuge*, in Jones's (2006: 189) terms, where the Highlands act as 'a convenient colonial refuge from modern urban life'. But in this most unreliable of films it is nothing of the sort. Our alien visitor is awakened in the bothy by The Logger, a man working in the area – with an English accent – who tries to grope her, before hunting her down to rape and murder her at the edge of the forest. Where Martin-Jones (2005), Jones (2006) and Caughie (2007) find that the Scottish Highlands are often represented as a sexually restorative place for English visitors, here the reverse is true. Not only is it the place in which our English female visitor finds that not only is sex not possible, but that its very prospect brings upon violence and murder. In Scotland's urban environs the alien's seductive power over men is total, and the film perpetuates her gaze in its modernist subjectivity. In the 'Highlands' the gaze abruptly shifts: 'it' becomes a 'she', and this dialectic other-self, between being human and female, also shows us Scottish other-selves: the aforementioned Scottish and/or British double consciousness, as well as the representational push and pull between Scotland's post-industrial hard-man heartlands (Glasgow) and its mythic, timeless, 'feminine' rural hinterlands (the Highlands).

Under the Skin, seen in the terms outlined in this chapter, offers the viewer a violent reversal of expectations. It offers a visually bracing reconceptualisation of the novel's end; however, this ending is primarily striking because it seems to offer a repudiation of the idea of the Highlands as a sexually restorative landscape for alien visitors. What is interesting here is that while the alien visitor is nominally 'English', the confrontation between modernity and pre-modernity is between Glasgow and its rural environs. While much of the literature around the film reiterates the idea that Glasgow is readable as a 'place out of time' because its inhabitants could not recognise Scarlett Johansson (Osterweil 2014), it is, in fact, in the film representative of modernity. The identity-assembling montage I discussed earlier uses a number of shots of people glued to their mobile phone screens, and the city is seen as populated with a vibrant mass of people, whether exiting a Glasgow Celtic football game,[7] or drinking and dancing excessively in a nightclub.

In *Under the Skin*, then, we have a Scotland represented through a city-urban landscape of industrial modernity that empowers its female protagonist. The shift to the pre-modernity of the 'Highlands' reveals an unsafe, and representatively unstable space, where national symbols are more frequent, and sexual liberation is rendered violently unattainable. What *Under the Skin*, then, seems to do is refract a tendency seen in other art-house films of the period which, to use Street's (2009: 143) terms, 're-place' Scotland. As with *Morvern Callar* (Ramsay 2002), which similarly uses a detached female subjectivity and avoids romanticised rural Scottish imagery, *Under the Skin* seems to destabilise and fragment traditional ways of thinking about gender, landscape and national identities. The film represents a devolutionary-era cultural milieu in Scotland that is confident enough to play around with shifting identities made possible by the loosening of ties with Britishness and the still-distant prospect of full statehood, the point made by Caughie (2007) in his analysis of *Morvern Callar*. Yet as Connor's analysis (2016), shows, this does not mean that the film's 'Scottishness' is not an important way in which to understand the film.

Conclusion

Under the Skin's innovative deconstruction of historically and representatively charged Scottish landscapes is one way in which this film adaptation offers a complex mediation on the dialectic between self and other. It offers its viewers a hall of mirrors, as contradictory and threatening as those in which Orson Welles finds himself at the end of *The Lady from Shanghai* (Welles 1947). At every turn the film seeks to reflect an image of the self that is distorted and fragmented by its incorporation of others. It details how the self and the other are engaged in a dialectic war, in which the power relations are not always equal; whether that be book and film, alien and human, human and female, Scotland and England or Glasgow and the Highlands. It stands as an example of how the process of producing film adaptations, with their inevitable textual gaps to be filled, can allow for imaginative and productive re-workings and re-readings of narrative and theme, related to the prominent and ever-shifting socio-political and cultural discourses of their era (in this case gender politics and national identities).

I have tried here to outline just some of the ways that *Under the Skin* offers the viewer the same insight into the development of self-consciousness that Burns's famous poem does. The film asks for questions of gender formation and power relations, as well as national iconographies, to be re-seen from an objective distance. I have argued that the film's development makes evident some of the ways in which adaptations are both 'self and other'. Their promotion and public discourse repeatedly reiterate and foreground their progenitor texts, and furthermore, one of the ways that Glazer's auteur status is articulated is precisely through the elevation of the film director's vision over the mechanics and themes of the novel. Subsequently, the film provocatively asks what it means to be human, and female, in the twenty-first century and finds, despite Glazer's pronouncements on its faith in humanity, that to be human and female is to be vulnerable to violence, and to be susceptible to expulsion for exploring sexuality and the female self. Finally, I turned to the film's invocation of the national, at a time when the concept of national cinema is often argued to be problematic (Bergfelder 2005; Higson 2000). I argue that *Under the Skin* shows how cinema need not be exclusively thought of as either transnational or national; and that while the realities of film production almost always necessitate transnational flows of capital and personnel, this doesn't necessarily mean that films cannot be understood as having themes that are both universal and nation-specific.

Notes

1. As Dillon (2011: 149) states: 'a female vodsel is repeatedly referred to as a "woman" for the first time in the novel (eleven times in pages 294–5)'.
2. For a detailed close analysis of the opening see Constable (2017).
3. Besides, Colin McArthur (2003) has already quite excellently and provocatively done precisely this.
4. Glazer frequently refers to the film as a 'political horror film' (Diaz 2014).
5. Lest we forget, Glasgow was one of the few Scottish local authority areas that voted in favour (54%) of independence for Scotland in the 2014 referendum.
6. A bothy is a place of communal shelter in rural Scotland, normally composed of a small stone- or wooden-roofed structure.
7. Though interestingly, the Glaswegian man picked up by the alien in the aftermath of the game is wearing the similar green and white colours of the great Edinburgh side Hibernian.

References

Aftab, K. (2013), 'Film review: Under the Skin – even Scarlett Johansson can't save Jonathan Glazer's laughably bad alien hitchhiker movie', *Independent*, London, 5 September, <https://www.independent.co.uk/arts-entertainment/films/reviews/film-review-under-the-skin-even-scarlett-johansson-cant-save-jonathan-glazers-laughably-bad-alien-8796596.html> (accessed 23 April 2017).

Bergfelder, T. (2005), 'National, transnational or supranational cinema? Rethinking European film studies', *Media, Culture & Society*, 27: 3, 315–31.

Bolton, L. (2011), *Film and Female Consciousness*, London: Palgrave.

Bradshaw, P. (2014), 'Under the Skin review – "Very erotic, very scary"', *The Guardian*, London, 13 March, <https://www.theguardian.com/film/2014/mar/13/under-the-skin-scarlett-johansson-peter-bradshaw> (accessed 17 May 2017).

Burns, R. (2001 [1786]), *The Canongate Burns: The Complete Songs and Poems of Robert Burns*, in A. Noble and P. S. Hogg (eds), Edinburgh: Canongate.

Caughie, J. (1990), 'Representing Scotland: new questions for Scottish cinema', in E. Dick (ed.), *From Limelight to Satellite: A Scottish film book*, Glasgow: Scottish Film Council, pp. 13–30.

Caughie, J. (2007), '*Morvern Callar*, art cinema and the "monstrous archive"', *Scottish Studies Review*, 8: 1, 101–15.

Collin, R. (2014), 'Under the Skin: "simply a masterpiece"', *The Telegraph*, London, 13 March <www.telegraph.co.uk/film/under-the-skin/review/> (accessed 24 April 2017)

Connor, J. D. (2016), 'Independence and the consent of the governed: the systems and scales of *Under the Skin*', *Jump Cut: A Review of Contemporary Media*, Fall, 7, <https://web.archive.org/web/20190403123106/https://www.ejumpcut.org/archive/jc57.2016/-ConnorSkin/index.html> (accessed 27 March 2017).

Constable, C. (2017), '*Under the Skin*: cosmology and individuation', *Movie: A Journal of Film Criticism*, 7, 31–4.

Diaz, A. C. (2014), 'Campbell and Glazer reunite on Scarlett Johansson alien flick', *AdAge*, <https://adage.com/article/agency-news/skin-reunites-walter-campbell-jonathan-glazer/292642> (accessed 20 March 2019).

Dillon, S. (2011), '"It is a question of words, therefore": Becoming-animal in Michel Faber's *Under the Skin*', *Science Fiction Studies*, 38: 1, 134–54.

Edensor, T. (2002), *National Identity, Popular Culture and Everyday Life*, Oxford: Berg.

Faber, M. (2000), *Under the Skin*, Edinburgh: Canongate.

FilmFour (2014), 'Under the Skin: the script', *FilmFour*, <http://www.film4.com/special-features/interviews/under-the-skin-the-script> (accessed 20 April 2017).

FilmNation (2014), *Under the Skin Production Notes*, <https://web.archive.org/web/20190408131214/https://static1.squarespace.com/static/4ff6691be4b0caef779fb186/t/5335cbb4e4b0d906f5019aea/1396034484635/UNDER+THE+SKIN+Production+Notes+FINAL.pdf> (accessed 9 April 2019).

Foundas, S. (2013), 'Telluride film review: "Under the Skin"', *Variety*, 30 August, <http://variety.com/2013/film/global/under-the-skin-review-telluride-venice-toronto-1200593111> (accessed 12 May 2017).

Gorfinkel, E. (2016), 'Sex, sensation and nonhuman interiority in *Under the Skin*', *Jump Cut: A Review of Contemporary Media*, Fall, 57, <https://web.archive.org/web/20190403122623/https://www.ejumpcut.org/archive/jc57.2016/-GorfinkelSkin/index.html#> (accessed 3 April 2019).

Higson, A. (2000), 'The limiting imagination of national cinema', in M. Hjort and S. Mackenzie (eds), *Cinema & Nation*, London: Routledge, pp. 63–74.

Hjort, M. (2000), 'Themes of nation', in M. Hjort and S. Mackenzie (eds), *Cinema & Nation*, London: Routledge, pp. 103–17.

Hogan, R. (2000), 'Michel Faber: "I think I've been writing ever since I was introduced to the English language",' *Beatrice*, <http://www.beatrice.com/interviews/faber> (accessed 17 April 2017).

Holden, S. (2014), 'A much darker Hitchhiker's Guide: Scarlett Johansson as a deadly alien in "Under the Skin"', *New York Times*, 3 April, <https://www.nytimes.com/2014/04/04/movies/scarlett-johansson-as-a-deadly-alien-in-under-the-skin.html> (accessed 20 October 2017).

Hutcheon, L. (2006), *A Theory of Adaptation*, New York: Routledge.

Jameson, F. (2011), 'Afterword: adaptation as a philosophical problem', in C. McCabe, K. Murray and R. Warner (eds), *True to the Spirit: Film Adaptation and the Question of Fidelity*, Oxford: Oxford University Press, pp. 215–33.

Jones, A. M. (2006), 'Enchanted places, land and sea, and wilderness: Scottish Highland landscapes and identity in cinema', in C. Fowler and G. Helfield (eds), *Representing the Rural: Space, Place, and Identity in Films about the Land*, Detroit: Wayne State University Press.

Leigh, D. (2014), 'Under the Skin: why did this chilling masterpiece take a decade?' *The Guardian*, 6 March, <https://www.theguardian.com/film/2014/mar/06/under-the-skin-director-jonathan-glazer-scarlett-johansson> (accessed 19 April 2017).

Marmysz, J. (2014), 'The myth of Scotland as nowhere in particular', *International Journal of Scottish Theatre and Screen*, 7: 1, 28–44.

Martin-Jones, D. (2005), 'Sexual-healing: representations of the English in post-devolutionary Scotland', *Screen*, Summer, 46: 2, 227–33.

McArthur, C. (1994), 'The cultural necessity of a poor Celtic cinema', in J. Hill, M. McClone and P. Hainsworth (eds), *Border Crossing: Film in Ireland, Britain and Europe*, London: BFI, pp. 112–25.

McArthur, C. (2003), *Brigadoon, Braveheart and the Scots: Distortions of Scotland in Hollywood Cinema*, London: I. B.Tauris.

Munro, Alice (1999), 'The Bear Came Over the Mountain', *New Yorker*, 27 December.

Osterweil, A. (2014), 'Under the Skin: the perils of becoming female', *Film Quarterly*, 67: 4, 44–51.

Osenlund, L. (2014), 'Interview: Jonathan Glazer', *Slant*, 3 April, <http://www.slantmagazine.com/features/article/interview-jonathan-glazer> (accessed 18 April 2017).

Pippin, R. B. (2010), *Hegel on Self-Consciousness: Desire and Death in the Phenomenology of Spirit*, Princeton University Press.

Robson, L. (2014), 'Scarlett Johansson in Under the Skin: "Prick her and she doesn't bleed"', *The Guardian*, London, 15 March, <https://www.theguardian.com/film/2014/mar/15/scarlett-johansson-under-skin-extraterrestrial> (accessed 17 My 2017).

Romney, J. (2014), 'Unearthly stranger'. *Sight & Sound*, April, 24: 4, 22–7.

Schalk, S. (2011), 'Self, other and other-self: going beyond the self/other binary in contemporary consciousness', *Journal of Comparative Research in Anthropology and Sociology*, 2: 1, 197–210.

Stasukevich, I. (2014), 'Alien ways', *American Cinematographer*, May, 95: 5, 44–53.

Street, S. (2009), 'New Scottish cinema as trans-national cinema', in J. Murray, F. Farley and R. Stoneman (eds), *Scottish Cinema Now*, Newcastle upon Tyne: Cambridge Scholars, pp. 139–52.

Tobias, S. (2014), 'Director Jonathan Glazer on Under The Skin's complex honesty', *Dissolve*, 4 April, <https://web.archive.org/web/20180724100504/https://thedissolve.com/features/interview/496-director-jonathan-glazer-on-under-the-skins-comple/> (accessed 18 April 2017).

Wigley, S. (2014), 'Film of the week: Under the Skin', *Sight & Sound*, April, 24: 4, 89.

Wiseman, A. (2014), 'Under the Skin: at any cost', *Screen Daily*, 24 March, <http://www.screendaily.com/features/under-the-skin-at-any-cost/5069904.article> (accessed 17 May 2017).

Filmography

Forsyth, B. (1983), *Local Hero*. 20th Century Fox.
Glazer, J. (2014), *Under the Skin*. Studiocanal.
Macdonald, D. (1954), *Devil Girl from Mars*. British Lion Films.
Mackendrick, A. (1949), *Whisky Galore!* General Film Distributors.
Mackenzie, D. (2002). *The Last Great Wilderness*. Feature Film Company.
MacKinnon, G. (1997), *Regeneration*. Artificial Eye.
Powell, M. and Pressburger, E. (1945), *I Know Where I'm Going!* General Film Distributors.
Ramsay, L. (2002). *Morvern Callar*. BBC Films.
Ulmer, E. G. (1951), *The Man From Planet X*. United Artists.
Welles, O. (1947), *The Lady from Shanghai*. Columbia Pictures.

7. BACK TO THE FUTURE: RECALCITRANCE AND FIDELITY IN *JULIETA*

Michael Stewart

False Start

Pedro Almodóvar's adaptation of three Alice Munro short stories – 'Chance', 'Soon' and 'Silence', which appear consecutively and as episodes in one character's life in the collection *Runaway* (2006) – was a much-anticipated project. Not only has Almodóvar noted frequently his great admiration of Munro's work, but the planned film (provisionally entitled *Silence*) was to be the director's first English language feature, and the first of his films to be set and shot outside of Spain – i.e. in Canada, the setting of the stories. The disappointment, then, was palpable when the director returned to Spain announcing that the project, in Canada at least, was off. Ignominy was then added to discomfort when, shortly before the Spanish release of *Julieta*, Almodóvar and his brother Agustín were embroiled in a tax scandal – leaked documents from a Panamanian law firm revealed that El Deseo (founded by the brothers) had set up an offshore company in the early 1990s (Romney 2016b).

The journey then from the excitement of the Munro-Canada pilgrimage project to the bruised and withdrawn figure that Almodóvar apparently became seems short. If, however, the director seemed to turn in on himself, this for Lange-Churion accords with his trajectory as a filmmaker and artist. Lange-Churion argues that Almodóvar's 'late style' (2016: 441) is characterised by inwardness, and an increasing tendency both to reference his own films, and imitate the classical language of Hollywood cinema. Lange-Churion suggests that a decline in Almodóvar's critical and artistic capabilities is evident from *Women on the Verge of a Nervous Breakdown* (1986) onward. Furthermore, Lange-Churion argues that La Movida, and by extension the films of Almodóvar, is more complicit with than critical of fascism in Spain. It (they) represents a superficial avant-garde, where history is neither confronted nor revised. The cultural transvesticism evident in La Movida and Almodóvar's films is a form of apathy and recycling, not radicalism. The contradictions and multiple valences of Spain's past – political, religious, ethnic and cultural – are repressed: 'This inability to reckon with the past resulted in a lost moment of social imagination and possible innovation, and ensured for the continuity of the most reactionary elements of Spanish political life' (2016: 444).

Lange-Churion's argument is important partly because *Julieta* does seem to represent a retreat; and also because it appears to be one of Almodóvar's most conservative films yet – featuring, for example, very little in the way of female solidarity or queer identity. However, not only is the version of modernism privileged by Lange-Churion familiar in ironic ways – i.e. familiar in its favouring of the art of white, male and European figures – but his argument about Almodóvar's decline depends on a stable and linear sense of trajectory. In this respect, any discourses around an artist's maturity and politics have to be treated with caution. Juan Carlos Ibáñez, for example, notes the frequent attacks on Almodóvar's work as 'apolitical' and 'ahistorical' (2013: 153), and the director's frustration in having to explain the consistency of his desire to speak to, not ignore, Spanish history and politics, and that this can be done in different ways: '(I)n my films there is no need for characters to talk about politics. The politics are implicit in the film' (Almodóvar, in Ibáñez 2013: 157). Ibáñez notes that Almodóvar changed his position somewhat in this respect, 'Twenty years ago . . . my revenge against Franco consisted in not recognizing his existence . . . Now I believe it is wrong to forget that era . . . ' (Almodóvar, in Ibáñez 2013: 160), and that from the mid-1990s onward Almodóvar has visited and revisited 'the problem of memory' (Ibáñez 2013: 158). *Julieta* revisits this problem in specific ways that I'll examine below. First, though, I want to consider what characterises the film's primary inspiration – *Runaway* (2006) and the work of Alice Munro.

Munrovian

That Alice Munro has been a source of inspiration for Almodóvar throughout his career may not be a surprise. A number of Munro's abiding themes are evident in Almodóvar's films. Munro consistently troubles the conventions of gender with regard both to narrative and character. As Tolan notes, while Munro's primary interest is women and the possibility of a 'female imaginary'

(2010: 171), her writing is as likely to subvert feminine norms as masculine ones. For example, while departures permeate Munro's work, these journeys seldom take the shape of the romantic masculine quest (solitary and moving outward), or more recognisably feminine versions of this form (spiritual, social and more oriented to home). Moreover, the ambiguous quests in Munro's work, Tolan notes, are as much about returns as departures, as well as the impossibility of escape.

This pattern is gendered, but is also about place. Tolan notes how the dispositions and identities of Munro's predominantly female protagonists are inescapably shaped by geographical location; and that a 'Canadian literary consciousness' (2010: 169) resonates in her work – in particular in *Runaway*, the focus of Tolan's article. This consciousness or 'aesthetic' (2010: 168) serves to invert the US version of the quest narrative, so that the house supersedes the road, and return supplants renewal. Working in tandem with this, Tolan suggests, is a peculiarly Canadian 'communitarian perspective' (2010: 173). The effects of this 'sensibility' (2010: 168), Tolan suggests, are strongly felt by the women in Munro's fiction, who also give it form. They evince an overwhelming desire to escape the strictures of rural Ontario small town life. However, the weight of social responsibility that compels them to return is doubled – in the combination of their gender with this specifically Canadian communitarian perspective. This combination, Tolan suggests, erases any liberal, individualised sense of self these women may have.

This social pressure, returning and apparent inwardness, however, are not without their own contradictions and potential productiveness. On more than one occasion, for example, Munro has commented on the metaphor of the house in her writing: 'I don't take up a story and follow it as if it were a road, taking me somewhere . . . I go into it, and move back and forth . . . It's more like a house' (Munro, in Tolan 2010: 168); and 'A story is not like a road to follow . . . it's more like a house . . . You can go back again and again, and the house, the story, always contains more than you saw the last time' (Munro, in Lister 2013: 45). Lister here connects Munro's compulsive return to the house not just to a Canadian aesthetic and sensibility, but to the writer's preference for the short story – or rather to her preference for the 'relativizing poetic' (2013: 45) most marked within the short story form. The short story, Lister suggests, is characterised by 'recalcitrance' (2013: 50). In Munro's stories, this is particularly evident. Meaning and interpretation are repeatedly made provisional; and her stories are dense with 'interruptions, turnarounds and strangeness' (Munro, in Lister 2013: 45).

Almodóvar's films are characterised too by turnarounds, interruptions and chance. This is equally true of much film melodrama. However, the director (and critics) describes *Julieta* as his least melodramatic film (in Romney 2016a), and this may reflect his attempt to capture something of the short story form – described by Lister (2013) as restrained as well as recalcitrant. Restraint is also in keeping with successful globalised film family melodrama in recent times, including, generally, those of Almodóvar. Whether *Julieta* is his most restrained film yet is debatable. However, there is no questioning the fullness and complexity of its engagement with *Runaway*, the collection's triptych, and the work and world of Alice Munro. In his deep desire to realise the project, Almodóvar seems to have taken on the qualities of a Munrovian protagonist, in particular the triptych and film's central character, Juliet/Julieta. His escape from the familiarity of home (Spain) was unsuccessful. He appeared to return without triumph, and underlined, then, that he had become a solitary and diminished figure. In his interview with Jonathan Romney, Almodóvar notes the frequency of his migraines, his deafness in one ear, his photophobia, and the infrequency of his sorties into high or public life: 'I stay at home. It's as simple as that' (Almodóvar, in Romney 2016a). I want to suggest, though, that however unplanned his return, and however beleaguered he may have felt, the process or journey has proved mysteriously productive. The figure of Julieta in Almodóvar's film is certainly his most solitary and inward-looking female protagonist. Why this should be so, what it means and how it's expressed, begins to tell us about the multiple nature of the triptych's journey from page to screen. Before I consider this, though, a summary of the film's complicated story might be useful.

Middle-aged Julieta (Emma Suárez, the younger version played by Adriana Ugarte) is in her Madrid flat packing, in readiness for a move to Portugal with her partner Lorenzo (Darío Grandinetti). On a final visit to the shops, she bumps into Bea (Michelle Jenner), a close friend of her daughter Antía (Priscilla Delgado/Blanca Parés). Bea has met Antía recently (Julieta has not seen Antía for twelve years) in Switzerland. This news (we learn) returns Julieta to a state of trauma. She splits with Lorenzo, telling him she can't go to Portugal, but does not explain why. She sells her Madrid flat and moves to a rented one in the same city – the flat she rented and shared years ago with Antía (or one on the same stair, at least). Though she has no address for her, she begins to write to Antía. It is the story of her life, a laying bare of the truth for her daughter, and for us. As a young woman, and supply teacher, she met Antía's father, Xoan (Daniel Grao), on a train. The journey, like their relationship, is marked by passion and guilt. Julieta moves to Galicia to live with Xoan, a fisherman, and soon afterward, Antía is born. Julieta visits her parents with the baby in Andalucia and is distressed by her mother's dementia and her father's relationship with her mother's young carer. When Antía is twelve, she goes to summer camp with her friend Bea. In Galicia, when the housekeeper Marian (Rossy de Palma) leaves the house for good, she takes pleasure in telling Julieta the truth of Xoan's infidelities (in particular with Julieta's friend Ava, played by Inma Cuesta). Julieta confronts Xoan, who admits to being unfaithful, but attempts to downplay its significance. Despite an impending storm, Julieta goes for a walk, upset and refusing to speak to Xoan. When she returns, the storm rages, but Xoan has gone out in his boat. Julieta is beside herself, and the next morning it is confirmed that Xoan has died in the storm. Julieta enters her first phase of traumatic grief – numb and ageing visibly. She keeps the truth of the night of the storm from Antía, not knowing that soon after Xoan's death, it is revealed to her in any case by the vindictive housekeeper. Julieta and Antía leave Galicia and rent a flat in Madrid. Julieta works at home (proof reading) and dedicates her life to her daughter. When Antía leaves home at seventeen to go to a retreat, Julieta is devastated again. When the period of Antía's retreat is over, Julieta drives, joyfully, to collect her. The head of the retreat tells her that Antía has already left and asked that Julieta should not be told of her new location. Angry and confused, Julieta withdraws into herself still further. She visits Ava in hospital. Ava has multiple sclerosis and is close to death. She tells Julieta that Antía has spoken to her on the phone. Antía blames both Ava and Julieta for Xoan's death. At Ava's funeral, Julieta meets Lorenzo, who is able to lift Julieta out of her depression and help her start her life again. She tells Lorenzo nothing of Antía and Xoan. All goes well until the first meeting with Bea at the street corner, after which Julieta and Lorenzo split (but we know Lorenzo continues to watch Julieta, unseen). A second meeting with Bea reveals that Antía was (and perhaps still is) a troubled and not altogether attractive person, and not the person Julieta thought she was. Julieta now appears more traumatised and confused than ever. In a daze, she walks into the path of a moving car. Lorenzo is nearby and accompanies her to hospitable. Her injuries are relatively minor. Lorenzo goes to Julieta's flat to find her some clothes. When he's there, he also collects her diaries/letters to Antía, and a letter. The letter is from Antía, and for the first time it has a return address – i.e. Antía's address in Switzerland. The letter is conciliatory, and is also about Antía's own grief – she recently lost one of her children in a drowning accident. Hesitant and still visibly traumatised, Julieta decides she will go by car with Lorenzo to visit Antía.

In Munrovian fashion, both the three stories and Almodóvar's film are marked by departures and returns. In 'Chance', readers are left to assume that Juliet has again departed from home (her parents' house and the house she grew up in in Ontario) to return to teach at Torrance House (a private girls' school) in Vancouver after a Christmas break. The three stories' biggest return, though, is to the parents' house, and this occupies almost all of the middle story, 'Soon'. *Julieta* does feature this same return, but it is given less narrative time. The two biggest returns in the film are Julieta's return to the flat in Madrid she rented and shared with her daughter, and her return to the events – via the letters and diaries she writes and narrates – that she believes prompted Antía to leave her forever. *Julieta* also ends with a departure to

Switzerland and begins with preparations for a departure to Portugal. The questing identified in Munro's work by Tolan (2010) is indeed ambiguous and hesitant in the three stories. But a sense of quest seems more obvious in *Julieta* than in the stories. At the start of the film, Julieta is in love, excited and determined about her new life in Portugal. This older Julieta does not seem too far removed from the bright, strong young woman we meet at the start of the film's fabula. In the early school sequence (the Torrance House equivalent not given a name or location), Julieta's confidence, desire and hunger for life are underlined.

The school sequence begins with Julieta in medium shot and centre-stage in the classroom. She is young and vibrant and charismatic (short, spikey peroxide hair, short skirt, busy jumper and black DM boots), with bright-eyed and highly engaged students. The lesson is about Greek vocabulary and myth. Julieta asks her students which type of sea we might associate with Ulysses. Via allusions to Hollywood stars and sex, she helps them to arrive at the right answer: Póntos is Ulysses's type of sea, 'the road to adventure and the unknown'. The classroom scene draws a strong parallel between Julieta and Ulysses as fearless adventurers, and this is endorsed by the final close-medium shot that tightly frames Julieta's luminescent face with the word Póntos on the blackboard. The school sequence then continues, and Julieta's potency and mastery of her environment are only heightened. A short but dynamic two-shot movement takes Julieta into the head teacher's office, where she is told that her standing with staff and students could not be higher, and that they are very sad to be losing her (her short-term replacement contract has expired). Julieta is not deflated, and the upbeat scene is joined by intrigue when the teacher hands her a letter. As we move with a cut from office back out into school corridors, Julieta's purposeful movement is joined by mystery music. This is the point in the sequence where Julieta is made most the adventurer on the high seas, entering the unknown without trepidation. The shot is medium-long in deep focus. Julieta walks towards us, filling the frame. She is smiling, contemplative, excited. The letter is from Xoan, the man she had a brief, passionate encounter with on the train. She is now walking in and through the tunnel of adventure, like the sea, strong and blue-grey in appearance. The building is modern, and the pillars Julieta walks through are large, square and geometric. This serves to heighten her purpose, and while the tunnel is in light and shadow, Julieta seems to bring light with her out of the tunnel. By the time we cut to her leaving through the school gates, she seems to know exactly where she's going. This powerful I-know-where-I'm-going sequence sets us up for the defeated, traumatised and greatly diminished version of Julieta we'll encounter later in the film, following the death of Xoan and departure of Antía. However, in the film and in marked contrast to the stories, Julieta does find a stronger version of herself again – wiping the past away via a new, modern, minimalist flat in Madrid, a new relationship and a planned new start in Portugal.

So questing and journeying are more complicated than they might initially appear in *Julieta*, and the same in some ways is true of Munro's triptych – where Juliet's vocation, clearly, is not teaching, and she also dismisses the notion of fate. Juliet's love of classical mythology, however, is presented as a constant. Classical stories are used in Juliet's romantic first encounter with Eric on the train, and also in her fantastic rewriting of Heliodorus's *Aethiopica*. In this story, Juliet has a perverse fascination for the 'ironclad devotion to purity of life and thought' (Munro 2006: 152) of the gymnosophists. She casts herself, though, as the queen of Ethiopia, who longs for the return of her kidnapped daughter. In Juliet's revised ending of the story, the daughter Charicleia, in a 'backward search' (Munro 2006: 152), renounces her learning with the gymnosophists, resists all fakers and charlatans, and is reconciled with the 'erring, repentant, essentially great-hearted queen of Ethiopia' (ibid.).

Juliet's love of learning and passion for the classics has stemmed from her parents, especially her father (this cultural formation and specific aspect of a complicated parental relationship is absent from the film). In the stories, it is Juliet's father who is the charismatic and inspirational teacher; and at the end of Juliet's journey, in 'Silence', she is pleased to have a tiny garden of her own – to be at last and for the first time a gardener 'as her father had been' (Munro 2006: 150). Her love for and admiration of her father endure, and she hopes her return home in 'Soon' will be a triumph in his eyes. This fantasy is confused and deflated by the all-pervasive social gaze of her home town (including her father) – the shame and pity of an unmarried mother – as well as by her disgust in the changes to her father – i.e. his clear affection for Irene (the young carer of Juliet's mother), and his decision to relinquish education for business.

Juliet's retreat into grief and loss and a tolerated unhappiness develops in stages in Munro's stories, such that, for all its relativising and shifts in tense and time and mode of enunciation, it exhibits a fairly clear linearity. This is less true of *Julieta*, which is more subject to melodramatic turnaround. Moreover, in Almodóvar's film, Julieta is as exiled and perhaps more homeless than Munro's Juliet. In the film, the family is given considerably less impact than in the stories – and in fact we never see the house in which Julieta grew up. One place of retreat and apparent peace (the modern Madrid flat) is given up when Julieta hears of her daughter's existence; and the key point of return, submission and potential repair (the writing in the old Madrid flat) seems to be dismissed when Julieta is rescued by Lorenzo and at last receives a letter from Antía. At the close of the film, Julieta is on the road, hesitant and scared, en route to an unknown person (Antía) and future.

Expanded Grief

Julieta's 'move(ment) back and forth' (Munro, in Tolan 2010: 168), then, is more marked, more Munrovian than in the three stories. To some extent this results from the conventions of the melodramatic form and its greater dependence on chance. In *Julieta*, Julieta's chance meeting with Bea is repeated, given greater narrative impact than in the stories, and also brought forward to the start of the syuzhet. But the backward and forwardness of *Julieta* has a meaning beyond the film's use of melodrama. It is also about trauma and history and a search for home. These themes and questions are articulated in different ways in the film, but are encapsulated in the street-wandering body of Julieta. This is a key visual expression of Munro's 'tortuous meanderings' (Tolan 2010: 176). The lead-footed figure of Julieta is not entirely absent from the stories, but Juliet does not walk repeatedly in a fugue through the streets of the city; and the most physical manifestation of her grief is a brief and devastating episode: 'So this is grief. She feels as if a sack of cement has been poured in to her and quickly hardened. She can barely move' (Munro 2006: 147).

This weight, this being weighed down, permeates *Julieta*, and in the terms of Mroz makes it a post-traumatic text, where 'the strange and heavy agony of grief . . . bends cinematic form and warps *mise en scène*' (2016: 4). This is a specific direction in which the film takes the three stories. As I've noted, the stories are not without trauma – the trauma of a sharp and unexpected attack of grief a short period after the death of Eric. What infuses the stories, however, is an increasing sense of loss, as well as a permanent tension between the individual and the social. *Julieta*'s expansion of trauma and post-trauma is expressed via the face and body of Julieta. In the first instance, the zombie-like figure of young Julieta is traumatised by grief following the death of Xoan. This appears to be straightforward mourning, and before the street-wandering begins is played out briefly via black clothing, a tearful identification of Xoan's body, and a scattering of ashes into the sea. Antía and Bea help Julieta to get through her mourning so she can function again in the world. But something remains, so that Julieta both stays indoors and dedicates all of herself beyond her new job to Antía. In Williams's (2009) terms, Julieta is a mourner and a melancholic, finding both the world and herself poor and empty. The film and Julieta at this point seem to anticipate the traumatic melancholia that will crush her following Antía's departure. However, while the initial loss of Antía is given its melodramatic moments – drinking and smoking alone in a barely lit apartment, followed by a fit of anger vented on Antía's bedroom and possessions – it does not descend to its traumatic depths until Julieta has her first chance meeting with Bea. Prior to this meeting, Julieta appears to be in a state of relatively even gender melancholia: 'the process by which the heterosexual ego assumes normative gender by giving up its forbidden homosexual attachments' (Williams 2009: 170–1).

However, as a melancholic, Julieta not only 'holds on to the object' (2009: 171), she also attempts to erase it, hiding it from Lorenzo, who it's revealed is ignorant of Antía's existence. The fallacy of this erasure is then shown when Antía's existence is confirmed by Bea. At this point, Julieta moves beyond the (heterosexual) norms of gender melancholia. She is consumed by a pathological mourning and excessive melancholia 'that fails to get over the loss of the love object' (Williams 2009: 168): attempting it seems to prolong indefinitely her cathexis to it.

This is what Julieta does when she turns away from Lorenzo and returns to the old flat in Madrid. It also describes the ending of Munro's three stories. Juliet's singular goal at the end of 'Silence' now has a perfect clarity and purity. As soon as she learns at the close of the triptych of Penelope's existence, she knows that she must turn away from any other possible associations and attachments (Gary) and wait and suffer in her own silence: 'She keeps on hoping for a word from Penelope, but not in any strenuous way. She hopes as people who know better hope for undeserved blessings, spontaneous remissions, things of that sort' (Munro 2006: 158). If this cathexis seems at odds with the characteristic recalcitrance of Munro's short stories (so vividly expressed in Juliet's version of the Ethiopia myth), it also has its own logic – because Penelope's existence serves to legitimate the absoluteness and finality of Juliet's rejection of anything that might divert her from this path. In this sense, while the ending of 'Silence' is enormously powerful in its ambiguity, its poetry and its philosophy, it is also highly melodramatic, in that Juliet's pure and motherly suffering is also a form of occulting – a kind of magic, a 'coin of virtue' (Williams 2009: 167), which Juliet vaguely but desperately hopes might yet be cashed in.

As I've noted, though, *Julieta*'s key differences in this respect are in the extent and multiple nature of its trauma. The weighed-downness of the film is evident from the start. What is also obvious from the opening is the inseparability in *Julieta* of mystery and trauma. Lister criticises Sarah Polley's adaptation of 'The Bear Came Over the Mountain' (Munro 1999) – *Away From Her* (Polley 2006) – because she believes it removes the 'Weltian mystery' (Lister 2013: 44) from Munro's short story, making clear, for example, the motivations of central characters. In the *Runaway* Juliet triptych, there is no particular mystery to Juliet's journeys, actions and motivations, however conflicted she is at points and throughout. The mystery is the reason for Penelope's failure to communicate or return, but even this is not dwelled on until the stories' close. Applying Lister's (2013) thesis to *Julieta*, it might be argued that the film succumbs to the demands of high-finance, widely distributed cinema via both the heavy-handed exposition scene in hospital just prior to Ava's death (when Antía's motivations for ex-communication and punishment are revealed to Julieta by Ava), and the fact that the film's ending points to a meeting and potential reconciliation between Julieta and Antía. I want to suggest, though, that *Julieta*'s mystery, like its trauma, exceeds that of the triptych, and moreover is not clearly solved by the film. Indeed what I'm calling the heavy-handed hospital scene proves to be a false resolution, in that it is shortly after Ava's shocking revelations that Julieta moves through her mourning and gets her life back on track – only then to be sent back downwards by the two chance meetings with Bea. Moreover, not only is Julieta still traumatised on her journey to Switzerland at the film's close, but she also tells Lorenzo that she does not intend to ask Antía why she excommunicated her.

Mystery and Shame, Writing and Voice

At one level, then, the mystery remains unsolved, and is also more generally overdetermined by the film. It is with us from the start and is all-consuming. It pervades the film and also peaks melodramatically at points. Two of the most obvious points, and scenes absent from the stories, are noirish nighttime scenes: the night of the storm and Xoan's death; and the night Antía returns with Ava to the house in Galicia and is told by Marian what she believes to be the true and accurate course of events on the fateful night. Along with the film's score, these are two of *Julieta*'s most Hitchcockian moments. They also feature a Hitchcockian figure (Marian, channelling, as it were, *Rebecca*'s (1940) Mrs Danvers), so maximised as to verge on parody. Kevin Sandler's analysis of Hitchcock's films helps us to understand the nature of the mystery in *Julieta*.

Sandler notes the argument of a number of theorists that 'guilt is the key to the complexity of Hitchcock's moral universe' (1997: 137). However in his analysis of Hitchcock's films – in particular what he considers to be the most unresolved and disturbing ones – *The Wrong Man* (1956), *The Paradine Case* (1947), and *Vertigo* (1958) – Sandler argues that shame, more than guilt, prevails. The two may converge, but they retain nonetheless significant differences:

> (T)he guilty self knows exactly what the punishment will be prior to the transgression. One never knows the path nor the outcome shame will take. By catching one off guard and unaware, the shamed situation is uncontrollable. Its unexpectancy creates an isolating and alienating experience . . . (and) sets one apart from the ordered world. (1997: 138–9)

Sandler finds *The Wrong Man* particularly powerful and disturbing in its articulation of shame. It is one of the most acute examples, he suggests, of Hitchcock's fascination with abjection and fear of abandonment. Its discomfort results from extreme fatalism and the powerlessness of the film's protagonists in the face of coincidence and bad luck. The great burden of shame and suffering in the film, Sandler argues, falls on Rose (Vera Miles). While society judges Manny (Henry Fonda) to be free at the film's close, 'Rose's inability to reconcile her perceived failure as a mother, a wife and a woman, is too much shame for even a "happy ending" to overcome' (1997: 146). Female suffering explains part of Hitchcock's attraction to Almodóvar. And for all her hatred of Mother Shipton's superior wisdom, it is Juliet's perceived failings as a mother that refuse to be banished at the close of 'Silence'. With regard to Sandler's analysis, though, it is shame, abjection, coincidence and fatalism that are amplified in the mysterious and traumatic world of *Julieta*.

Shame, mystery and trauma, I've suggested, are overdetermined in *Julieta* via score and a weighed-down body and *mise en scène*. They are also expressed and equally overdetermined by writing and voiceover, the latter connecting in part with Sandler's (1997) argument regarding fatalism and Hitchcock and shame. On her first entry to her letter/diary/confession to Antía – the 'hazardous journey through the "tunnel of memory"' (Ibáñez 2013: 163, quoting Almodóvar) – Julieta's voice and aural and visual arrangement powerfully evince noirish fatalism. This continues the move in Almodóvar's films into 'dark melodrama . . . (and) stormy *film noir*' (Ibáñez 2013: 169) that Ibáñez suggests begins with *All about My Mother* (1999). In this scene, Julieta seems at once to be cutting through and submitting to a web of investigation. This is how Karen Hollinger describes voiceover in the woman's film: 'She has possession of the voiceover narration but in a sense is also possessed by it as its object of inquiry' (1992: 35). Hollinger breaks the woman's film down into four sub-genres (maternal melodrama, medical melodrama, love story and paranoid gothic woman's film), and notes that while female voiceover is rare in, for example, 1940s gothic melodramas, in the woman's film more generally it is 'extensive' (1992: 50).

Marsha Kinder describes Almodóvar as the master of maternal melodrama (2013: 293), and looks in detail at his use of voice and sound. Kinder's assessment of Almodóvar contrasts significantly with that of Lange-Churion (2016). Kinder argues that the director's use of voice and sound is one indicator of his artistic growth. The maternal voice in particular, Kinder argues, is a key feature of Almodóvar's 're-trial' (2013: 299) and dialogic approach to his films – a 're-visiting and improving what he has already done' (ibid.). The voice – a 're-envoicement' (2013: 284) – reverberates across his macro-melodrama. Frequently, Kinder notes, the mother's voice in Almodóvar's films is a source of grace – forgiving the unforgivable and offering the possibility of rebirth. Sometimes it will confess crimes against the father; always it will produce an 'audio fetish that binds mother and daughter' (2013: 294). In this respect, Kinder argues, Almodóvar's use of sound and voice is profoundly feminised, and acutely aware of the 'gendering of sound-image relations . . . within Hollywood classical cinema' (ibid.).

Kinder notes that one of the key films of Almodóvar featuring a mother's voice as a source of grace is *The Flower of My Secret* (1995). This film, she argues, marked a shift in Almodóvar's work to a more sombre form of melodrama, and featured 'fashionably lean writer Leo (Marisa Paredes)' (2013: 292). Leo is saved from suicide when she hears internally the voice of her mother. This also helps her to move from a form of writing that restricts her to a more expressive and liberating form of writing. In *Julieta*, too, writing is voiced-over and inseparable from a mother's voice. The letter in the 'literary film', Vidal argues (2006: 425), is overvalued and has a meaning beyond its material presence. It points to a subject 'always already alienated in the Symbolic order' (2006: 426):

> [Its] cluster of signifiers . . . (the voice, the face, the writing hand, the paper, the quill) . . . suggest that the letter constitutes . . . an unstable, composite sign. Rather than a metaphoric, 'deep' object, the letter – the presence of writing within the film text – creates relations between subjective positions and, at the same time, stresses their unstable status, their performativeness. (Ibid.)

Julieta is not a literary film in the way Vidal's examples (*The Age of Innocence*, 1993; *Onegin*, 1999) are literary films, but it is a film equally overdetermined by writing (and voiceover). However, I follow the work of Isaacs to suggest that is it is not enough or accurate to describe Almodóvar's film as haunted by Alice Munro and her writing. Cinema, Isaacs argues, 'is indelibly imprinted with the expressive modalities of writing (whether short story, novel or screenplay) that traverses literary and imagistic significatory fields' (2016: 437). Isaacs' example in this part of his analysis is Annie Proulx and the strong interrelation between her short story and the film of it directed by Ang Lee (*Brokeback Mountain*, 2005). Similarly, I want to suggest that *Julieta* and Munro's stories share a 'method' (Isaacs 2016: 441) and an expressive modality of which writing and voice are key parts.

This language of recalcitrance, of unknowability and, especially in Almodóvar's case, mutability, is shared by *Julieta*, and given its strongest expression in writing and voiceover. In the film, and progressively in the stories, the narrative voice is compelled by misplaced guilt and a longing for an imagined past. It occupies 'the domain of the inexpressible that nurtures the melancholy for an imaginary (lost) world' (Vidal 2006: 429). The most obvious loss in the stories and in the film is Penelope/Antía, and the melancholia that ensues is, in Williams's (2009) terms, for the pre-oedipal world of mother and daughter. I suggested that at the close of the triptych, Juliet resorts to a certain type of occultism is the hope of returning Penelope to her mother. In the film, when Julieta first sits down to write, it is a powerful ritual; a no less desperate attempt to magic Antía and the past into existence. The writing in a sense is Antía and is Julieta, and voiceover and image work to give this idea form. In Cixous' terms, Julieta's writing produces a 'memory of the flesh' (Cixous, in Delgado-Poust 2016: 1569). For Belén Vidal, this will to reanimate is a familiar function of the letter in film:

> '[T]he very fact of addressing someone in an epistle ... transforms the addressee from an absent figure into a presence, which hovers in the text's interstices.' The letter ... begs the exploration of the *writing effect* as one such interstitial inscription of absence in the plentitude of the illusionist cinematic text. (2006: 419–20, Vidal here quoting Naficy 2001)

The absences in *Julieta* are multiple and unstable, and the film makes little attempt to hide the fetish it makes of writing and voice. As I've begun to suggest, the clean writing sheet represents a submission of sorts to monsters as well as demons. The clean white sheet, as Kinder (2013) suggests of the aural parts of Almodóvar's films, reverberates within and beyond the film. The modern Madrid flat is a failed attempt to wipe clean and start afresh. The unnaturally clean white sheet in the over-conventionalised mourning scene struggles to conceal something broken, deformed, monstrous – and connects with other heavy, brutal, dismembered and broken figures throughout the film, not least the zombie-like and, at one point, two-headed Julieta. In this respect, Julieta's diaries, narration and street-wandering represent what Delgado-Poust calls 'traumatic body memory ... *le corps morcele* ... that ... disables the efficacy and implies the dissolution and fragmentation of the intact body and identity' (2016: 1565). The multiplicity of the absences and the presences in the interstices and the monstrosity are important because they take *Julieta* beyond blankness and erasure. Erasing difficult historical and political questions is, as I've noted, what Lange-Churion (2016) argues is achieved by Almodóvar's late films. Again, here, Kinder understands Almodóvar's work in a markedly different way:

> Although Almodóvar had deliberately acted (especially early in his career) as if Franco had never existed, he boldly replaced those official voices with an outrageous cacophony of commentaries, speeches, and songs from his own subculture of the *Movida* and from other foreign underground movements. (2013: 285)

Obscene Virtue and Fidelity

From this quote, in Kinder's terms, Franco and Spain's past are inescapably absent and present: they never existed, but they nonetheless inform his work. At one level, it is this inescapability, this impossibility that Almodóvar revisits in *Julieta*, and that Julieta speaks to when she writes. If at the start of the film

Julieta boxes away and erases Antía and the past, then as she admits herself, as an 'addict' (see the writing scene I refer to below), part of her knew she would always return. But as well as being characterised as an illness and pathology, the writing begins as if it were the resumption of a mysterious, dangerous courtship. Typically, Vidal notes (2006: 428), the letter in film is an occulted and fetishised object, a fantasy of and compensation for an absent other – classically, in Lacanian terms, an impossible, courted lover, a union endlessly deferred. This courtship in *Julieta* seems to end in flat disgust in a hospital room when Julieta tells Lorenzo to destroy her diaries. This disgust, it appears, results from the second meeting with Bea, where she reveals a truer, and in Bea's terms, uglier, more monstrous side to Antía.

Julieta feels betrayed and foolish that she could have devoted so much of herself to something or someone she barely knew or understood. At this point in the film, as at the close of the stories, there is a thin line between devotion and pathology, purity and monstrosity – between perhaps what Lange-Churion calls courtly love and obscene virtue. These terms in Lange-Churion's analysis (2016: 445) of Almodóvar's films, translate only into patriarchy and conservative morality; and he opposes these to the subversive potential of the Bakhtinian carnival. The virtue in *Julieta* is obscene indeed in its perversion of saintliness and purity, and of mothering as self-abnegation. However, the excesses of Julieta's devotion and pathology go beyond the terms of Lange Churion's analysis. Two moments in *Julieta* exemplify this. The first is when Julieta is immersed in her obsession after her first chance meeting with Bea but not as traumatised as she will be after the second meeting. She is writing her diaries/letter to Antía and narrates this for viewers: 'When a former addict relapses just once . . . the relapse is fatal. I abstained from you for years . . . Your absence fills my entire life and destroys it.' These fatal, noir-ish lover's words are spoken over a beautifully arranged shot that does not match them entirely. This is the companion shot to the earlier tunnel shot (to which I refer above: when young Julieta leaves the school). The earlier shot, as I note, is the tunnel of adventure. The companion shot that I'll look briefly at now is the tunnel of memory and love.

The shot is of Julieta writing in the old Madrid flat. It begins as a beautiful medium shot, where there is an ontological harmony between Julieta and writing. The camera is at knee-height and it appears to be midday. Sunlight streams into the large, almost empty room in broad shafts via two tall French windows. While some shadow remains, the effect is one of light and air. This is matched by Julieta's pose and appearance. She perches on her chair, but is not precarious. She is settled but weightless – weightless at last, if fleetingly. She wears cream light linen shorts and a matching shirt open at the neck. She writes on a glass table that we can see through from our low perspective. She is framed by one of the large windows that is open onto a sunny street. Wisps of steam rise from the coffee cup at her elbow. The shot is elegant and simple and employs a graphic match between legs – Julieta's bare bent legs, the crossed wooden legs of the glass table and the steel legs of her chair. This heightens the sense of harmony and flow. Julieta is lit in sun and shadow, slender, purposeful and ageless. While she describes herself in the narration/writing as a broken addict, the image before us is a more benign spirit. The camera then starts to slowly recede and the shot becomes more congruent with the weight of the narration. It remains beautiful, but is now more of a mystery and a tunnel. The receding shot is through dark doors and down an unlit hallway. Julieta remains our focus in a longer shot, until there is a cut to a close-up of the words 'la destruye' on the page in front of her as she narrates it. The receding shot is in marked contrast to young Julieta striding towards us in the tunnel of adventure shot. It, the receding shot, might also be conceived of as one of the most potent moments of the film's 'backward search' (Munro 2006: 152).

The second moment is an excessive display of singular love. It is a warmly lit bedroom scene on the evening that Julieta returns from visiting her parents with the infant Antía. In a medium-close tableau, Julieta settles the child in her cot while Xoan in foreground-left takes off his top to become semi-naked. As Julieta turns from the cot to come more fully into shot, she notices a new tattoo on Xoan's upper-left arm. The tattoo is a red heart. Inside the heart is a boat on the seas and on either side of it two capital letters in black: A and J. When Xoan confirms that this is Antía and Julieta, Julieta is thrilled and bends to kiss the tattoo. Xoan tells her to be careful as the tattoo is still tender, confirmed by the angry skin surrounding it. We then cut to an extreme close-up of Julieta kissing the tattoo – so close as to cede eroticism to monstrosity. Mysterious thriller music meets the kiss, and the shot finishes and is held on an open, wet, red mouth very close to the red, raw tattoo.

The lines of devotion and obscenity are more complicated in *Julieta* than Lange-Churion (2016) suggests of Almodóvar's work. In both the stories and the film, fidelity is one of the key mysteries, and this is especially so with regard to *Julieta*. Fidelity in the film is snare and monster. After the briefest of exchanges, it prompts a fateful trip and a death with apparently endless repercussions. It prompts the vindictive telling of the perceived truth by a monstrous figure (Marian) who acts out of fidelity to Xoan, Antía and an anachronistic sense of family honour. That fidelity is so expanded and complicated and played across women in Almodóvar's version of the stories is perhaps no surprise. Julia Biggane's work points to a specific but widely felt feature of Spanish history and culture which arguably is one part of *Julieta*'s dialogue and dense network of associations.

Biggane has researched Spanish political memoirs published until at least the mid-1980s. Her specific focus is the memoirs and autobiographies of male and female members of the Falange movement. Her findings, however, are supported by her broader secondary research of 'female life writing' (2015: 518). Male memoirs, Biggane finds, follow a *Bildungsroman* trajectory with emphases on agency and autonomy. They are dissolute, distancing themselves in the post-war period first from Falangism, and then from state fascism more broadly. Female memoirs, Biggane finds, are markedly different. They are classically organic rather than dissolute. They are characterised by their recurring references to confinement and impotence, but are also highly relational and frequently visual. Their primary 'obsessive' (2015: 520) focus, though, is loyalty, continuity, lineage and fidelity. This emphasis, Biggane argues, is a 'political affect' (2015: 523) in which it is difficult to separate the personal and familial from specific historical circumstances. Indeed, while Biggane argues that there are clear historical reasons why the need for continuity and fidelity is most felt by women in late-modern Spain, she also finds, in the women's memoirs and autobiographies, that the target of the fidelity is less clear – and that there is evidence of

> chinks of doubt, disavowal and indications of the chafing constriction of post-Unification female Falangism . . . (F)or all that Primo de Rivera places her faith in family lineage as the key to preserving the political integrity of Spain, there seems to be a disavowed recognition that lineage, however pure and tightly clung to, is also fragile and easily lost. (Ibid.)

Biggane's research helps to show the complexity and the deep-rootedness of the relationships among women, fidelity and writing in Spanish culture. How applicable these findings and ideas are beyond Spain is debatable; but I would suggest there is a connection here to the power and mystery of Munro's triptych that so attracted Almodóvar. In the stories, it is clear that Juliet's strongest connections are with her father and daughter. At the close of 'Silence', Juliet speculates and hopes that something of her father might endure in Penelope, and that it might be this 'purity' and 'rock-hard' (Munro 2006: 158) quality that explain why the daughter no longer has any use for her mother. Exactly what this purity in Penelope might be is hard for readers of the stories to judge, as so little time is spent with the daughter. But we know what Juliet imagines it to be; and it is given form in her journey and her thoughts, in her recasting of the Ethiopia myth and, especially, in her relationship with her father, Sam. The 'rock-hard honesty' (Munro 2006: 158) of Sam's thought and actions set themselves in Juliet's imagination against vulgar provincialism and smallmindedness – against what Tolan (2010) calls the Canadian communitarian ethos. This is consistent in the stories, but slips in its focus – a deep fidelity to the father that, following Biggane (2015), struggles to keep a purchase: Sam foregoes the heroic integrity of teaching for the dirty commerce of market gardening; Sam teaches Juliet how to discretely separate herself from the herd, but, like her, most wants to be just like it; Sam tears down the only place Juliet has ever thought of as home. But for all the fragility, absence and unknownness of the objects of Juliet's fidelity – or perhaps because of these qualities – Juliet holds fastest to some principle of purity, in so doing increasingly isolating and impoverishing herself.

Fidelity, then, is a key part of the stories and is related in complex ways to gendered and social identities and the Canadian communitarian perspective. Fidelity in *Julieta*, as in the memoirs examined by Biggane (2015), is central to the point of obsession. Its connection to the social is less obvious than in the stories. Instead, its inextricability from gendered and political Spanish history is amplified. This amplification is evident in various ways in the film and is articulated via women, writing, voice and silence. It reaches a point of melodramatic excess in the hospital scene (Julieta's final visit to Ava), but its focus here is not clarified. The reasons for Antía's departure are revealed as grotesquely unfair and disastrously familiar. Ava is shamed by Antía as a 'whore' for sleeping with her father; Julieta is shamed by Antía for driving Xoan to his death by failing to forgive him for his infidelities. Even this interpretation lends too much coherence to Antía's reasoning. What most gives the scene form is obscene fidelity to absent and imagined figures. This is the difficult and inescapable fidelity that gives shape to Almodóvar's adaptation of Munro's triptych. It is a deeply Spanish fidelity that is most felt and least finished, perhaps, for women. It is also Munrovian, sharing with Munro's stories an expressive form that underlines recalcitrance and mutability. Looking at *Julieta* as Almodóvar's most Munrovian film allows us to see that, yes, it is indeed a very inward-looking text, but that this is not a disavowal of the past. Equally the film is about departures, and this may seem to take it out and beyond the highly centripetal triptych. This however misses the productive obsessions and enduring method of Almodóvar and Munro. For both these writers, the journey and the quest and change are evident and marked, but not paramount: difficult knowledge and resonance – Barthes' 'thousand entrances' (in Kinder 2013: 300) – involve going back – back into the house, bravely, painfully, to find the door or room missed, and always 'more than you saw the last time' (Munro, in Lister 2013: 45).

References

Biggane, J. (2015), 'Loyal subjects: gender, fidelity and the post-Franco Falangist memoir', *Bulletin of Spanish Studies*, 92: 8–10, 511–23.

Delgado-Poust, A. (2016), '(It's) all about the mother: scarred memories and amnesic bodies in Rosa Montero's *La Hija del Caníbal*', *Bulletin of Spanish Studies*, 93: 9, 1555–70.

Hollinger, K. (1992), 'Listening to the female voice in the woman's film', *Film Criticism*, 16: 3, 34–52.

Ibáñez, J. C. (2013), 'Memory, politics, and the post-transition in Almodóvar's cinema', in M. D'Lugo and K. M. Vernon (eds), *A Companion to Pedro Almodóvar*, Malden, MA: John Wiley, pp. 153–75.

Isaacs, B. (2016), 'Literary images: towards a phenomenology of cinematic writing', *Screen* 57: 4, 431–45.

Kinder, M. (2013), 'Re-envoicements and reverberations in Almodóvar's macro-melodrama', in M. D'Lugo and K. M. Vernon (eds), *A Companion to Pedro Almodóvar*, Malden, MA: John Wiley, pp. 281–303.

Lange-Churion, P. (2016), 'Pedro Almodóvar's *La Piel Que Habito*: of late style and erotic conservatism', *Bulletin of Spanish Studies*, 93: 3, 441–53.

Lister, R. (2013), 'Adapting the short story: fidelity and motivation in Sarah Polley's *Away From Her*', *Journal of Adaptation in Film and Performance*, 6: 1, 43–54.

Mroz, M. (2016), 'Framing loss and figuring grief in Pawel Pawlikowski's *Ida*', *Screening the Past*, 41.

Munro, A. (2006), *Runaway*, London: Vintage Books.

Naficy, H. (2001), *An Accented Cinema: Exilic and Diasporic Filmmaking*, Princeton: Princeton University Press.

Romney, J. (2016a), 'Pedro Almodóvar: "Nobody sings. There's no humour. I just wanted restraint"', *The Observer*, 7 August 2016.

Romney, J. (2016b), 'Reviews: *Julieta*', *Sight & Sound*, 26: 9, 80.

Sandler, K. S. (1997), 'The concept of shame in the films of Alfred Hitchcock', *Hitchcock Annual*, 6, 137–52.

Tolan, Fiona (2010), 'To leave and to return: frustrated departures and female quest in Alice Munro's *Runaway*', *Contemporary Women's Writing*, 4: 3, 161–78.

Vidal, B. (2006), 'Labyrinths of loss: the letter as figure of desire and deferral in the literary film', *Journal of European Studies*, 36: 4, 418–36.

Williams, L. (2009), 'Melancholy melodrama: Almodóvarian grief and lost homosexual attachments', in B. Epps and D. Kakoudaki (eds), *All About Almodóvar: A Passion for Cinema*, Minneapolis: University of Minnesota Press, pp. 166–92.

Filmography

Almodóvar, P. (1986), *Women on the Verge of a Nervous Breakdown*. Laurenfilm/El Deseo.
Almodóvar, P. (1995), *The Flower of My Secret*. CiBy 2000/El Deseo.
Almodóvar, P. (1999), *All about My Mother*. El Deseo.
Almodóvar, Pedro (2016), *Julieta*. Echo Lake/El Deseo.
Fiennes, Martha (1999), *Onegin*. 7 Arts International.
Hitchcock, A. (1947), *The Paradine Case*. Selznick International Pictures.
Hitchcock, A. (1956), *The Wrong Man*. Warner Bros.
Hitchcock, A. (1958), *Vertigo*. Alfred J. Hitchcock Productions.
Lee, A. (2005), *Brokeback Mountain*. Focus Features.
Polley, S. (2006), *Away From Her*. Foundry Films.
Scorsese, Martin (1993), *The Age of Innocence*. Columbia Pictures.

PART IV

THE LOCAL, THE GLOBAL AND THE COSMOPOLITAN

8. *EL PATRÓN DEL MAL*: A NATIONAL ADAPTATION AND *NARCOS* PRECEDENT

Ernesto Pérez Morán

Introduction

The research project *Historias locales, visiones globales* (*Local Stories, Global Visions*) financed by the University of Medellín (Colombia) in collaboration with two other Spanish universities, the Pontificia of Salamanca and the Carlos III of Madrid, commenced in 2017. The project's goal was the comparative study of two television series, *Narcos* and *El Patrón del Mal* (*EPDM*). The idea was to scrutinise both productions in order to elucidate their main similarities and differences, as well as whether or not their countries of origin had conditioned the way the respective stories were articulated. For that, nine hundred scenes were selected (out of a total of 4,154 between both) and analysed from different perspectives: script, staging, sound and the connection between the narrated events and the way they were actually presented.

I have decided on a slightly different and provocative approach here, given that my main objective was based on two separate understandings of *adaptation*: on the one hand, there is the *adaptation* of *EPDM* from Alonso Salazar's *La Parábola de Pablo* (2001), which has led to a compared analysis between the two series and the book. The series obviously had different audiences in mind – this was reflected on the perspectives they adopted and that conditioned their discourses, especially when measuring how true-to-life they were to the actual events, as well as the 'degree of similarity between the characters and the events found in the film and the book' (Sánchez Noriega 2000: 63). On the other hand, even though *Narcos* does not have a direct literary reference, it adapts Colombian reality and history in accordance perhaps with what audiences around the world expect. Thus, I aim to clarify this adaptation manoeuvre of extreme currency through the lens of postcolonial studies.

Starting with the latter objective, let me consider a few lines taken from an obscure, albeit intriguing, article written by Von der Walde (1998), in which she establishes a stimulating analogy between magical realism and postcoloniality: 'Both discourses about otherness have had held positions of privilege in the academia of the so-called First World partly because they have been provided by the Other,' The author is thinking of Spivak (1990), when she defends the 'canonization of magical realism as a literary paradigm of Third World production' (1998: 161). She goes on to develop a useful argument:

> Magical realism, understood as a version of otherness rendered by the Other, once incorporated by First World academia, detached from its historical context and converted into a formula, accomplishes very little. It finally merges into a process of colonization through discourse ... and converts into a hegemonic discourse, doing away with the differences and placing them abroad, in another culture. (1998: 161)

To conclude, the author claims that 'drug trafficking is the phenomenon in which the colonial experience most dramatically crosses paths with capitalism ... at the same time that its lack of presence in academic circles is symptomatic' (ibid: 171).

Digging Deeper

> Magical realism is defined as what happens when a highly detailed, realistic setting is invaded by something too strange to believe. There is a reason magical realism was born in Colombia.
>
> (*Narcos*, 2015–)

Thus begins *Narcos*, as if ascertaining a mainstream transmutation of Von der Walde's postulates, juggling two of the most commonplace clichés about Colombia – magical realism and drug trafficking. It is misleading because, in reality, magical realism is a terminology that was created in 1925 by the art critic Franz Roh, who utilised this label to define a certain type of post-expressionist painting (Bautista 1991). Exemplifying colonial tradition in its truest form, the narration starts (we here adopt the point of view of the Other) showing a Centra Spike[1] airplane flying over the Medellín skies at the same time that we hear Steve Murphy's voiceover about the United States government and about Colombian drug lords. It highlights the intention to tell a story about something alien, about these Others, that will be translated into the types of characters, the scenes and the storytelling from an American perspective, all funded by Netflix – it also includes an extremely misleading note of disclosure at the start of every episode, stating two things in just a few lines:

> This television series is inspired by true events. Some of the characters, names, businesses, incidents and certain locations and events have been fictionalized for dramatization purposes. Any similarity to the name, character or history of any person is entirely coincidental and unintentional. (*Narcos*, 2015–)

There is little truth in this statement – *Narcos* is, as I will demonstrate, a manifestation of colonial discourses, an adaptation of history according to ethnocentric and hegemonic standards.

EPDM begins with a quote that goes in a different direction altogether: 'Those who don't know their own history are doomed to repeat it', attributed to the Spanish philosopher Jorge Agustín Nicolás Ruiz de Santayana. It implies a moral warning, a revisionist declaration from the producers and a way to connect with the Colombian spectator, at whom this series is directed. The different target audiences play an important role in the production process – *Narcos* is global, *EPDM* is domestic. *Narcos* also features some questionable casting decisions: a Brazilian actor (Wagner Moura) plays Pablo Escobar, Colonel Carrillo is played by a Cuban-American (Maurice Compte), and a Puertorriqueño (Luis Guzmán) plays the role of El Mexicano. Besides, the several artistic licenses taken by the series, often favouring the American protagonists, create a wide gap between the narrative and the Colombians who are familiar with Pablo's history – the production once again makes decisions with the global market in mind, creating a chronicle that is alien to most Colombian audiences. Omar Rincón was one of many critical voices that brought it forward. His diatribe 'Narcos da risa' (*El Tiempo*, 2015) was only one of the attacks, which have come from all directions, even from abroad. Sarah Gibson (2016) accused the series of 'cultural imperialism', very much like Michelle Klein (2016). At the same time, Juliana Martínez maintains that '*Narcos* has very little of the nuance and complexity that the real story of Escobar has' (2015). These intentional and oversimplified artistic concessions are present in *Narcos*, whose main characters, real-life agents Steve Murphy and Javier Peña who played a major role in the pursuit of Pablo – the hunt is the driving force behind the series plot – are not even present in the Colombian *telenovela* (soap opera). What moves the story forward here is Pablo Escobar, himself, his rise and downfall. This paradox reifies the conflict that will be dealt with forthwith.

Postcolonial Studies

I will continue by covering the postcolonial attempts at doing away with alien and ethnocentric points of view – I will also contemplate how the aforementioned panorama reflects on both series. This time, I will use a different starting point, in the words of Robert Guédiguian (2002), a filmmaker from Marseille: 'Men, (or) any community of human beings, need to fabricate their own image.' If I look backwards, postcolonial studies originated in North American universities between the 1960s and the 1970s as a reaction to the most distinguished school of thought of the time, which, in turn, sprouted from imperialism. The heads of the movement were scholars from several old colonies who questioned the legacy left by the empires and denounced how this hegemony denied formerly colonised countries a meaningful voice – their existence is seen only through the lens granted by First World countries. Galcerán goes straight to the point when she affirms:

> The colonial discourse portrays locals by always endowing them with negative traits or, at least, not as positive as Europeans'. The critical study of this discourse offers the very starting point of postcolonial and decolonial studies. (2016: 22)

With that in mind, it is not incidental that in *Narcos* the *sicarios* (hired assassins) are presented in such a Manichean way: the characterisation of Poison, one of Pablo's hitmen, is flat and lacking in nuance, regardless of the considerable weight he has in the narrative (he appears in 9.7 per cent of the scenes analysed). From him, we learn only of his obsession with the number of murders on his tab. There are no meaningful feelings or conflicts that help the development of his character, something that is extensive to the other *sicarios*, none of which fit the requisites (Egri 1960; Seger 1990) of deep and complex characterisation: they have no private lives, no background, they have no motivations, nor are they granted the slightest description or depth established by the aforementioned authors. The opposite happens in *EPDM*: Chili, like Poison, has a similar presence in the storytelling (6.4 per cent), however, he is meticulously construed through several plot twists and narrative threads dedicated to him. They show his aspirations to rise in the organisation, his friends and enemies inside the cartel, and even his purchases once he reaches a certain status. The same can be said about other hitmen, such as Topo, who will undergo his own transformation, or Popeye, whose name was changed to Marino in *EPDM* (avoiding possible legal problems), which is something Genette (1982) calls heterodiegetic transposition. Marino, for instance, will start as Regina Parejo's (Virginia Vallejo) personal driver and will evolve into one of Pablo's most infamous henchmen. His conflict lies in his feelings for

Yesenia and he will eventually play a major role in Pablo's downfall. This comes direct from the Alonso Salazar's novel, which will be seen later when I discuss *EPDM*'s adaptation.

Narcos uses a different path by painting an ideal picture of the American agents involved, Murphy and Peña, as well as of the Unites States ambassador, who will counsel all of the Colombian presidents and candidates in the first season. Murphy will fail to save the Minister of Justice but will successfully prevent president César Gaviria from boarding the Avianca plane (according to news articles of the time, this really never happened), which was carrying a bomb planted by Pablo. Returning to the topic of postcolonial studies, Edward Said's *Orientalism* (2008 [1978]) is a major reference work. It sharply reveals how the Western world has, throughout history, construed the East as the Other, and denounces its colonising and homogenising practices. Known for its fierce criticism, Frantz Fanon's *Los condenados de la tierra* (*The Wretched of the Earth*) (1961) is another crucial work. Fanon, a philosopher and a psychiatrist, charges against colonialism, which he considers a force that denies the subdued their very authenticity. The aforementioned Spivak coins the term *essentialism* as a strategic manoeuvre that creates stereotyped representations of subordinate identities. Silva (2016) adds to it, claiming that 'the postcolonial, subordinate, and decolonial studies proposed questioning the perspective of a Western-devised map layout of the Other'.

This map takes shape in *Narcos*'s very first shots and reveals itself in other aspects. The aesthetics chosen for Medellín, for example, portray a city that is far from its empirical reality: it is pictured as colourful and exotic (alien perspective) when, in fact, it's more on the cold brownish-grey side as the bricks and concrete of its backbone. Also, the choice of using the camera propped on the shoulder, especially in dialogue scenes shot in close-ups, conveys the idea of an artificial realism, particularly due to its point of view, emphasised by the voiceover of the protagonist, an American whose position of authority contradicts his knowledge of his surroundings. Rarely is the perspective of the Other so explicit as it is here, more so due to the dogmatism and Manichaeism present in these claims: In only two episodes of *Narcos* (the first and the fourth) can we find more than ten incidences of the aforementioned good versus evil polarisation. The first episode's prologue, which tells the origins of Pablo's rise to power, revolves around the binary, black-and-white confrontation between the good and the bad guys, including Nixon in the former group and Pinochet in the latter – although 'sometimes bad guys also do good things' (scene 10). Murphy's discourse is certainly ironic, nevertheless, this distance is non-existent in any of the seven references to the good and the bad guys found in episode 4. For instance, when Murphy talks about the judges in scene 20, 'For the first time in the history of Colombia it was the good guys who had to hide their faces behind the masks', or about law enforcement officers on scene 26, 'There were a lot of good cops in Colombia', about himself and his rivals on scene 39, 'The bad guys need to get lucky every time. The good guys just need to get lucky once', or, on scene 41, when he emphasises the message from the first episode, this time without a hint of irony, 'And sometimes, bad people help you do good things'.

Once more Said asserts that any report about the East given by an external source reveals that these representations are indeed only representations, 'not "natural" depictions of the Orient' (2008: 45). On the contrary, this against-the-grain postcolonial reading starts with the colonised subjects themselves, often present as lower-ranking theoreticians created by American academia. The education of a body of researchers born in the old colonies is a classic Trojan-horse-style strategy that strengthened their resistance and survival against colonialism. At the same time, it generated an inverted point of view by salvaging narrations and other cultural elements that can explain their own points of view, which, in turn, had the side effect of helping confront Eurocentric discourses.

The fact that *EPDM* eliminated almost all the foreign characters stresses its (unconscious) intentions of decolonising the discourse as a means to tell its own story in accordance with Guédiguian's first claim – it's no coincidence that it's told through a *telenovela*, a purely Latin-American narrative style. It is important to point out that this 'local formula' used in the Latin-American *telenovela* has little resemblance with the schemes employed by Netflix – at least in theory, given that there is some hybridisation present. *EPDM*'s format comprises of 113 episodes, with a total length of 3,185 minutes (28.2 per episode), whereas *Narcos*'s twenty episodes average 48.6 minutes (a total of 972). This difference is explained by the fact that a Latin-American *telenovela* has a standard length of half an hour (although *EPDM*'s first and last episodes are longer), it can last indefinitely (there is no specified maximum number of episodes), and it does not follow American TV's season structure (which is used in *Narcos*, as expected). Thus, the differences in format are more than evident, placing *EPDM* into the structure of what came to be known as *narcotelenovela* (Rincón 2009).

Martín Barbero (1992: 46) establishes two habitual operations in the *telenovela*: 'The outlining is understood by the majority of analysts in terms of lack of psychology . . . and the Manichaean polarisation and character simplification into good and bad is ideological blackmail'. This way, character building in *Narcos*, as seen above, fits Barbero's outlining better. Another defining element of the *telenovela* is its limited budget, since, according to Mazziotti, 'it is traversed and weaved in three separate instances: its industrial production, textuality, and audience expectation' (1996: 13). *Telenovelas*' lower budgets, if compared with *Narcos*'s, usually translate into longer scenes, fewer locations (especially outdoors), and fewer pulses, or according to Pérez

Morán, 'dramatically relevant actions' (2017: 19). All of these together tend to confer *telenovelas* a slower pace. Let us check if this is, indeed, true in our comparative analysis.

EPDM's step outline is comprised of 3,024 scenes, averaging 26.7 scenes per episode, whereas *Narcos* has 1,130 scenes, 56.5 per episode. Each scene lasts an average of less than a minute (0.94) in *EPDM* has an average of 1.16 minutes in *Narcos*. The length of each shot also favours *EPDM*'s pace, averaging 5.1 seconds, as opposed to 6.2 seconds in *Narcos*, when one would expect that the latter would cut the shots shorter. With regards to shooting locations, considering that *Narcos* is a larger production and that *telenovelas* usually have more indoor studio shots, one could imagine that there would be a considerable difference between them in the number of outdoor shots. However, statistics show that *Narcos* shot 33 per cent of its scenes outdoors, whereas *EPDM* shot 36 per cent. Also, even though it is a smaller production, *EPDM* has more shots on location (161) than the Netflix series (154).

All of these elements contribute the *telenovelas*' often morose rhythm; consequently, it does come as a surprise that *EPDM* has more pulses than *Narcos*. It would not be far-fetched to presume that a longer *telenovela*, with more episodes, would have fewer of them – *Narcos* has 213 and the Colombian production has 251 pulses. *EPDM*'s dynamic tone and its already-mentioned hybrid nature prove that any preconceived ideas regarding its format are no more than common misconceptions. Neither is *EPDM* a *telenovela*, nor is *Narcos* too far from being one.

A Local/National Adaptation

There is something, notwithstanding, that places the two series at opposite sides of the spectrum – and here we go back to one of the goals I set at the beginning – for *EPDM* is an adaptation from a novel by Alonso Salazar, who, at one point in the past, had been mayor of Medellín. This reference contrasts the structures adopted by *EPDM* and *Narcos*, highlighted even more by the employed points of view and the target audiences. There will be the three cornerstones upon which I will lay our arguments (the last two, related with the first part of this text). In Alonso Salazar's novel, written in 2001, Escobar's story is told chronologically, documentary-style, in ten chapters. It's based, from the beginning, on the testimonies of Arcángel (a fake name), who had been a collaborator of Pablo Escobar, thus structuring the start of the text – his voice fades with the turn of the pages only to regain its strength towards the end.

In *Narcos*, Pablo is already working as a smuggler in the magnificent breakout scene on the bridge when his truck is intercepted by the police. This incident never really happened – Salazar stages a much less spectacular happening.

Narcos, on the other hand, effectively portrays a Pablo who knows by name every police officer present at the checkpoint. The Netflix series starts by focusing on the most dramatic period of Pablo's life, whereas *EPDM* takes up way before that, with him as a child, bullied by his cousin and his brother. The goal in this first episode is to unveil his youth, a part of his life that is less known to the public, through extracts from Salazar's book, word by word. The idea is to explain the origins of the monster, how he comes to be, and inquire about his motives once and for all. Thus, it pays special attention to his relationship with his parents (2001: 41; scenes 17 to 20), his grandfather's beginnings as a smuggler (2001: 37; scenes 32 to 34), the incidents of violence in Colombia (2001: 42; scenes 21 to 23), the way he drops out of school, which, for Salazar (2001: 44) is the key moment in Pablo's decision to start a life of crime, and the preamble of the relationship with his wife to be, Victoria, here called Patricia (2001: 58; scene 39).

Furthermore, the *telenovela*'s first episode – *EPDM*'s second episode takes place during *Narcos*'s first – introduces some classic quotes made famous by Pablo, his family and collaborators. Many of these lines had already become part of the Paisa's idiosyncrasy, forewarning his drug empire. For example, Pablo's promise (2001: 34; scene 38): 'If I don't have a million pesos in five years, I'll shoot myself'; or his mother's famous advice ('The day you do something bad, do it well. Don't be stupid and allow yourself to get caught', in scene 29). There is one in particular, extracted from the book, that was acted out slightly differently in the *telenovela* for dramatic purposes: in the novel Pablo threatens 'I'm gonna kill this *sonofabitch*, and I'm gonna kill his family up to his last generation, if his grandma is already dead, I'm gonna unbury her and kill her again' (2001: 335–36), whereas on screen it is heightened to, 'I'll kill you, your daddy, your mommy, your uncles and aunts, your wife María, the little boy Santiago, the little girl Pilar, in other words, even your grandma ... and in case she's already dead, I'll unbury her and will kill her again' (scene 7, chapter 24).

Alonso Salazar's book delves into Pablo Escobar's daily routines as a means of humanising him – his habit of smoking pot, his fascination for Vito Corleone in *The Godfather*, the warmth in the treatment of his family (2001: 162) – as well as providing the character with depth, both of which – i.e. both efforts after authenticity – are maintained by *EPDM*, often through extracts from the novel. *Narcos* does not employ this recourse with the same frequency, although we do witness Pablo singing in the shower (scene 1, episode 12), waking up in the cathedral (scene 4, episode 10), and his moments of intimacy with his wife Tata develop one important subplot.

Pablo's weakness for women and his extramarital affairs are well documented and told in detail in Alonso Salazar's novel: for example, the one with Yesenia (2001: 165), the one with journalist Virginia Vallejo (2001: 100–1), among others. It's intriguing that these romantic escapades serve the purpose of showing Pablo's darkest side in *EPDM* – his treatment of these women is cruel and merciless whenever they try to distance themselves from him. This is only circumvented in *Narcos*, which could be construed as contradictory – even though *EPDM* is a soap opera, in this aspect, it cuts much deeper than the clichéd approach in the Netflix series, as I have stated before. Using E. M. Forster's distinction between flat or well-rounded characters (1927: Chapter 4), the ones in *Narcos*, from Escobar to Murphy, should be grouped with the former. The characters from *EPDM*, on the other hand, are imbued with vividness and depth, even though they come from a *telenovela*, a format that regularly makes use of stereotypical, easily recognisable characters.

Both series, however, introduce some of Pablo's little quirks, such as his habit of never tying his sneakers or his coolness under pressure – he would wait until the last moment to abandon a safe house before it was hit by the police or the army (2001: 265). Some of these getaways were so spectacular that none of the series show them, probably because they wouldn't look too credible or due to the poor reliability of the eyewitness, none other than Pablo's own mother:

> There was this one time, recalls *doña* Hermilda, that when Pablo was doing some writing in his office at El Poblado, some 100 policemen show up. 'Good morning, sir', (one of them greets Pablo). 'Good morning, gentlemen, go on right ahead', replies him. 'Would you be so kind as to tell us the whereabouts of Pablo Escobar?' 'Oh, yes, I'd be more than glad to do so', he says as he goes for the front door, opens it and yells, 'Pablo, some people here need you!' and takes off right away. Another time, he was on the run when he stumbles, at a cornfield, upon an old lady clearing off the weeds. He tells her 'Look, give me some clothes and a scythe and I'll pay you right back'. When the cops arrive they ask 'You haven't seen this guy come this way, have you?' 'I've got no time for anything but my crops and the harvest of my *little corn* (maicito)', replies Pablo, throwing them off, this way. This is, I believe, a veritable proof of intelligence. (2001: 265)

Besides painting a picture of Pablo on a very personal level, the shows also focus on historical events. Here, again, they diverge in completely different paths. The book stresses that drug trafficking was already present in Colombia before Pablo (2001: 71),[2] but the series identify him as either the one who introduced it in the country (*EPDM* shows his trips to Ecuador) or the one who was responsible for its establishment (*Narcos* starts with a Chilean trafficker and Pablo teaming up to smuggle cocaine). The Netflix series, however, barely mentions – compared with *EPDM* – that Pablo was the sponsor of Colombia's first paramilitary movement, the group Death to Kidnappers (Muerte a Secuestradores) (2001: 83), upon the kidnapping of Marta Nieves

Ochoa, whose two brothers, known as the Ochoas, alongside Pablo, were some of the founding members of the Medellín cartel.

Narcos ignores these types of contextualisation, focusing instead on the bizarre and outlandish, as well as the questionable. Alonso Salazar, for example, states that the attack on the Palacio de Justicia performed by the M-19 guerrilla group was in no way aimed at burning documents that incriminated Pablo Escobar (2001: 141), likewise, *EPDM* holds its distance from making such claims. On the other hand, *Narcos* does not hesitate in Murphy's voiceover:

> Some escaped . . . but not before accomplishing their true goal: setting fire to the room that contained 600,000 pages of evidence against Escobar. The entire case against him turned to ash. In the United States the Mafia makes witnesses disappear so they can't testify in court. In Colombia, Pablo Escobar made the whole court disappear. (Episode 4, scene 64)

Episode 4 ends with Pablo's hitmen murdering the head members of the M-19 group in their own house, an event that, as far as can be judged, never took place. It portrays the guerrilla group as ragged psychos (a very American perspective, coming from a government who is used to dealing with these movements through fearful and illegal death squads). *EPDM* concentrates on Pablo's love–hate relationship with them, which is explained in depth by Alonso Salazar (2001: 104), and in the links among the guerrilla, land reform and the narcos (2001: 111). Of course, *Narcos* does not even mention any of this.

Finally, Alonso Salazar comes to the conclusion that Pablo's downfall could be partly blamed on his own *sicarios*, who would constantly pester him for jobs – more targets, more money (2001: 295 and 313). *Narcos* doesn't raise this question, perhaps because it would undermine its singular representation of Pablo. *EPDM*, in this respect, sticks to Salazar's storyline. The endings of the two series veer away from Salazar's novel, though, which dedicates several pages to revealing different reactions to Pablo's demise (2001: 346 ff). *EPDM* goes on to show an extremely tearful summary, and *Narcos* jumps forward to introduce season three, in which Peña is sent away to fight the Cali cartel. It could be claimed, then, that *EPDM*, regarding the adaptation typologies, is exactly what its creators set themselves to make, an adaptation with no strings attached, which adopted a different path from the documentary format of the book (no developed plots nor subplots – it forces a quasi-constant dramatisation). This is what Genette (1982) would call *continuation*, in this case, of the paraleiptic sort (the series fills the silence and the gaps) developing secondary plots (*interpolation*, in Genette's words).

I use Doležel's concept of *literary transduction* (1998) to explain *EPDM*'s translation of the story into something of its own, separate from the original narrative. I could also use Sánchez Noriega's *expansion* (2000: 70) to describe how new elements were added to the already lavish world of the original text in the 113 episodes of the series. And according to Leitch, Caracol's Colombian production would be a *superimposition* (2007: 102) because the requirements of popular culture – it is a *telenovela*, after all – influence the adaptation process with its very own generic conventions. Later on, Leitch would also consider the concept of *colonisation*, which could also no doubt be extended to *Narcos*, since it is an adaptation filled with 'filmic spirits' (2007: 109). Finally, Estermann (1965) talks about a category coined by him, *filmkunstwerk*, when something new is created out of the original literary work that can then be replaced by the adaptation in people's imaginary due to the nature and degree of the changes made, very much like what happened in Colombia with *EPDM*. At any level, the series maintains what some authors refer to 'faithfulness to the essence'.[3]

If *Narcos* were an adaptation from *EPDM* (it isn't, but let's consider it) it would, again according to Genette (1982), both be an *intramodal transformation* owing to its variation in perspective, and fit the concept of *transvalorisation*. According to Gil and Pardo (2018: 45), it also influences 'the value attributed to a single or a group of actions and to the character in them, improving or worsening him, changing him from a secondary role to the main part, etc.'. This is clear in *Narcos* when Murphy is converted into the protagonist.

Narcos, however, is a different sort of adaptation. Morin (1966: 46) states: 'The adaptation creates a homogeneous style – a universal style – and this universality includes the most diverse contents.' This is a manoeuvre that leads, undoubtedly, to standardisation: 'This homogenising tendency is at the same time a cosmopolitan tendency that gravitates towards the weakening of national cultural differences in favour of the culture found in the great supranational areas' (1966: 55). If I return to the aforementioned authors when discussing postcolonialism, Morin leads us directly to my object of study, when he concludes that:

> This cosmopolitanism irradiates from a development point that ascertain its domination over all others: The United States. That is where mass culture was born, and that's where its most powerful and globalizing energy can be found. (1966: 56)

Conclusion

It has been proven that the nationalities of the series and their goals, as well as their respective countries of production, condition certain transcendent elements, such as the plot (in *Narcos*, where the main plot is different and the subplots carry more weight) and the presence or absence of characters – even though they are not present in *EPDM*, the protagonists in *Narcos* are real-life characters, which is a production choice that helped create an American hegemonic perspective on a Latin-American country. Consequently, they generates another type of characterisation, one that endows more weight and depth to the Americans, and another type of discourse, a Manichaean polarisation of good versus evil.

Other aspects undergo relevant alterations, with similar and far from naive purposes, such as the staging – with the beautiful settings and the camera-on-shoulder in *Narcos*, whereas *EPDM* employs a more conservative and local, *telenovela-style* formula (Corral 2007; Rocha 2018) – or Murphy's voiceover, endowing the American discourse with authority. These factors should not be ignored, as Sergio del Molino warns in his magnificent fictional chronicle *La España vacía* (*Empty Spain*): 'The change in narrator is a moral question . . . The difference between telling a story or having a story told on your behalf is the same as between being in control or being controlled' (2016: 565). I believe this quote perfectly summarises the difference between both discourses, a *sui generis* literary adaptation designed with the audience in mind, like *EPDM*, and a global adaptation of local history, like *Narcos*, which relies on the global cliché of the local.

Notes

1. An American top-secret surveillance unit that played a quintessential role in the capture of Pablo Escobar. Its operation is described in detail in Mark Bowden's book *Killing Pablo: The Hunt for the World's Greatest Outlaw* (2002).
2. Alonso Salazar had already written a book about it in 1998 called *La Cola del Lagarto*, and previously had offered a remarkable explanation of *paisa* idiosyncrasy in *No nacimos pa' semilla* (1990).
3. For a more in-depth look, I suggest Frago Pérez (2005: 66–7).

References

Barbero, M. (1992), *Televisión y melodrama*, Bogotá: Tercer Mundo Editores.
Bautista, G. (1991), 'El realismo mágico: historiografía y características', *Verba hispanica*, 1, 19–26.
Bowden, M. (2002), *Killing Pablo: The Hunt for the World's Greatest Outlaw*, New York: Penguin.
Corral, M. J. (2007), 'Amor en custodia. Una telaraña sentimental', *Chasqui*, 99: 60–5.
Del Molino, S. (2016), *La España vacía. Viaje por un país que nunca fue*, Madrid: Turner.
Doležel, L. (1998), *Heterocosmica: Fiction and Possible Worlds*, Baltimore: Johns Hopkins University Press.

Egri, L. (1960 [1946]), *The Art of Dramatic Writing: Its Basis in the Creative Interpretation of Human Motives*, New York: Simon & Schuster.

Estermann, A. (1965), *Die Verfilmung literarischer Werke*, Bonn: H. Bouvier u. CO, Verlag.

Fanon, F. (2001 [1961]), *Los condenados de la tierra*, México: Fondo de Cultura Económica.

Forster, E. M. (1949 [1927]), *Aspects of the Novel*, London: Edward Arnold.

Frago Pérez, M. (2005), 'Reflexiones sobre la adaptación cinematográfica desde una perspectiva iconológica', *Comunicación y Sociedad*, 18: 2, 49–82.

Galcerán, M. (2016), *La bárbara Europa: Una mirada desde el postcolonialismo y la decolonialidad*, Madrid: Traficantes de Sueños.

Genette, G. (1982), *Palimpsestes. La littérature au second degree*, Paris: Seuil.

Gibson, S. (2016), 'How 'Narcos' is just another form of cultural imperialism', *The Guardian*, 28 September, <https://www.highsnobiety.com/2016/09/28/narcos-cultural-stereotypes/> (accessed 27 January 2019).

Gil, A. J. and Pardo, P. J. (eds) (2018), *Adaptación 2.0. Estudios comparados sobre intermedialidad*, Binges: Orbis Tertius.

Guédiguian, R. (2002), 'Un desastre antropológico', *El País*, 31 March, <https://elpais.com/diario/2002/03/31/opinion/1017529210_850215.html> (accessed 17 April 2018).

Klein, M. (2016), 'Netflix's Narcos: America's cultural imperialism retells history', *McGill International Review*, 18 October, <https://www.mironline.ca/netflixs-narcos-americas-cultural-imperialism-retells-history/> (accessed 28 January 2019).

Leitch, T. (2007), *Film Adaptation and Its Discontents: From Gone with the Wind to The Passion of Christ*, Baltimore: Johns Hopkins University Press.

Martínez, J. (2015), 'Netflix "Narcos": "cultural weight" or cultural maquila?' *InSight Crime*, 27 November, <https://www.insightcrime.org/news/analysis/netflix-narcos-cultural-weight-or-cultural-maquila/#Alejandro> (accessed 29 January 2019).

Mazziotti, N. (1996), *La industria de la telenovela. La producción de ficción en América Latina*, Buenos Aires: Paidós.

Morin, E. (1966), *El espíritu del tiempo*, Madrid: Taurus.

Pérez Morán, E. (2017), *Antimanual de guion*, Medellín: Sello Editorial Universidad de Medellín.

Rincón, O. (2009), 'Narcoestética y narcocultura en Narcolombia', *Nueva Sociedade*, 122: 147–63.

Rincón, O. (2015), 'Narcos da risa', *El Tiempo*, 6 September, <https://www.eltiempo.com/archivo/documento/CMS-16346263> (accessed 27 January 2019).

Rocha, S. M. (2018), 'Narcotelenovelas e um relato de nação: aproximações da cultura e da política colombianas através do estudo de recepção de Escobar, el patrón del mal, por audiências brasileiras', *Palabra Clave*, 21(1): 58–85.

Roh, F. (1925), *Nach-expressionismus (Magischer Realismus): Probleme der neuesten europäischen*, Malerei, Leipzig: Klinkhardt & Biermann.

Said, E. (2008 [1978]), *Orientalismo*, Barcelona: Debolsillo.

Salazar, A. (1990), *No nacimos pa' semilla. La cultura de las bandas juveniles de Medellín*, Bogotá: CINEP.

Salazar, A. (1998), *La cola del lagarto. Drogas y narcotráfico en la sociedad colombiana*, Santafé de Bogotá: Editorial Proyecto Enlace, Ministerio de Comunicaciones y Corporación Región.

Salazar, A. (2001), *La parábola de Pablo. Auge y caída de un gran capo del narcotráfico*, Bogotá: Planeta.

Sánchez Noriega, J. L. (2000), *De la literatura al cine. Teoría y análisis de la adaptación*, Barcelona: Paidós.

Seger, L. (1990), *Creating Unforgettable Characters*, New York: Henry Holt and Company.

Silva, V. (2016), 'Poscolonialismo, crítica y subalternidad', *LaFuga*, 18, <http://2016.lafuga.cl/poscolonialismo-critica-y-subalternidad/792> (accessed 11 April 2018).

Spivak, G. (1990), 'Postestructuralism, Marginality, Poscoloniality and Value', in P. Collier and H. Geyer (eds), *Literary Theory Today*, Cambridge: Polity Press: 219–45.

Von der Walde, E. (1998), 'Realismo mágico y poscolonialismo: Construcciones del otro desde la otredad', in S. Castro-Gómez and E. Mendieta (eds), *Teorías sin disciplina (latinoamericanismo, poscolonialidad y globalización en debate)*, México: Miguel Ángel Porrúa.

9. CONSTRUCTING NATIONHOOD IN A TRANSNATIONAL CONTEXT: BBC'S 2016 *WAR AND PEACE*

Carol Poole and Ruxandra Trandafoiu

War and Peace is a BBC [British Broadcasting Corporation] Cymru Wales drama production, in partnership with the Weinstein Company and BBC Worldwide/ Lookout Point. It was first broadcast on BBC One in January 2016, attracting six million viewers per episode. Although the BBC may be famous for its costume drama adaptations, which have become an intrinsic part of its brand appeal, adapting a giant of Russian and world literature would have been a challenging task. The 2016 adaptation had a lot to prove, after the BBC's previous 1972–3 adaptation of *War and Peace*, starring Anthony Hopkins, which numbered seventeen episodes. On the big screen, King Vidor's 1956 celebrity-studded Hollywood extravaganza and Bondarchuk's 1965–7 Oscar-winning definitive Russian take on *War and Peace* left emblematic imprints. Producer Julia Stannard and writer Andrew Davies thus had the challenge of entering a busy space of 'dialogic intertextuality' (Stam in Burry 2016: 6) and an ongoing symbolic dialogue between various high-profile intertexts.

The chapter uses a limited comparative approach. Bondarchuk's four feature films made in the 1960s have become a key reference point for any Tolstoy adaptation, since they were adapted from inside Russian culture. The BBC's 2016 adaptation, on the other hand, takes the viewpoint of an outsider looking into the specificities of Russian culture at a sensitive time in European politics. Bondarchuk's adaptation of *War and Peace* can thus illuminate and aid the analysis of Davies's adaptation, although the focus must remain on the 2016 television text. Comparisons between adaptations produced for cinema and television respectively, are not new, as Sarah Cardwell attests (2005). She analysed the challenges Davies faced in 2002 when he adapted *Doctor Zhivago* for the BBC, in the shadow of David Lean's big feature film from 1965. Cardwell expertly moved the analysis between the two adaptations, showing how Davies shifts emphasis in his more modern take for the small screen and makes references to Lean's film and other adaptation sources (Cardwell 2005: 173). 'I would argue for intertextual criticism as a viable alternative to fidelity criticism', Cardwell proclaimed (2005: 173), and we have heeded that call.

Methodologically, we have also inched towards capturing voices from the production side of adaptations. Over the last decade, more and more academics have moved away from a purely textual based analysis. Cardwell's interviews with Andrew Davies that sit at the origin of her 2005 book on the writer, as well as subsequent interviews with the same Andrew Davies by Cartmell and Whelehan (2007a), are examples of a new interest in what Cardwell calls 'critical practice' (2005: 173). More recently, Simone Murray called for a 'sociological approach' to adaptation, 'foregrounding those issues usually pushed to the margins of adaptation studies work: the industrial structures, interdependent networks of agents, commercial contexts, and legal and policy regimes' (Murray 2012: 6). Murray argues that because the adapted texts 'illuminate the contexts of their own production' (Murray 2012: 5), we need to move away from exclusively textual analysis towards 'alternative methodologies' (Murray 2012: 17). We have taken a similar sociological approach in our recent analysis of BBC's *Death Comes to Pemberley* (Poole and Trandafoiu 2018). Although Murray discusses the role of the producer in turning an initial concept into 'commercial artefact' (Murray 2012: 159), she takes the discussion into aspects of marketing without dwelling for too long on the producer's specific role and perspective. We aim to remedy the lack of attention offered to the production side of adaptations and we are quoting from an interview with Julia Stannard, the producer of *War and Peace*, conducted by Carol Poole in August 2018 and reproduced with kind permission.

The comparative and production-focused approaches illuminate certain shifts in the adaptation industry, such as the one from ethnic to more civic and post-national representations of nationalism. They also allow us to analyse the repositioning of the BBC from a public service provider, anchored in the national cultural space, to a universally relevant content producer driven by commercial imperatives. This new position confirms the BBC as a post-national player with a cosmopolitan outlook, entailing almost equal relevance given to other cultures and increased focus on global audiences. The chapter also makes the point, in its final part, that the trend for a more cosmopolitan or transnational approach in heritage television and costume drama has redefined the relationship that these productions have with the notion of authenticity, by offering an homage to authenticity but not actually being 'a slave to authenticity'. *This* approach reveals the ideological and cultural task of bringing adaptation productions into contemporaneity.

INDUSTRY ADAPTATIONS: THE BBC AS A COSMOPOLITAN PLAYER

In the 1980s, the British heritage film, within which costume drama was subsumed, was identified as essential to the new enterprise culture in the creative industries, and integral to its revival. The industry shifted from a focus on national cinema to productions suitable to attracting worldwide audiences. The emergence of home video, satellite and cable in the last two decades of the century, as well as the indigenous and international success of British drama, spearheaded by productions such as *Brideshead Revisited* (1981) and *Chariots of Fire* (1981), which received awards and drew large audiences and good reviews, created a bigger market for quality costume drama.

In the 1990s, this trend continued under successive governments and especially New Labour, who revived 'Cool Britannia' both as a form of soft nationalism and a way of using culture to drive economic revival. Although coming under criticism for its uneven effect on the British cultural industries and the gap between rhetoric and evidence especially when we consider the regional and local levels (Oakeley 2004), the investment paid off for those players that were located at the centre of cultural policy concerns, such as the BBC.

While looking forward, the BBC also maintained an interest in the past; a renewed concern with history is usually part and parcel of processes that aim to re-instil national pride. A steady flow of costume dramas ensued, which continued well into the new century. The trend was cemented by productions such as Andrew Davies's *Pride and Prejudice* (1995), which famously sparked Austenmania. Adaptations began to be defined by the crossing of boundaries between 'pastness' and 'presentness' (Cardwell 2002: 92), in a 'televisual synthesis of represented past and contextual present' that might account for 'the programmes' appeal to their audience' and 'the genre's wider cultural significance' (Cardwell 2002: 98). According to Andrew Higson (2003), these dramas had specific features: they delved into the past or adapted canonic literature; they featured beautiful landscapes, stately homes and costumes and the lives of the middle and upper classes; there was a focus on character development and a preoccupation with love stories, family relationships and social issues; camera work and editing were defined by fluidity and rhythm; and they often had a classic soundtrack. Such productions showcased a certain technical artistry and carried out an aesthetic function, allowing the BBC to use its soft power to remain an active agent in a market that was becoming increasingly competitive. Today, we might also see them as a nostalgic attempt to recuperate a past that never was and re-propose whiteness as the norm, against contemporary realities. However, the retrograde elements of this historical outlook were about to get a makeover at the turn of the millennium, also evident in more recent adaptations such as *War and Peace* (2016).

The survival of costume drama and heritage television more generally, was only possible in the context of subtle shifts towards a cosmopolitan vision, both at the macrolevel, in terms of commercial expansion, and at the microlevel, in terms of production practices. Cosmopolitan attitudes entail universal values, respect and consideration for the equal other and expressing oneself on a global multicultural stage (Yilmaz and Trandafoiu 2015). National concerns do not disappear, but the nation becomes just one of many players in a global playground. The BBC may still be viewed symbolically as the embodiment of what is great and good about British culture, but it is also trying to consolidate its footing in a global network of media players.

Market and industry demands have brought fluidity and complexity to television production. The BBC is now chasing global competition and has the strategic imperative to create value. A shift has therefore occurred in the way the role of costume drama is envisioned, from 'faithfully' adapting great works of literature, to tackling great stories that have the potential to attract global audiences (such as love, sex, betrayal, failure, triumph), and are spectacularly produced (using dramatic editing, compelling musical scores, great architecture and fashion). Sexed up and commercialised without eschewing quality, BBC's costume drama is an important weapon in the competition war. National pride is maintained, but productions like *War and Peace*, that are transnational in scope and design, show that the BBC is proud to put on a good show that sells well worldwide.

The BBC's main competitors are not within the national market any more; its challengers are global giants like Netflix or Amazon Prime (Sillito 2018). The BBC now needs to strike the right balance between its public service remit and increased investment in commercial activities, via its commercial subsidiaries. Both are dependent on the strength of its brand. The merging of BBC Worldwide and BBC Studios in Spring 2018 was part of the strategy to make the BBC more competitive, while maintaining the brand and its perceived quality. The launching of BritBox, a joint BBC–ITV streaming service of quality British drama in February 2019, follows the regulator Ofcom's call for collaborations in the internal market that would allow British broadcasters 'to keep pace with global players' (Waterson 2019).

The strategy seems to be working. A recent report highlighted that 'BBC Worldwide accounted for approximately 90 per cent of the BBC's commercial revenue in 2016–17, mainly from the sale and distribution of TV content and formats internationally and in the UK. In 2016–17, it generated the largest turnover of any UK media distribution company' (National Audit Office 2018: 5). Revenue amounting to £1.2bn generated from the BBC's commercial activities in 2016–17. Between 2012 and 2017 BBC Commercial Holdings paid £312m in dividends to the BBC Group for spending on public service broadcasting. It is therefore important for the BBC to be commercially successful to be able to reinvest the profit. Public service and commercial viability, national pride and the BBC brand – as well as being relevant universally via cosmopolitan practices – go hand in hand.

At the microlevel, internationally relevant productions have financial stakes, which feed into key production decisions for individual dramas. Pre-sales, which are based on the strength of the brand and the reputation of British costume dramas, are essential for securing the production quality necessary to satisfy global audiences. Julia Stannard, the producer of *War and Peace*, pointed out that producers must envisage an 'international' audience 'used to watching international co-productions'. The outcome of such a vision is that 'you will already have European pre-sales, you will have hopefully US pre-sales, all of this can feed into your budget, so you could be looking at three times your licence fee in terms of the working budget'. She made the point that having the ambition to target an international audience results in financial rewards that are 'liberating', from a creative viewpoint. She observed: 'it's slightly a different world in terms of how you produce the shows and you just have to adapt – what is your audience and what is your budget and generally the two do align' (Julia Stannard interview, 29 August 2018).

International pre-sales allow producers to seek diverse international locations, employ an international cast and pay experts to bring an aura of 'authenticity' to the production. As Julia Stannard pointed out:

> That's why you go to Russia, because we're not experts on Russia, so who do you talk to? The Russians! So, we worked very closely with historical advisors, cultural advisors, there are so many things that we never would have got right if we hadn't filmed it in Russia. (Interviewed 29 August 2018)

War and Peace showcases the cosmopolitan approach now taken by the BBC: fitting diverse parts into a coherent puzzle that transcends the national. Productions have become transnational in outlook and practices to achieve, as producer Julia Stannard observed, the best balance between costs and gains. Audiences have become international while productions have become transnational in a chicken and egg scenario. Potentially, there is a moral conflict between the BBC, as a national public service provider, and the BBC as a cosmopolitan broadcaster, responding to the needs of transnational and transcultural audiences with a renewed cosmopolitan outlook. However, productions such as *War and Peace* show that the BBC can meet that challenge, by pleasing both British and international audiences.

Fifty Years of *War and Peace*: From Nationalism to Transnationalism

In the current context of a competitive global market and cosmopolitan productions, it is significant that the BBC has turned towards adapting classics of universal (and not just British) literature and in 2016 the trio Andrew Davies (writer), Tom Harper (director) and Julia Stannard (producer) took on Tolstoy's epic *War and Peace*. Davies had already adapted *Doctor Zhivago* for the BBC in 2002, when he started from the same premise that the novel was a British classic, despite being a Russian novel (Cardwell 2005: 162).

War and Peace is not just a work of literature, it is also a historical novel, and history often has global ramifications. The novel's account of family tribulations, its love stories and its explorations of the class system are framed by the Napoleonic wars (1793–1815), which had widespread European relevance, engaging not just Tolstoy, but also other great European writers of the time, such as Stendhal, Thackeray and Hugo. Following the trend for historicisation, also displayed by other greats like Darwin and Marx (Zorin 2015), *War and Peace* showed how the national was always framed by the European and the transnational. This is evident in the tensions that the novel references, between Russian traditionalism and modernity, national specificity and European aspirations, strong local identity and universal expansionism. Tolstoy's novel could be read therefore as 'an international story', which accounts for the BBC wanting the adaptation to 'feel like an international production' (Julia Stannard interview, 29 August 2018).

Accordingly, the BBC's six-part adaptation was, from its inception, destined to cross not just diverse media and historical periods, but also cultures and traditions, and represent a 'plurality of voices' and 'changing boundaries' (Della Colletta in Burry 2016: 7). As Burry points out, 'the transportation of Russian texts across borders into new cinematic territories' shows how 'cultural texts become adaptable through semantic shifts as they enter different temporal, spatial, social and historic contexts' (Burry 2016: 7). The BBC's 2016 production became therefore a different proposition from Sergey Bondarchuk's 1965–7 *War and Peace*. The two entirely different historical and ideological perspectives originate from the requirements and practices of Soviet 'propaganda' film of the 1960s and British heritage drama in the new millennium, respectively.

Produced at a time of change in Soviet politics and Russian film between 1961 and 1967, in the context of de-Stalinisation and escalation of Cold War tensions during the Brezhnev era, Bondarchuk's production was an important propaganda weapon in the symbolic cultural Cold War with Hollywood and an answer to King Vidor's 1956 *War and Peace* (Youngblood 2014). As Youngblood points out, a Soviet adaptation was necessary to properly represent the artistic and national values of Tolstoy's text (2014: 10–28). While any adaptation could be seen 'as a political act' (Burry 2016: 2), for Bondarchuk there were additional and more acute considerations of fidelity and respect for both the letter and spirit of Tolstoy's text. In an interview available in the accompanying DVD collection released by Mosfilm, Bondarchuk tells about the letter received from a citizen in which he was reminded: 'You have a great responsibility, try to live up to it. We, the millions of viewers, are waiting.' The pressure was caused not just by the Russian disdain for Vidor's Americanised version, but also the internal political context in a communist Soviet Union whose expansionism was based on Russian nationalism. For Bondarchuk therefore, the drive was not just aesthetic, but also deeply ideological (Norris 2014). Nationhood was about a moral victory, about the symbols of unique Russian identity expressed in deeply felt cultural identity markers, the old way of imagining nationhood and especially Russianness (*War and Peace*, Mosfilm DVD 1965–7). As Catriona Kelly points out, for Russians history provided the binding material that connected the 'chosen people', whose common destiny was and is still defined by suffering (in Bragg 2014).

Consequently, Soviet Russia poured unlimited imperial resources into the production, which cost a reported $700 million in today's dollars (Youngblood 2014: 1). Bondarchuk's cluster of films remain the biggest ever made in terms of manpower and scope. The writer, director and actor was offered 20,000 extras (12,000 of them soldiers) and the pick of any artefact in any museum in the Soviet Union, and whole factories became involved in the production. As Karen Shakhnazarov, General Director of Mosfilm, comments in the additional materials that accompany the DVDs, it could have only been done in Russia 'at that time'.

The Bondarchuk production is of its time, not just in terms of resources, but also in relation to approach, filming technique and special effects (Youngblood 2014: 92). The 'voice of God' voiceover makes audiences feel they are looking in on a world that they are not part of. They are being educated about war, politics and big philosophical ideas. The voiceover is not only a convention of the time, but also a propaganda tool. Bondarchuk therefore takes a more 'ethnic' approach, spending most of the time on the serious matter of Napoleon's invasion, the plight of the Russian people, their heroism and survival. Battle scenes are given much more running time (Borodino is over twenty minutes long in Bondarchuk and about six in Davies), while great historical figures like Field Marshal Kutuzov are given much more prominence. The war itself becomes a separate story, a separate character and a huge spectacle. This is emphasised by a separate focus on war in one of the films (Part 3: 1812), the pyrotechnic effects, the vivid depiction of carnage and the small number of close-ups, which indicate a reluctance to focus on characters' individual inner conflicts at the expense of the bigger national story.

At the other end of fifty years, in a different historical and political context aimed at an international audience, with an international cast and crew, the Davies–Harper–Stannard undertaking offered an opportunity for a 'panoramic historical reconstruction' (Zorin 2015) through reimagining the Napoleonic wars (1793–1815) from a contemporary understanding of European history (Foster 2013), a strategy that, as both Zorin (2015) and Foster (2013) infer, recent text-to-screen adaptations tend to be very good at. Despite working with fewer resources (about £2 million per episode), the 2016 adaptation had a few distinct advantages: it was ideology-free, apart from ratings concerns – Davies could see Tolstoy through the lenses of contemporary politics; logistic and financial constraints redistributed attention towards the domestic sphere; and the more generic, less ethnically specific approach constructed universally relevant visuals.

Politically, the 2016 reproduction of a key event in Russian history allowed Davies to also reflect the current tensions between Russia and the rest of Europe. This is evident in the dialogues between the Tsar (Alexander I) and the positively represented Field Marshal Kutuzov, the first embodying ethnic nationalism in its extreme form, the latter a more progressive civic patriotism. Visually, we also have a more post-national 'European' take on identity. We lack the potentially alienating visual markers of Russian Orthodoxism with its Slavic and Oriental roots, which only makes rare appearances. Landscape and architecture have a more generic 'Eastern' feel in line with many other productions now filmed in Eastern Europe and visually connect the viewer with recognisable European-style urban architecture. Even visually, nationalism, in its most acute ethnic form, had been replaced with a more civic version, informed by post-national ethos. As Habermas explains in his analysis of emerging post-national 'constellations' (2001: 66), although we can observe the 'hardening of national identities as different cultural forms of life come into collision' (Habermas 2001: 72), cultures are also 'softened' in the 'wake of assimilation into a single material world culture' (Habermas 2001: 72–3). Davies represents this vision in the 2016 adaptation, in which the war is less about ethnic difference and more about the political ambitions and greed of despots. It is not just a Russian war, it could be anyone's, in the same way as the Napoleonic wars heralded other continent-wide conflicts. In this sense, Napoleon is no different from Alexander I, just maybe smarter, and a savvy viewer might even see certain connections with Putin's leadership style. In true cosmopolitan fashion, the production crosses geographical and political boundaries to focus on connections, not hard borders.

To bring the story into contemporaneity, Davies engineered some important emphases and, equally, elisions, because in contemporary adaptations meanings 'must be redefined to correspond with the new spatial and temporal territories' (Burry 2016: 7). Andrew Davies's script, in a slight departure from previous adaptations, emphasises the need for equality and individual emancipation, a sign of the contemporary imperative of 'cosmopolitan solidarity' rooted in the 'universalism of human rights' (Habermas 2001: 108). As a Brit and as a Welshman, Andrew Davies would have been very much aware of contemporary and universal conceptions of equality and rights. Two main examples invite attention: the emancipation of women (where Tolstoy and Bondarchuk were more ambiguous) and the egalitarian effect of war and nationalism on the class system.

War has a democratising effect on women, enabling them to cross an invisible fault line between the domestic and public spaces. External forces pressurise Natasha Rostova to seek to reverse the ill fortunes of her family and she obtains (limited) agency in the process. Marya Bolkonskaya comes alive when she is pushed out of her confined domesticity by having to flee from war, bury her father and control the anger of her peasants. These stories are emphasised in the 2016 adaptation, where we are invited to empathise with these romanticised, but also modern heroines, who take their destinies and love interests into their own hands. Julia Stannard, the producer, explained how emphasising this aspect was important for the adaptation:

> Marya . . . is empowered by her father's death . . . she's a brave and fearless woman. In a way, she is less concerned by the trappings of femininity and probably she thinks she will never marry. She fights off Anatol's advances because she can see that he is not going to bring any love and happiness into her life. He might be gorgeous, but he's not going to make her happy. And finally, she finds true love with Nikolai. In the book she is the one who sort of instigates their union, which is so bold for those days. (Julia Stannard interview, 29 August 2018)

War has always been a social opportunity because mobilisation, propaganda, state organisation, and the professionalisation of state and army can all contribute to strengthening feelings of nationhood (Smith 1981). In 1812 Russian officers and soldiers spent a long time in close proximity. Officers discovered folk culture, but also, on the way back from Paris, learned of new political ideas in the salons of Western and Central Europe (Jahn 2004: 58–9). At the end of the war, the upper classes had to reward lower classes with social reforms and in the relationship between count Pierre Bezukhov and peasant Platon Karataev we have the ultimate symbol of 'social reunification' (Adamovsky 2010: 66). Karataev also becomes the embodiment of the authenticity of the people (the Russian *narod*). While Bondarchuk removed much of Pierre's dalliance with the masonry and in so doing, the intricacies of his relationship with Karataev, Davies makes Karataev a key character. His role is to give Pierre depth, making him a man ahead of his time, entering history from a position of marginality and thus able to understand the inequalities of the class system. As producer Julia Stannard observed: 'The most interesting character has got to be Pierre, he is classless, he is a kind of existential hero before existentialism was a philosophy. He is just actually looking for the meaning of life' (interviewed 29 August 2018).

While the specific historical context and its associated philosophies may be lost to television audiences, changes in class hierarchy would be relevant, which is why the 2016 adaptation uses several opportunities to make this point, such as officers dying alongside soldiers and thus being made equal in suffering and death and naked men bathing alongside one another. The 2016 adaptation takes audiences on a visual journey, with the sharp contrast between the opening scene in Anna Plavovna's chic and gilded French style salon, with characters decked in high collars, smart uniforms and bejewelled Regency dresses, and the bucolic ending, with the Bolkonskys, Rostovs and Bezukhovs gathering in their new Arcadia, with their *rubashka*-inspired tunics, fur trims and traditionally patterned shawls. Some of the characters, unhappy in the opening scene, have gained happiness by the final one, as they make the journey from a formalised, hierarchical society, to a simpler and equalising one. Modern (for the time) haircuts and fashions make room, towards the end of the series, for the more traditional headscarves worn by Natasha Rostova in episode 6 and Pierre Bezukhov's peasant clothes, visually a democratising and unifying symbolic gesture.

Storywise, Davies takes the narrative indoors more often than Bondarchuk did. He had used the same tactic of moving the focus away from big (expensive, cast-heavy) cinematic scenes and towards highlighting the intimacy of relationships in *Doctor Zhivago* (Cardwell 2005: 170). As Isaiah Berlin (2013) observes, one of the most interesting contrasts in Tolstoy is that between private and public life. Andrew Davies underlined this duality in his script for the BBC: the micro stories of family life taking place alongside the backdrop of the national story unfolding during Napoleon's invasion of Russia in 1812. Bondarchuk could film in Moscow and could use the vast expanses of the Russian landscape for his war scenes. Legal and financial imperatives restricted the 2016 production in this respect, although they also allowed Davies to strike a better balance between domestic and public life. Female characters are given more depth in Davies, while Bondarchuk diminished some of the characters to focus mainly on Natasha, Pierre and Andrei. Producer Julia Stannard agreed that 'the starting point for *War and Peace* is a story about love; it's a story about familial love, romantic love, divine love, love for your country, love for yourself, love for your friends' (interviewed 29 August 2018), which makes the production more universally appealing.

There are different kinds of political premises and different commercial imperatives at the heart of the two productions. These juxtapositions are evident in

Russian audiences' responses: 'The new series ... is inferior to Sergei Bondarchuk's famous *War and Peace*, as it lacks the latter's reverent attitude to the text, great casting choices and empathy towards the protagonists', wrote Alexander Alekseyev in *Rossiskaya Gazeta*, quoted by *Russia Beyond* (26 January 2016). Although other critics praised its quality and respect for the novel, the majority thought it oversimplified and disliked Davies's 'additions' (in *Russia Beyond*, 26 January 2016). 'Andrew Davies immediately puts a little *Game of Thrones* into the sacred cow entrusted to him', a Novosibirsk culture site wrote, quoted by *The Guardian* (Elgot and Luhn 2016). Vladimir Tolstoy, the author's great-great-grandson, thought that the adaptation was 'done carefully enough'. The accessibility and entertainment value of the BBC adaptation was largely seen as positive, but the series did not feel Russian enough and was maybe 'too English' (in Elgot and Luhn 2016).

The word 'sacred' used in relation to Tolstoy, the complaints about being 'too English' and not 'Russian enough', indicate that Davies and the BBC had achieved their objectives. Fidelity and authenticity are the concern of identity symbolism preoccupied with the uniqueness of ethnicity, of blood and belonging. The BBC, on the other hand, had to consider a transnational audience. These comments encapsulate the difference between a national and a postnational approach and the shift from propaganda, to the new ideology: entertainment.

Adaptations must provide both 'entertainment and quality', with public service television 'turning towards the popular' to 'rejuvenate' itself (Kleinecke-Bates 2009: 113–19). In giving prominence to the story and the everyday, Davies decouples *War and Peace* from some of its more particular, specifically Russian foundations, to imbue the televisual texts with themes that have preoccupied him as a writer time and again. As Cardwell observes in her definitive text on Davies, themes reoccur in his adaptations, such as 'education, history and the past, freedom versus conformity, the individual within the institution' (2005: 188), which amount to a contemporary worldview. In so doing, he 'places an emphasis on the ordinary, the everyday – the people, relationships and situations that are quotidian and shared by many' (Cardwell 2005: 195), those general ingredients that contemporary television routinely works with.

Over a fifty-year period, as the two adaptations demonstrate, *War and Peace* has shifted from a nationalistic proposition crafted by ideological concerns from inside Russian culture, to a post-national one. The adaptation industry has moved into transnational territory from the point of view of values, systems and practices, working with international resources to satisfy global audiences. It is a proposition that has moved away from the ethnic weight of 'blood and belonging', towards a more cosmopolitan conception of humanity sharing the same emancipatory rights. BBC's 2016 *War and Peace* is transnational in its purpose, planning and execution. In the following section we elaborate on the transnational characteristics of the 2016 production, to show that transnationalism does not eschew a quest for authenticity, but it transforms it.

Transnationalism as Homage to Authenticity

The industry shifts detailed in the first part of this chapter show why specificities are being reinterpreted and adapted for the new post-national and global roles that public service broadcasters, like the BBC, need to adopt. There is a fine line to be walked between providing a credible 'authentic' cultural experience, and the imperative to entertain and be universally relevant. Following Higson, Cartmell and Whelehan (2007b: 2–3) have criticised the 'discourse of authenticity' that still permeates 'ignorant' film reviews, and have advocated a move away from adaptations seen as 'sycophantic' and 'derivative', a prevailing trend in the case of the heritage genre. Consequently, the authenticity of experience has replaced, to a certain extent, the pursuit of fidelity, so typical of adaptation studies at one time.

Stand-in locations, the fluid interpretation of localism and the aesthetic eclecticism of objects, music and costumes, give *War and Peace* an air of mimicked authenticity and approximate identity that purists would reject, but transnational audiences can better respond to. In this sense, the 2016 *War and Peace* pays homage to 'authenticity' and historical reconstruction, within the limits of contemporary production concerns and resources and without unreasonable authenticity claims. Producer Julia Stannard initially thought: 'If we're going to do *War and Peace* we have to shoot in Russia, because it is about Russia and why would you not'. However, after taking into account the actual logistics and the nature of Russian bureaucracy she had to say 'let's start as close to Russia as we can because we'll get the architecture that feels appropriate to Russia' (Julia Stannard interview, 29 August 2018).

Some filming did take place in St Petersburg and Veliky Novgorod in Russia, especially to make the most of the Dutch, Danish and Swedish influences that began to characterise St Petersburg's architecture when it became a capital in 1712, under Peter the Great, who abandoned the Byzantine tradition. The Western European look provides subliminal recognition for audiences and eliminates the threat of visual alienation or cultural shock. Most of the filming took place nevertheless in Lithuania and Latvia, where architecture that could stand in for both the Eastern Byzantine style, but also the more European-inspired architecture, was available. Vilnius and Rumšiškės (a town now functioning as an ethnographic museum) in Lithuania and Rundale Palace in Latvia were chosen, the last one 'because it looks like St Petersburg', explained producer Julia Stannard (in Webb 2016). The choice to film in the Baltic countries was also due to the quality of the infrastructure and lower production costs than in Russia, and the similarity in architecture as well as tax incentives available in Lithuania.

As director Tom Harper explained: 'it was the combined effect of it all' (Van Roon 2016).

The hybrid style was also reflected in the musical score, which features the Latvian State Choir, because the logistics did not permit recording with a Russian church choir. 'They can all sing in Russian and they've got that very Baltic, open-throated sound, not like a Western classical choir', composer Martin Phipps told Billboard (in Newman 2016). His approach to producing the score was eclectic overall: 'I wanted to do a very Russian choral sound mixed with Rachmaninoff meets Vangelis and see if we could mix those elements together' (in Newman 2016).

Eclecticism, with its mix of familiarity and exoticism, is mirrored in some of the costumes, which combine Eastern designs (the occasional fez or turban and Oriental patterns) and Regency-style ball gowns worn by the younger women. The jewellery was designed by Petr Axenoff, a Russian designer who takes inspiration from Russian folklore and fairy tales but produces very modern pieces. According to media reports, costume designer Edward K. Gibbon reflected that it was 'a huge responsibility to honour the amazing writing. We didn't want to reinvent the period, but we did bring something modern to it. It's a very modern piece' (in Kendra 2016).

Critics nevertheless took issue with some of the costumes. Kendra (2016), a fashion historian and writer, applauded the production for putting wigs on older men and servants, the oversized collars, older men's lounging wear and military uniforms, as well as reflecting Oriental influences in the prints, embroidery and jewellery. However, she also criticised some historical inaccuracies that, in her view, included hair fringes (motivated by making female actors look younger), technologically advanced fabrics, sexy dress cuts, including one-shoulder backless dresses, V-neck cleavages and the total absence of corsets.

In contrast, producer Julia Stannard defended the way the production paid attention to historical accuracy:

> Anna Pavlovna was dressed how she would have been. She almost represented St Petersburg society. So that was very much about distancing themselves from the Muscovite heartland, which was much more Asian influenced, Eastern. And this was all very much about recreating themselves with the French language, European fashions . . . So that's a very deliberate choice we've made, to do credit to how she would have been dressed, which is very much the new Russia. (2018)

She also discussed how the choice of costumes had to speak metaphorically about class and space divides between the high society in the capital and 'the Russian countryside, Uncle Mikhail and the lodge and Natasha's dance and all of the true folklore of Russia, so it's exactly about that, the complete divide and conflict and contrast between those two worlds, the old and the new Russia' (Julia Stannard interview, 29 August 2018). The mix of styles was therefore motivated by creating meaning for international audiences, while also communicating an enactment of authenticity, an authenticity that was shaped by production and audience needs.

The homage to authenticity was confirmed by director Tom Harper, who talked about how the production consulted a panel of literary, military and architectural experts to create a near-authentic look for the piece (in Van Roon 2016). The objects and furniture were locally sourced in order to mimic the aristocracy's Russophile and historicist trend (Roosevelt 2003) under Nicholas I (1825–55), so just before Tolstoy's novel was published in 1869. Furniture, food and tableware served to give the production a recognisably Russian feel and contributed to characterisation. This is particularly obvious in the home of the Rostovs, the archetypal Russian family, where much attention is given to decorative motifs (elk heads, bearskin rugs and gold samovars), patterns and colours, as well as furniture.

Architecture and design always speak more broadly about the cultural, social and political aspects of a historic period and the dialogue between Slavic and Western styles is poignantly captured on screen, at a time of important shifts. These elements were important not just to showcase the contrasting aspects of Russian culture, between West and East, modernity and tradition, but also create a certain symbolism in the private lives of the main on-screen families, from the comfortable riches of the Bolkonskys, to the shabbier but warm home of the Rostovs and the sterile, cold palace belonging to unhappy Pierre and *Hélène*. Viewers are thus transported from the opening panoramic view of St Petersburg, where late Peter the Great baroque dominates, to the Rostovs' traditional but relaxed home style and Uncle Mikhail's wooden cabin in the forest, during a scene where the characters return to the source of Russian culture, the land and its peasants. An homage to authenticity is enacted here, which works visually and symbolically for global audiences.

It would have been wrong to become 'a slave to period detail', Julia Stannard explained, because the effect is 'that the characters don't inhabit their space in a comfortable way. You want them to sit on the sofa with their feet on it, because that's how people are if they want to be comfortable; you want people to take their jackets off and throw them on the bed; you want people to inhabit their space in a way that it belongs to them' (Julia Stannard interview, 29 August 2018). This means that authenticity needed to be reinterpreted for production needs and audience expectations. 'What we went out to do was not to create a museum piece where everything was exactly like in the book, but to take the book as our guide and try to tell this story as truthfully as we could for a modern audience', Tom Harper clarified (in Van Roon 2016).

The concepts of authenticity and fidelity have to be envisioned henceforth within the new framework for producing transnational adaptations. Authenticity has to be enacted as part of a more hybrid, universal approach, where the pursuit of accuracy and fidelity are replaced by an homage to authenticity that audiences can better connect with. In adapting *War and Peace* in 2016, the BBC had to take certain political and creative decisions to ensure that history, particularly concerning a different nation, and literature, rooted in the peculiarities of Russian culture, remained relevant to both British and international audiences. This represented quite a challenge, since the BBC was working from outside the target culture and with the 1965–7 Russian adaptation of *War and Peace* still looming large, but met it by refashioning Russia and Russianness for transnational appeal. Authenticity therefore had to be recalibrated into homage as a strategy for drawing transnational audiences into a story that had national specificities.

Conclusion

The 2016 adaptation of *War and Peace* tells the story of the new challenges and complexities that characterise the screen industries today. Public service broadcasters like the BBC have had to adapt to contemporary industry conditions, increased international competition and the pressure to generate income that could be reinvested in future quality productions. Heritage costume drama, when adapted to contemporary audience tastes and refashioned from a transnational perspective, have an important role to play within the new economic model.

As a result, the 2016 *War and Peace* proposes a contemporary reinterpretation of the novel, with its own inflections and subtractions that make the text relevant to contemporary transnational audiences, interested less in the trappings of authenticity and in being 'of the place' and more in a good story, captivatingly told through character, dialogue and *mis en scène*, linked by production considerations that see transnationalism coupled with financial gains. A transnational approach has not dismantled a quest for authenticity but has transformed its meanings. This approach allows the BBC to remain competitive and financially viable, and to maintain its brand appeal and soft power credentials.

References

Adamovsky, E. (2010), 'Pierre Bezukhov becomes (really) Russian: some issues of national identity in Tolstoy's narrative and life experience', *Fragmentos*, 38: 59–69.

Berlin, I. (2013), *The Hedgehog and the Fox: An Essay on Tolstoy's View of History*, Princeton: Princeton University Press.

Bragg, M. (2014), *In Our Time*, with A. N. Wilson, C. Kelly and S. Hudspith, BBC Radio 4, broadcast 21 December.
Burry, A. (2016), 'Introduction: filming Russian classics – challenges and opportunities', in A. Burry and F. H. White (eds), *Border Crossing. Russian Literature into Film*, Edinburgh: Edinburgh University Press, pp. 1–16.
Cardwell, S. (2002), *Adaptation Revisited. Television and the Classic Novel*, Manchester: Manchester University Press.
Cardwell, S. (2005), *Andrew Davies*, Manchester: Manchester University Press.
Cartmell, D. and Whelehan, I. (2007a), 'A practical understanding of literature on screen: two conversations with Andrew Davies', in D. Cartmell and I. Whelehan (eds), *The Cambridge Companion to Literature on Screen*, Cambridge: Cambridge University Press, pp. 239–51.
Cartmell, D. and Whelehan, I. (2007b), 'Introduction – Literature on screen: a synoptic view', in D. Cartmell and I. Whelehan (eds), *The Cambridge Companion to Literature on Screen*, Cambridge: Cambridge University Press, pp. 1–12.
Elgot, J. and Luhn, A. (2016), 'Russia's verdict on BBC's War and Peace: "a classic with cleavage"', *The Guardian*, 26 January.
Foster, C. (2013), 'Adapting history and the history of adaptation', in L. Raw and D. E. Tutan (eds), *The Adaptation of History: Essays on Ways of Telling the Past*, Jefferson, NC: McFarland, pp. 117–28.
Habermas, J. (2001), *The Postnational Constellation*, Cambridge: Polity.
Higson, A. (2003), *English Heritage, English Cinema. Costume Drama since 1980*, Oxford: Oxford University Press.
Jahn, H. F. (2004), '"Us": Russians on Russianness', in S. Franklin and E. Widdis (eds), *National Identity in Russian Culture*, Cambridge: Cambridge University Press, pp. 53–73.
Kendra (2016), 'Top 5 costume inaccuracies – and accuracies – in War & Peace', *Frock Flicks*, 26 February.
Kleinecke-Bates, I. (2009), 'Historicizing the classic novel adaptation: *Bleak House* (2005) and British television contexts', in R. Carroll (ed.), *Adaptation in Contemporary Culture. Textual Infidelities*, London: Continuum, pp. 111–22.
Murray, S. (2012), *The Cultural Economy of Contemporary Literary Adaptation*, London: Routledge.
National Audit Office (2018), 'The BBC's commercial activities: a landscape view', Report by the Comptroller and Auditor General. HC721.
Newman, M. (2016), '"War and Peace" composer explains his fresh approach to scoring the Russian classic', *Billboard*, 18 January.
Norris, S. M. (2014), 'Tolstoy's comrades: Sergei's Bondarchuk *War and Peace* (1966–67) and the origins of Brezhnev culture', in L. Fitzsimmons and M. A. Denner (eds), *Tolstoy on Screen*, Evanston: Northwestern University Press, pp. 155–78.
Poole C. and Trandafoiu, R. (2018), 'Migration, symbolic geography and transforming identities when Death Comes to Pemberley', in D. Cutchins, K. Krebs and E. Voigts (eds), *Routledge Companion to Adaptation*, London: Routledge, pp. 194–206.
Roosevelt, P. (2003), 'Russian estate architecture and noble identity', in J. Cracaft and D. Rowland (eds), *Architectures of Russian Identity 1500 to the Present*, Ithaca: Cornell University Press, pp. 66–79.

Russia Beyond (2016), 'How Russians react to BBC's War and Peace', 26 January.
Sillito, D. (2018), "'Netflix effect' poses challenge to British TV', BBC, 17 July, <https://www.bbc.co.uk/news/amp/entertainment-arts-44862598> (accessed 9 November 2018).
Smith, ad (1981), 'War and ethnicity: the role of warfare in the formation, self-images and cohesion of ethnic communities', *Ethnic and Racial Studies*, 4: 4, 375–97.
Stannard, J. (2018), Interview by Carol Poole, conducted 29 August.
Van Roon, D. (2016), 'War and Peace director Tom Harper: "I felt like an army general myself, but with less severe consequences"', *DELFI – Lithuania Tribune*, 25 January, <https://en.delfi.lt/lithuania/culture/war-and-peace-director-tom-harper-i-felt-like-an-army-general-myself-but-with-less-severe-consequences.d?id=70212940> (accessed 9 November 2018).
Waterson, J. (2019), 'BBC and ITV team up to launch Netflix rival BritBox', *The Guardian*, 27 February, <https://www.theguardian.com/media/2019/feb/27/bbc-and-itv-team-up-to-launch-netflix-rival-britbox> (accessed 28 February 2019)
Webb, C. (2016), 'Where to find the dazzling palaces in War and Peace', *Radio Times*, 10 January.
Yilmaz, A. and Trandafoiu, R. (2015), 'Introduction', in A. Yilmaz, R. Trandafoiu and A. Mousoutzanis (eds), *Media and Cosmopolitanism*, Oxford: Peter Lang, pp. 1–28.
Youngblood, D. J. (2014), *Bondarchuk's War and Peace: Literary Classic to Soviet Cinematic Epic*. Lawrence: University Press of Kansas.
Zorin, A. (2015), 'Tolstoy replays history', *Times Literary Supplement*, 18 March.

Filmography

Bondarchuk, S. (1965–7), *War and Peace*. Soviet Union: Mosfilm.
Chadwick, J. and White, S. (2005), *Bleak House*. UK: BBC.
Harper, T. (2016), *War and Peace*. UK: BBC.
Hudson, H. (1981), *Chariots of Fire*. UK: 20th Century Fox.
Langton, S. (1995), *Pride and Prejudice*. UK: BBC.
Percival, D. (2013), *Death Comes to Pemberley*. UK: BBC.
Sturridge, C. and Lindsay-Hogg, M. (1981), *Brideshead Revisited*. UK: Granada Television.

10. *THE BEAUTIFUL LIE*: RADICAL RECALIBRATION AND NATIONHOOD

Yvonne Griggs

Travelling Stories

ABC Australia's *The Beautiful Lie*, an adaptation of Leo Tolstoy's *Anna Karenina*, takes an adaptive pathway that foregrounds adaptation's capacity for textual migration and evolution, shifting the narrative into a very fertile yet different temporal, geographical and cultural locale. Unlike many prior film and TV costume drama adaptations of Tolstoy's canonical nineteenth-century text, it operates within what Della Coletta terms the 'agoraic domain' (2012: 2) – a 'domain' that is defined not by the historical parameters of the text it adapts but by its propensity to migrate to another space, in this instance to a contemporary Australian setting that enters into a 'cross-cultural dialogue' with its precursor text (2012: 3). In its migration to an Australian context, notions of national identity of relevance to a contemporary Australian audience take precedence over lip service to the kind of costume drama treatment that has become synonymous with screen adaptations of the realist novel of this literary period. Hutcheon reminds us that the kind of transcultural adaptation envisioned in an adaptation like *The Beautiful Lie* is 'nothing new' (2006: 145): stories continue to migrate across the centuries, many of them in a notably different guise, and yet they remain indelibly connected to earlier migratory narratives that speak to what Rose identifies as ongoing 'anxiety-provoking issues' – issues that transcend the geography of time, place and cultural proclivity as they evolve into something often markedly different though intertwined at a thematic level with the 'anxieties' that have informed not just one specific narrative but many (1996: 2). *The Beautiful Lie* revolves around the fictional exploration of 'anxiety-provoking issues' related to family and love in its many forms, all of which are of central import to Tolstoy's nineteenth-century Russian story. While the textual politics of Tolstoy's nineteenth-century Russia inevitably find no traction in the story's relocation to contemporary urban Australia, the narrative's complex exploration of love and family relationships is convincingly revisioned for its new national audience. If, as Palmer argues, all texts are 'fragments' awaiting further 'gestures of continuation' (2017: 94) that are both 're-creative' and inherently 'summative' (2017: 104–5), this adaptation of *Anna Karenina* represents an innovative 'continuation' of Tolstoy's exploration of the human condition that is of universal relevance. It should thus prove to be an exportable TV product, especially given the classic status of Tolstoy's world-renowned text, but in an intensely competitive TV industry dominated by its preoccupation with the global market, the production of 'quality' drama has become synonymous with brand image. For some TV broadcasters that image is linked to particular TV genres that employ constructed notions of the host nation's national identity: both image and product migrate with ease across transnational and transcultural borders. However, the image and products of other national broadcasters often face a more problematic pathway to global transferability.

It is difficult for a contemporary Australian adaptation of a canonical nineteenth-century novel that has traditionally been presented as costume drama fare to find traction within the global market place, especially when competing within an export market that has historically favoured the British TV costume drama serial adaptation. These British TV dramas present a specific construct of nationhood that finds a global audience, despite the predominantly British nature of both the content and its treatment. Deemed the most 'British of all TV genres', TV costume drama adaptations are realised on screen through a certain kind of 'complex fiction-heritage aesthetic'; characterised by country houses and period detail they are, argues De Groot, immutably 'intertwined with a British national identity' that is capable of 'expor[ting]' so-called 'British values around the world' (De Groot 2015: ix–x). This manufactured image of Britishness has become an anticipated trope of its generic identity, its selective and romanticised presentation of a past creating what Voigts-Virchow terms a 'globalized fanta[sy]' of what 'national identity' entails (2007: 135). Even when the narratives being adapted are geographically and culturally 'Other', the British TV costume drama adaptation creates a monopoly around what has become synonymous with its own exportable brand of British heritage, cultivating a 'Britishness' that remains an ingrained and exportable part of the genre's DNA. Nevertheless, the current popularity of TV series that offer a more radical recalibration of canonical literature suggests the appeal of traditional TV costume drama adaptation is on the wane. Series like Showtime's *Penny Dreadful* (2014–16) are indicative of how far the boundaries are shifting away from the conservative British offerings that have historically monopolised the TV landscape (Griggs 2018: 23). The BBC and ITV have also produced a more experimental mode of costume drama adaptation in recent years, marked by the arrival of series like *Sherlock* (2010), *Jonathan Strange and Mr Norrell* (2015), and *The Frankenstein Chronicles* (2015).

ABC Australia's *The Beautiful Lie* is, like these more playful and decidedly less reverential adaptations, a daring outlier. For the first time in its adaptive history *Anna Karenina* is presented as a contemporary reimagining resituated within the national context of antipodean Australia. The series is not defined first and foremost by its relationship with a pre-existing text; instead it takes a pathway that foregrounds adaptation's capacity to relocate to not only a very different cultural, temporal and geographical framework, but to a decidedly different national space. Tolstoy's nineteenth-century Russian tale is reimagined within a contemporary context set in twenty-first century Australia, St Petersberg and Moscow being transformed into modern day Melbourne. While protagonist Anna and her husband are constructed as the 'perfect' sporting celebrity couple, Anna's cavalry officer lover, Count Vronsky, is given a similarly modern equivalency, appearing in this adaptation as a bohemian record producer. The series' construction of the Ivins as sporting heroes whose private lives play out across various public media platforms is particularly telling given the status of such heroes within an Australian context: they are set up as 'national role models', Anna's inevitably public betrayal of husband Xander, 'the golden boy of Australian tennis', construed here according to Australian TV critic Rosemary Neill as an offence against 'the nation as a whole' (2015). Issues addressed in the series reflect twenty-first century concerns, from eating disorders and body image to the sexual and gender politics of our era; and yet, as in Tolstoy's novel, 'universal' issues related to familial structures and love in all of its forms remain central to its narrative momentum. The regularity with which Russian classics are adapted to screen is, according to Burry, in part a consequence of their capacity to engage 'to an unusual degree' with the contemporaneous 'problems of modernity' (2016: 1–2), even as screen adaptations of these narratives bring to the fore their own contemporaneous and cultural concerns in matters of love, fidelity and family (7).

However, from the early days of its adaptation to screen, the novel's preoccupation with family is superseded by the construction of its central romance. Film adaptations starring Greta Garbo serve to illustrate this narrow focus. In the 1927 adaptation tellingly titled *Love*, Garbo stars alongside her lover John Gilbert, their off-screen romance forming part of the film's publicity materials. Garbo reprised her role in MGM's 1935 adaptation in which this Russian narrative is presented as 'yet one more Hollywood adulterous love story of the

1930s' (Makoveeva 2001: 118). Both Garbo films also come with an alternative 'happy ending' that rewrites Anna's tragic demise, her suicide replaced here by the lovers' reunion. Given the time constraints of cinema and the romantic appeal of the narrative's tragic love story, the decision to focus on the relationship between the titular Anna Karenina and her lover is a commercially astute strategy. Though some films, like the 1947 British adaptation, provide a sense of the social cohesion envisaged in Tolstoy's novel (Makoveeva 2001: 121), most do not venture beyond the confines of the Anna/Vronsky relationship. Furthermore, all film adaptations to date present the story as a lavish costume drama, but despite attention to period detail and location, Leitch argues that there is a tendency to construct Russia and Russianness as 'Other' when adapting Russian stories to screen space: on-screen 'Russia', in both MGM's 1935 adaptation and the 1947 British adaptation, devolves into what Leitch terms a 'site of exotic tourism' rather than a meaningful construction of place and of Russian identity (Leitch 2016: 20–35). Joe Wright's *Anna Karenina* (2012) represents a refreshing challenge to costume drama's ongoing capacity to dictate adaptive terms of reference by parodying the tropes of the genre through its highly stylised theatrical mode of presentation; however, as with its cinematic predecessors, the destructive love between Anna and Vronsky forms the narrative focus of this film, and though Wright's treatment of the period costume genre deconstructs the artifice of heritage cinema, it is tethered to the genre by association and generic expectation. Like earlier adaptations of the 1930s and 1940s, it remains a 'site of exotic tourism' dressed here in a theatrical garb that further dilutes any meaningful construct of nationhood. There have also been several British TV serialisations of *Anna Karenina*, all of which are costume drama adaptations that, like their film siblings, employ a heritage aesthetic. The BBC's *Anna Karenina* (1977) ventures beyond the relationship of Anna and Vronsky, engaging with the relationship stories of Dolly and Stiva, Kitty and Levin during its ten-episode run, and within the parameters of a four-part mini series format, Channel 4's *Anna Karenina* (2000) is able to present the complexities of Anna's demise, but like their cinematic counterparts, in each series the narrative lens is firmly focused on destructive love that leads to an inevitably tragic close. Though the most recent TV serialisation, a Russian costume drama adaptation released in 2017, offers a decidedly male-centric approach to the narrative, it also focuses on the torrid love affair of Anna and Vronsky, even if from a very selective, patriarchal standpoint. Nevertheless, director Shakhnazarov's meticulous reconstruction of Russian period history in the two eras depicted on screen does ensure that this production, unlike its predecessors, is reflective of a Russia that is not merely another 'site of exotic tourism' produced for the entertainment of an export market.

The desire to avoid the tropes of costume drama is fundamental to *The Beautiful Lie*; from the outset, producer John Edwards envisaged a contemporary

Australian take on the narrative rather than one that reconstructs what often amounts to a flawed representation of Tolstoy's contemporary Russia. What Edwards and his writing team seek to retain instead is the novel's exploration of 'anxiety-provoking issues' (Rose 1996: 2) that are as relevant to contemporary Australians as they were to Tolstoy's Russian contemporaries. Producers Edwards and Imogen Banks, along with scriptwriters Bell and Jonathan Gavin, approached the series as 'a study of love' (Edwards, quoted by Bell in Griggs 2015), but as in Tolstoy's story, it is not simply a study of destructive love epitomised by Anna Karenina and Vronsky; as in the novel, the series explores the many kinds of 'love' that underpin relationships. It is a story 'about obsessive, erotic love, brotherly love, parental love: all these aspects of love' that 'play themselves out in a multi-layered way across the story' (Edwards in Enker 2015). It is also about the familial structures that support all kinds of 'love'. In *Anna Karenina*, what Tolstoy 'loves' is 'the idea of a family' (Tolstoy in Morson 2010: 358), the prominence of which is written into the novel's opening lines:

> All happy families resemble one another, but each unhappy family is unhappy in its own way. (1999 [1877]: 1)

While film adaptations of Anna Karenina focus on the torrid love affair of Anna and Vronsky, almost to the exclusion of other relationships within the narrative, as in Tolstoy's novel, *The Beautiful Lie* explores all kinds of love within the social networks of family and community. Its numerous story arcs unfold in a manner that is structurally akin to that of its precursor text. Tolstoy devotes as much of his prose to the build-up of the relationship between Levin and Kitty as to the unravelling of the relationship between Anna and Vronsky. This is mirrored at a structural level in *The Beautiful Lie* in which the parallel relationships between not only Anna, husband Xander and lover Skeet, but Kitty and Peter (the novel's loyal Levin), and Dolly and Kingsley (its unfaithful Stiva) are all central to narrative momentum and to its thematic preoccupation with matters of love and family. Even if the social context must inevitably change due to the conscious shift in the narrative's locale and era, 'there is' maintains Banks, 'universality in the emotional core of the story' (Banks, in Mercado 2015) that translates to the time-rich and more expansive storytelling parameters of TV serialisation.

Nationhood and the Global Market

However, whether this or any screen narrative can produce a quintessential depiction of 'nationhood' is debatable. Writing back in the 1980s Rowse and Moran question the very possibility of defining 'nationhood', asking 'How much reflection is adequate reflection' thereof (1984: 232). The issue of what constitutes an 'adequate reflection' of 'Australianness' remains a contemporary one that is further complicated by the fact that the medium of television is, unlike the 'higher arts', invariably charged with the task of instilling something definitive about national identity into its programming (232). Jacka notes that television has played a major role in 'nation building' throughout the twentieth century (2004: 31) while, speaking in 2015, former ABC managing director Mark Scott argues that the national broadcaster is still charged with delivery of 'Australian stories' that 'underpin Australian identity, culture and society', citing shows like *Puberty Blues* (2012–14), *The Time of Our Lives* (2013–14), *Redfern Now* (2012–13), and *The Slap* (2011) as Australian TV products that engage audiences in 'thinking and talking about Australian families and different life experiences in our shared nation' (2015). To this list I would add Australian TV shows like *The Secret Life of Us* and *The Beautiful Lie* as series of a similar leaning, even though the latter series has its genesis in a Russian nineteenth-century canonical text.

Despite this ongoing desire to ensure national representation through the telling of distinctly Australian stories, within the global context of the twenty-first century, nation building on screen is increasingly tempered by an equal desire to generate screen products that are able to transfer to an international market with ease. The current industry view is that TV programmes should be viewed as 'transnational cultural commodities'; nevertheless, they must also retain their appeal to the domestic market of origin (O'Regan and Ward 2011: 34). Some nations have created and continue to create niche programming that meets the demands of both its domestic and its international audience without compromising their identity as the products of that particular nation; the longevity of the British costume drama as a 'transcultural commodity' attests to this, as does the ongoing success of the Nordic Noir crime brand of programming: both retain markers of cultural and national specificity that then serve to distinguish them within the global marketplace, and both have built their reputations around certain TV genres. Australian TV programming is less clearly defined within the context of a particular TV genre but it is similarly associated globally with certain distinctive cultural and national markers that have come to represent a particular construct of Australia's 'national image' (O'Regan and Ward 2011: 35). As a public broadcaster, part of the ABC's remit is to provide programming that is reflective of not only national identity but also of cultural diversity (Jacka 1990: 25), but while this may ensure the visibility of the ABC's domestic audience it does little to facilitate the smooth transition of Australian drama to a global market. Rowse and Moran argue that to view culture in general as a marketable commodity and TV programmes in particular as 'indices of nationality' can lead to a dilution of 'Australianness': within the wider context of Australian TV production, local authenticity is often sacrificed in pursuit of internationally recognisable signifiers of Australia and 'Australianness' (1984: 272), some of which have little cultural currency for the domestic audience and are decidedly dated.

Part of the mismatch between perceived notions of Australia and the reality thereof stems from earlier attempts to generate specific images of Australia and Australianness on screen. Working to undermine perceptions of Australia underscored in a series of Australian films of the early 1970s that construct a 'mateship' culture, the Australian Film Council actively sought to build a very different image of nationhood through its support of films adapted from literary texts that presented a more 'decorous' image of Australiana (McFarlane 2014: 12). Films like *Stork* (1971), *The Adventures of Barry Mackenzie* (1972), and *Alvin Purple* (1973) that perpetuate an image of the macho 'Aussie Ocker' stand in stark contrast to the body of work consciously supported by the Australian Film Council and now collectively known as the AFC genre of films (Dermody and Jacka 1988: 28–37). While Ocker films and to a lesser extent Ocker TV series like *Number 96* (1972–8) are characterised by a crass representation of a specifically working-class strand of the 'Australian way of life' within an urbanised Australia (O'Regan 1995), AFC film adaptations like *Picnic at Hanging Rock* (1975), *The Getting of Wisdom* (1977), and *My Brilliant Career* (1979) serve to reconstruct the Australian image through their evocation of period and place (Dermody and Jacka 1988: 32), the urban Australia of Ocker film and television being superseded by what has become an on-screen aestheticisation of a certain kind of imposing rural landscape. Epitomised by films like Peter Weir's *Picnic at Hanging Rock*, such landscapes have become iconic signifiers of 'Australia' that remain a prominent feature in many Australian films and TV dramas; though now viewed as period films that had limited capacity to reflect the lived realities of 1970s Australia (Rowse and Moran 1984: 237) they have, nevertheless, had a longstanding impact on the way Australia is perceived by an international audience. The AFC genre and the films defined as belonging to that genre may have corrected the exaggerated caricature of the Aussie Ocker but it left a legacy of a different kind, that, according to Turner, 'retrojected "Australian nationhood"' instead of dealing with the 'complex contemporary realities of an urban "multicultural" society' (1989: 115). This 'fetishisation' of Australia as a site of 'exotic landscapes' remains synonymous with overseas perceptions of the Australian lifestyle: in today's global market the 'more familiar and more subdued landscapes of home' that appeal to the domestic audience have to be negotiated (O'Regan and Ward 2011: 44). Just as Tolstoy's Russia can become an 'exotic site of tourism' in some film adaptations of *Anna Karenina*, commercial pressure to produce the anticipated exotic landscapes that have become cultural signifiers of 'Australianness' prevails in the current TV landscape.

This kind of 'landscape exhibitionism' remains an important unique selling point that can be exploited in pursuit of export markets (O'Regan and Ward 2011: 36–44), and many contemporary Australian TV series that attain a global market are, like the AFC genre films of the 1970s, adaptations. Some, like TV series *Mystery Road* (2018) and *Wolf Creek* (2016–), are adaptations of films that already have an established international audience familiar with the iconic outback Australia setting of these screen narratives. Similarly, as a series that adapts what has become part of the Australian film canon, TV's *Picnic at Hanging Rock* (2018) draws on the cultural kudos of Joan Lindsay's novel but it is Weir's film and the haunting Australian landscapes lensed in that film that ensured the series' global release and a presence at international festivals. What these adaptations also share, as a consequence of an already established international presence acquired through their cinematic precursors, are well established distribution networks that orchestrate global release. For Moran, distribution is 'the master element in the circuit across the field of television' (Moran 2009: 12) and an increasing awareness of the significance of establishing such 'circuits' of communication and distribution is leading to ventures that are bringing Australian drama to an international audience as joint ventures between Netflix and the ABC demonstrate. *Pine Gap* (2018) is one such venture that according to ABC's director of television, David Anderson, is 'an Australian drama that can resonate both locally and with a global audience' (Anderson, in Otterson 2017).

'Everyday' Australians

The Secret Life of Us (2001–6), set in urban Australia rather than in the iconic Australian outback, also established a dedicated overseas audience by foregrounding instead an articulation of 'Australianness' through 'a traditional kind of Australian realism' that, unlike either the AFC genre films of the seventies or contemporary TV adaptations that capitalise on the landscape currency of their cinematic forerunners, is 'modest' in its 'invocatio[n] of the national', and is inflected through 'language, cultural routines' and everyday 'characteristic environments' (Craven 2008: 59- 60). Despite its high art affiliation with canonical literature, it is to this variety of TV drama that *The Beautiful Lie* is indebted: both 'landscape exhibitionism' and the traditional costume drama treatment of canonical narrative are pressures that are resisted. Like *The Secret Life of Us* it 'rehear[ses] new ways of seeing the Australian setting' (Craven 2008: 61). The story's relocation to the cityscapes of Melbourne and its more affluent suburbs becomes a defining feature of the series. Cinematographer John Brawley and director Glendyn Ivin see its urban locale as an essential part of the story's identity; aerial shots of Melbourne's cityscape are frequently employed to reinforce the reality of the contemporary scene within which the story unfolds (Brawley 2016). Brawley's use of a hand-held camera underscores the series' realism by creating 'an aesthetic that [isn't] polished' (Brawley 2016); in accord with Ivin's intent, the ever-moving camera establishes an intimacy with the audience, providing what Ivin describes as the series' 'heartbeat' (Ivin in Brawley 2016). Treatment of iconic signifiers, like the train that is the instrument of Anna's death in both novel and screen adaptations to date, is similarly indicative of the ways in which this production seeks to ground events in real terms.

Historically, the train has become a metaphorical allusion to Anna's 'sexual drive' (Leving 2016: 114) but in *The Beautiful Lie*, it becomes a prominent part of an urban landscape that is intrinsically connected to the evolving love of Anna and Skeet, as sound-sensitive Skeet teaches her to hear and appreciate the rhythms of the city through the static of its street lights and the ticking noise of cold train tracks (episode 2). Trains become part of the visual landscape too. Recurring shots of trains at red light crossings punctuate the narrative, signalling the ominous role the train will play in the series' closing moments (episode 5). In contrast to a closing flashback to that earlier moment of ordinary intimacy with Skeet, Anna now stands alone by the tracks, unable to hear anything (episode 6). By employing a colour palette that references the 'vivid and supersaturated colour work' of photographer Nan Golding (Brawley 2016), Brawley attains a visual realism that the more traditional costume drama adaptations of Tolstoy's tale are unable to realise on screen, and while Anna here, as in other productions, is associated with the colour red through her costuming (Leving 2016: 118), this colour becomes a more embedded part of her presence in the final moments, the red lights of the approaching train referenced throughout, saturating the screen before editing to a black screen that denotes her death. The iconic signifiers are retained, but they become an organic part of the narrative's realism rather than abstract allusions; they are synonymous with an everyday urban landscape rather than the 'fetishiz[ed]' and 'exotic landscapes' (O'Regan and Ward 2011: 44) that overseas viewers have come to associate with 'Australia'.

It is in the minutiae of relationships rather than the grandeur of the epic costume drama that this adaptation of *Anna Karenina* excels. While its adaptive predecessors are preoccupied with reproducing period detail within what is ostensibly presented as nineteenth-century Russia, this series explores universal issues that transcend period and nationhood in favour of a detailed study of the human condition, revolving here, as in Tolstoy's novel, around matters related to the relationships that define us. Like the aforementioned series noted by Scott as so central to Australian TV drama, *The Beautiful Lie* explores Australian culture, identity and experience through the familiar lens of the contemporary Australian family. In its treatment of narrative content and in its on-screen presentation thereof, it aims for what Ivin deems 'truthful storytelling' (Ivin in Brawley 2016). Though a producer-driven creation championed by Edwards and his desire to present this as a 'study of love', Bell's way in to the process of adapting the novel to a long-form serial format was very much character driven, with plot and themes feeding into story arcs that focus on relationships within the re-visioned cultural landscape of a metropolitan contemporary Australia (Bell, in Griggs 2015). Though this adaptation, like its predecessors, is ostensibly concerned with Anna's story arc, the script explores in detail the novel's three central relationships: Anna and Vronsky, Dolly and Stiva, and Levin and Kitty. However, Bell acknowledges that 'there's a lot of change and intervention' at work here (Bell, in Mercado 2015) and while such change and intervention are inevitably due in part to the story's temporal, geographical and socio-cultural relocation, it is Bell's interventions at the microlevel that are most telling. Dolly is, according to Morson, the real heroine of Tolstoy's novel (Morson 2010: 361). Her 'heroism' is reconfigured in *The Beautiful Lie* through small acts of everyday living illustrated not only through the love of her children, as in Tolstoy's novel, but through a detailed, light-hearted exploration of the complexities of her relationships with younger sister Kitty, family nanny Gabriella and repentant husband Kingsley. But it is her ongoing relationship with Kingsley that forms one of three central story arcs: the hedonistic Stiva of Tolstoy's imagining is re-visioned as a momentarily unfaithful yet steadfastly repentant husband who values family and the love of his wife above all else. His charm lies in his capacity to endure, to atone and to declare his undying love of the woman he still regards as 'the most interesting in the room' (episode 5). Tolstoy's aim was to urge his readers to 'question the romantic ideal' and to show that 'romantic love is but one kind of love' (Morson 2010: 362); here, the love between Dolly and Kingsley is framed as a long-lasting love – one that can overcome the pressures of contemporary family life. It is a happy, and eventually a dependable love that evolves during the story arc afforded to Kingsley and Dolly who, unlike Anna and Xander, choose to work through their problems to the point where Dolly allows Kingsley to return to the marital bed, stating simply 'I love us' (episode 3).

The relationship between Kitty and Peter provides another variant of happy, dependable love that stands in stark contrast to the toxic, destructive 'love' epitomised by Anna and Skeet. Like the enduring love of Dolly and Kingsley, the love of Kitty and Peter is conveyed as one that builds from a position of weakness to one of strength. Initially presented as characters defined by an unrequited love, they emerge as the story's most romantic yet most grounded couple. Though couched in a tragi-comic narrational mode, Kitty's narrative trajectory is of a particularly complex nature as she slowly transforms from the petulant, self-absorbed, therapy-dependent girl who hates her own body to the woman who marvels at that same 'imperfect' body's capacity to create life (episode 6). Like Tolstoy's Levin, Peter is 'in love' with the whole idea of family, and his story arc is built around his 'journey towards becoming a family man' (Bell, in Griggs 2015). His pursuit of love is an integral part of that journey, his undying love for Kitty expressed most convincingly in a moment of simplicity and understatement during an unspoken exchange facilitated by fridge magnets during a post-dinner party clean up in Dolly's kitchen (episode 3). Co-scriptwriter, John Gavin scribes it as an epiphanal moment for Kitty, set within the very ordinary rhythms of everyday life. It is an extended and carefully choreographed scene in which the audience is invited to become part of an exchange in which Brawley's ever-moving camera becomes its 'heartbeat'. We move with each of them to and from the fridge, waiting to see what has been written and how they respond, simple phrases mapping out their emotional positions, and culminating in a poem that demonstrates the depth of Peter's love and constancy:

> Kitty: You are sad.
> Peter: Yes but I am strong
> Kitty: Why sad
> Peter: You are in my heart
> Kitty: I was mean
> Peter: Through storm seas'/mist and night rain/I am a tiny ship/you are the moving star. (Episode 3)

This and the following scene, in which Dolly and Kingsley finally resume their sex life, are presented as moments infused with a warmth and intimacy bred of normalcy. They are scenes that are strategically positioned to stand in stark contrast to an earlier scene between Anna and Skeet as they engage in awkward car sex at Anna's home; the close-ups of Anna's face signal her distress, and Xander's realisation that this is taking place within the confines of his own familial territory frames the moment as one that signals the end of any semblance of their normal family life (episode 3). Morson claims the narrative threads of Tolstoy's tale revolve first and foremost around family life, the moral worth of each character being dependent on his or her capacity to 'understand and appreciate family' (2010: 358). While other adaptations of *Anna Karenina* on screen couch Anna's betrayal in terms of 'romantic' inevitability, in this series – in her abandonment of her family – Anna is cast as one whose 'moral worth' is questionable, particularly in light of the moral choices made by others within the narrative. The romantic excesses of Anna's claim that '[w]ith Skeet [she] fee[ls] like a starving person given food' is swiftly undermined by brother Kingsley's observation that 'cheating is cheating' (episode 3).

Like *Puberty Blues*, a series produced by the same creative team and seen as its 'tonally similar sibling' (Bell, in Griggs 2015), *The Beautiful Lie* is grounded in environments and cultural rhythms that reflect a contemporary urban

Australia; Tolstoy's novel shares a 'tonally' similar approach to the presentation of his contemporary scene and despite the tragic narrative outcome of novel and series, the journey towards that outcome is realised through understatement that often employs a gently humorous treatment of story content. Bell takes her lead from Tolstoy and his prose, arguing that:

> He was famously grumpy . . . but he still makes me laugh. Just these little comments that he makes; there's one here about Dolly, where she says she'd never leave her husband because she'd got into the habit of loving him. So clever . . . only a few words in a whole paragraph of stuff . . . understated and still so true. (Bell, in Griggs 2015)

Using this as their adaptive starting point, Bell and Gavin script a drama that plays to the story's comedic strengths without sacrificing its tragic undertones. This textual duality is acknowledged by numerous TV critics: Neutze (2015) sees it as 'essentially a comedy' that follows 'an almost Chekovian template, where tragedy and comedy work in concert'; Enker (2015) describes it as 'a beast with tragically existential undertones which are unavoidably humorous'. The humorous treatment of the narrative informs not only selection of content but of cast. Bell cites the importance of casting comedian Celia Paquola in the role of Dolly Faraday; Paquola exploits the comedic potential of the script in her on-screen realisation of the relationship between Dolly and her unfaithful husband Kingsley, ensuring her prolonged 'revenge' and his endurance thereof, can still translate as 'love' (Bell, in Griggs 2015). The Dolly/Kingsley/Gabriella 'love triangle' is a comedic strategy that serves to illustrates this. In a scene in which Dolly and Gabriella share a bed in Kingsley's absence, our suspicion is that Kingsley's inability to make it home from work on this particular evening is due to further infidelities, but when Dolly, as part of her 'revenge', sends him a 'selfie' that shows her in bed with Gabriella, we see him alone in his hotel room, laughing out loud at his wife's audacious stunt (episode 3). The casting of Sophie Lowe as the vulnerable yet feisty Kitty is similarly significant: her 'tragicomic moment of self-implosion' as she is seen sprawled on the floor gorging on the leftovers from her disastrous engagement party (episode 2) is swiftly followed by the disturbing realisation that she is a recovering bulimic whose fragile self-worth has yet again been undermined (Bell, in Griggs 2015).

Bell sees Tolstoy's story as one that is as much about family as it is about love, and the series' story arcs present as an interconnected network of familial bonds. Through her love of Peter, Kitty learns the value of family and though initially cast in the role of over-indulged and self-centred younger sister of older, more worldly-wise Dolly, she embraces motherhood and is instrumental in helping Dolly see that her dependency on Gabriella – a dependency comically referred to by Dolly as a case of 'Stockholm Syndrome in reverse' – is no longer necessary (episode 3). In a clever structural turn, Bell engineers closing scenes that place all but Anna within the confines of a family unit: three generations of the Ballantyne clan are gathered at Peter's family home, and in a scene that mirrors an earlier moment of family togetherness shared by Anna, Xander and Kasper on board a flight to visit family in episode 1, it is Helen, Xander and Kasper who are now seen sharing family time as they jet off on a family holiday. In striking contrast to these comforting images of dependable love, at this point in the narrative Anna is seen alone and contemplating suicide, having abandoned both her initial and her newly acquired 'family'. Abandonment of family, and in particular abandonment of her son, is at the heart of her downfall in this production: it plays to contemporary anxieties about maternal commitment, with even Skeet's seemingly dispassionate mother accusing Anna of the ultimate motherly betrayal, her damning words – 'I would never tell you to choose a man over your child. You always choose your children' (episode 6) – compounding Anna's guilt. Unable to come to terms with her betrayal of her first child, Anna is incapable of loving her second, her distress couched here in contemporary terms of reference as post-natal depression. The revelatory momentary lapses that Anna experiences during childbirth return her to an emotional dependency on the safety and comfort of 'family' and her affiliation with Xander (episode 4), but the tragic course of her narrative is already in place, the opening voiceover of the series leaving viewers in no doubt that she will ultimately return to her fatal, all-consuming relationship with Skeet.

Anna's voiceover frames the narrative: it is a storytelling device that is employed during the opening and closing moments of every episode as she maps out not only her own demise but the narrative trajectories of Dolly and Kingsley, Peter and Kitty, and Xander and Skeet. Bell deems her use of this strategic storytelling device a 'practical' yet 'essential choice' – one that ensures Anna is not 'lost' in this 'ensemble cast' where 'so much screen time' is dedicated to the relationships of those around her (Bell, in Griggs 2015). It is an unusual choice: the transition of the first person narrative voice of a prose text to the visual canvas of screen space is a notoriously problematic part of the adaptation process. Voiceover has been introduced to telling effect in some film adaptations of canonical texts: in Heckerling's *Clueless* (1995) and Cuarón's *Great Expectations* (1998) its usage is more than tokenistic, but in most instances it is a device that struggles to give any extra dimension to either the on-screen storytelling or the inner psyche of its speaker. Garcia notes that voiceover is rarely used in TV drama and often to less telling effect; though utilised with greater frequency of late (*Desperate Housewives*, 2004–12; *Narcos*, 2015–; *Mr Robot*, 2015), voiceovers are used to 'complete the psychology' of the speaker: these are not 'storytellers' who 'play with the details' of the tale (Garcia 2016: 18). The distinctive voiceover introduced in *The*

Beautiful Lie has a very different function: it marks a radical shift away from TV norms. While it may be a 'practical' choice used here as a means to keeping Anna to the forefront of the narrative, it is also a choice that hands the control of the narrative to the story's doomed protagonist, her commentary extending beyond inner reflection of the kind most often employed in voiceover to moments she would have no first-hand knowledge of. Here, through a discourse on the nature of 'love' that opens and closes each episode, Anna recounts events as they unfold for all of the characters involved, taking on an omniscient narrational role that affords her control of the narrative and the capacity to comment on the emotional state of others. Her role as overseer of the narrative is given credibility since the audience is made aware from the outset that Anna is already dead, affording her voiceover a more reflective and fatalistic dimension: in her opening commentary Anna notes 'By the time my boy turns seven I'll be dead' (episode 1). For Bell, this voiceover is 'all about keeping [the] humanity' of a character whose 'bad decisions' make it difficult 'to watch and to read her': it is a strategy that provides 'a way for people to stay connected to her' on her journey of 'self-implosion' (Bell, in Griggs 2015). It is an adaptive intervention that translates the novel's omniscient third person narration into more intimate voiceover mode, monopolising on what Cardwell sees as the TV medium's 'greater capacity for intimate equality with the viewer' (2007: 194). Anna's voiceover gives the viewer privileged access not only to her inner thoughts but also to her reflections on the thoughts and actions of others central to the narrative. It further provides a cyclical narrative structure that leads to an inevitable point of closure that nonetheless posits the idea that 'love' remains a cultural anxiety that will continue to inform the decisions we make, the lives we choose to build, regardless of the story's geographical, temporal or socio-cultural frame of reference. Anna's opening discourse on love is revisited almost verbatim in the moments leading up to her suicide at the close of the series:

> Love can be strange. Love is familiar. Love can be broken.
> It can be fixed. Love can be lost and then found again.

Her closing voiceover functions as a sound bridge, playing over scenes that juxtapose her current solitary position with those of others who have been central to the tale: with the exception of Anna and Skeet, all are framed as members of a convivial family unit in the midst of everyday situations, the normalcy of their relationships standing in stark contrast to the drama of Anna's impending demise. In a swift edit to a black screen in the closing seconds before her death, the viewer is denied access to not only Anna's on-screen presence but to the established intimacies of her voiceover commentary.

Conclusion

Tolstoy's tale of 'unhappy families' has traditionally been adapted as costume drama within established historical and geographical boundaries that are at least in part grounded in the cultural climate of a nineteenth-century Russia; however, *The Beautiful Lie* demonstrates the text's capacity to transcend the geography of time, place and cultural proclivity by exploring the story's preoccupation not, as is the adaptive norm, with romantic love but with love as a reflection of the human condition. It does what all good adaptations should do: it 'evolve[s] and mutate[s] to fit new times and different places' (Hutcheon 2006: 176). It is in essence a family drama that explores issues of universal concern, and yet it also inscribes a sense of nationhood, not through any preconception of what constitutes 'Australia' and its iconic landscapes but through its exploration of and engagement with the familiar and familial, producing instead a story that is reflective of the lived experience of contemporary Australians. It re-visions Tolstoy's *Anna Karenina* without compromising its Australian credentials or the cultural identity of its intended Australian audience, taking a fresh approach to the adaptation of the nineteenth-century canonical text that is so often mired in the kind of prestige costume drama branding epitomised by British TV serial adaptations. It is poised to monopolise on current trends that suggest a move away from the popularity of staid TV costume drama adaptations to a more experimental terrain that is no longer solely the purview of British TV production. However, its pathway to global transferability remains problematic: even though it is a series with literary cultural currency that should, at least in part, contribute to its smooth transition to a global platform, in this current golden age of TV drama an affiliation with a work of canonical literature as a marker of global audience appeal is not enough, even when, as is the case with *The Beautiful Lie*, the adaptive approach is innovative and engaging. While this is a series that adapts a much loved text that thus has the potential to attract an established audience of international reach, finding traction for any product within an increasingly competitive global marketplace is challenging. Scott notes that the media industry's ability to continue to 'create and tell and share Australian stories' is dependent upon a better understanding of the impact of digital technologies and their reach (2015); though *The Beautiful Lie* is a series that successfully represents Tolstoy's classic tale as an Australian story replete with cultural signifiers of 'Australianness', without the all-important distribution networks alluded to by Moran, Australian series like this will remain first and foremost products consumed by a domestic audience.

References

Brawley, J. (2016), '*The Beautiful Lie*: a love story', John Brawley blog, 7 February, <https://johnbrawley.wordpress.com/2016/02/07/the-beautiful-lie-a-love-story/> (accessed 22 January 2017).

Burry, A. (2016), 'Introduction: filming Russian classics', in A. Burry and F. H. White (eds), *Border Crossing: Russian Literature into Film*, Edinburgh: Edinburgh University Press, pp. 1–16.
Cardwell, S. (2007), 'Literature on the small screen: television adaptations', in D. Cartmell and I. Whelehan (eds), *Literature on Screen*, Cambridge: Cambridge University Press, pp. 181–95.
Craven, I. P. (2008), 'Southern stars and secret lives: international exchange in Australian television', *Continuum*, 22: 1, 51–67.
Della Coletta, C. (2012), *When Stories Travel: Cross-cultural Encounters between Fiction and Film*, Baltimore: Johns Hopkins University Press.
Dermody S. and Jacka, Liz (1988), *The Screening of Australia: Anatomy of a Film Industry* (Volume 2), Sydney: Currency Press.
De Groot, J. (2015), 'Foreword', in J. Leggott and J. Taddeo (eds), *Upstairs and Downstairs: British Costume Drama from the Forsyte Saga to Downton Abbey*, Lanham: Rowman & Littlefield, pp. i–xi.
Enker, D. (2015), '*Anna Karenina* gets modern makeover', *Sydney Morning Herald*, 7 October.
Garcia, Alberto N. (2016), 'A storytelling machine: the complexity and revolution of narrative television', *Between*, 6: 11, 1–25.
Griggs, Y. (2015), 'Alice Bell, interview with author', 15 December.
Griggs, Y. (2018), *Adaptable TV: Rewiring the Text*, Basingstoke: Palgrave Macmillan.
Hutcheon, L. (2006), *A Theory of Adaptation*, London: Routledge.
Innocenti, V. and Pascatore, G. (2014), 'Changing series: narrative models and the role of the viewer in contemporary television seriality', *Between*, 4: 8, 1–15.
Jacka, L. (1990), 'ABC television drama: policy and ideas of national broadcasting', *Metro Magazine*, 83, 23–6.
Jacka, L. (2004), 'Doing the history of television on Australia: problems and challenges', *Continuum*, 18: 1, 27–41.
Leitch, T. (2016), 'Across the Russian border', in A Burry and Frederick H. White (eds), *Border Crossing: Russian Literature into Film*, Edinburgh: Edinburgh University Press, pp. 17–39.
Leving, Y. (2016), 'The eye-deology of trauma: killing Anna Karenina softly', in A. Burry and F. H. White (eds), *Border Crossing: Russian Literature into Film*, Edinburgh: Edinburgh University Press, pp. 102–20.
Makoveeva, I. (2001), 'Cinematic adaptations of *Anna Karenina*', *Studies in Slavik Cultures*, 2, 11–134.
McFarlane, B. (2014), 'The long shadow of Hanging Rock', *Screen Education*, 75, 9–12.
Mercado, A. (2015), 'Bringing *The Beautiful Lie* to television', *Mediaweek*, 16 October, <https://mediaweek.com.au/bringing-the-beautiful-lie-to-tv/> (accessed 20 October 2015).
Moran, A. (2009), *New Flows in Global TV*, London: Intellect.
Morson, G. (2010), 'Marriage, love, and time in Tolstoy's *Anna Karenina*', *Journal of Family Theory & Review* 2, 353–69.
Neill, R. (2015), 'The Beautiful Lie transplants Tolstoy to Australia', *The Australian*, 17 October.

Neutze, B. (2015), 'The Beautiful Lie: review, arts and culture', *Daily Review*, 19 October, <https://indaily.com.au/arts-and-culture/2015/10/19/the-beautiful-lie/> (accessed 20 October 2015).

O'Regan, T. (1995), 'Australian film in the 1970s: the ocker and the quality film', Centre for Research in Culture and Communication (Murdoch University), *AustLit*, <https://wwwmcc.murdoch.edu.au/ReadingRoom/film/1970s.html-1> (accessed 15 October 2019).

O' Regan, T. and Ward, S. (2011), 'Defining a national brand: Australian television drama and the global television market', *Journal of Australian Studies*, 35: 1, 33–47.

Otterson, J. (2017), 'Netflix partners with Australian Broadcasting Corporation on spy series *Pine Gap*', *Variety*, 13 September, <https://variety.com/2017/tv/news/netflix-australian-broadcasting-corporation-pine-gap-1202557126/> (accessed 30 October 2018).

Palmer, R. B. (2017), 'Continuation, adaptation studies, and the never-finished text', in J. Grossman and R. B. Palmer (eds), *Adaptation in Visual Culture: Images, Texts, and Their Multiple Worlds*, Basingstoke: Palgrave Macmillan, pp. 73–100.

Rose, Brian A. (1996), *Jekyll and Hyde Adapted: Dramatizations of Cultural Anxiety*, Westport, CT: Greenwood.

Rowse, T. and Moran, A. (1984), '"Peculiarly Australian": the political construction of cultural identity', in S. Encel (ed.), *Australian Society: Introductory Essays*, Melbourne: Longman Cheshire, pp. 229–77.

Scott, M. (2015), 'The future of the Australian story', *The Inaugural Brian Jones AO Lecture*, Macquarie University, 15 September, <http://about.abc.net.au/speeches/the-future-of-the-australian-story/> (accessed 14 October 2015).

The Beautiful Lie (2015), Australia: Endemol/Southern Star Entertainment.

Tolstoy, L. (1999 [1877]), *Anna Karenina*, Ware: Wordsworth Editions.

Turner, G. (1989), 'Art directing history: the period film', in T. O'Regan and A. Moran (eds), *The Australian Screen*, Victoria: Penguin, pp. 99–117.

Voigts-Virchow, E. (2007), '*Heimat* and Heritage', in D. Cartmell and I. Whelehan (eds), *Literature on Screen*, Cambridge: Cambridge University Press, pp. 123–38.

PART V

REMAKING, TRANSLATING: DIALOGUES ACROSS BORDERS

11. IN ANOTHER TIME AND PLACE: TRANSLATING GOTHIC ROMANCE IN *THE HANDMAIDEN*

Chi-Yun Shin

The Handmaiden (Ah-ga-ssi/아가씨, 2016)¹ is the tenth feature film by the South Korean director Park Chan-wook, who is mainly known for his highly stylised and visceral tales of vengeance that include the Cannes Film Festival prizewinner *Oldboy* (Oldeuboi 2003). An eagerly awaited film since his English language thriller *Stoker* (2013), *The Handmaiden* was very much promoted worldwide as the work of Park Chan-wook, an acclaimed international auteur. 'From the director of *Oldboy* and *Stoker*' is indeed the top line that adorns the film's UK theatrical poster. Upon its international release, the film garnered critical and commercial success. Among its many accolades, the film was in competition for the Palme d'Or at the 2016 Cannes Film Festival, and won the 2018 BAFTA (British Academy of Film and Television Arts) Award for Best Film Not in the English Language. According to the 2016 Korean Cinema Yearbook, it was also 'sold to a record 175 territories (besting the previous high of 167 for Bong Joon-ho's 2013 feature *Snowpiercer*)', and reportedly grossed over US$37.7 million (Paquet 2016: 7).

In the UK, *The Handmaiden* enjoyed a particularly successful release. Over the first six weeks of play, its gross reached £1.25 million and it became the best-performing Korean film at the box office by a wide margin, beating Park's own *Oldboy* at £316,000 (Gant 2017: 9). As Charles Gant points out in his *Sight & Sound* report, 'that's a remarkable result', considering the relatively poor box office track record of Korean films as well as the fact that foreign language films rarely hit £1 million in the UK market.² Then again, as Gant puts it, 'The Handmaiden offered an altogether different proposition for UK audiences', and one of the salient aspects for its UK distributor Curzon Artificial Eye was the film's 'connection to Sarah Waters' novel Fingersmith' (2002: 9). Indeed, to all intents and purposes, The Handmaiden is an adaptation of British writer Waters' third novel Fingersmith, even though the film transports a gothic tale of crime set in nineteenth-century England to Korea of the 1930s when the Korean peninsula was under Japanese occupation. Furthermore, notwithstanding the cultural relocation, The Handmaiden is in steadfast and evident dialogue with Fingersmith, and it is this inter-medial relationship between the original novel and the film adaptation that is the main concern of this article. In particular, it focuses on the sensual eroticism of the central lesbian couples in both texts.

Enter the Author: Sarah Waters on The Handmaiden

Published in 2002, Waters' Fingersmith is an example of Neo-Victorian historical fiction that consciously replicates some of the details of Victorian 'sensation' novels, particularly of Wilkie Collins, which are full of intense melodrama and intrigue.[3] To give a truncated preview of the novel, it tells the story of Sue Trinder, the eponymous fingersmith (pickpocket), who is roped into helping Richard 'Gentleman' Rivers seduce a wealthy heiress, Maud Lilly, sequestered in a big country house called Briar with her uncle. Sue is to pose as a lady's maid, to gain Maud's trust and to persuade her to elope with Gentleman. Once they are married, Gentleman plans to have Maud committed to a lunatic asylum and to take her fortune for himself. Unexpectedly, however, the two women are attracted to each other, and there ensues a complicated tale of love and deception that involves Sue's incarceration in the madhouse. Full of its own twists and turns, the novel made the bestseller list, becoming a mainstream breakthrough for Waters, and was shortlisted for both the Man Booker and the Orange Prize – two of the most prestigious literary prizes in Britain. A BBC television serialisation soon followed in 2005, manifesting its commercial and critical success.

Back in 1998, Waters had made a sensational debut with a novel called Tipping the Velvet, which was hailed as signalling 'a powerful new voice in lesbian fiction', along with her second novel, published in 1999, Affinity (Armitstead 2017). Although she has since written novels set at different times,[4] with her first three novels all being set in the Victorian era – the quasi-trilogy that includes Fingersmith – Waters has marked her career with what she calls 'lesbo Victorian romps'. Of being labelled as a lesbian writer, Waters said, 'I'm writing with a clear lesbian agenda in the novels. It's right there at the heart of the books' (Lo 2006), indicating a pivotal part the topic of same-sex passion plays in her novels. Paulina Palmer, for instance, evaluates 'her ability to combine the representation of lesbian history with an awareness of the interests and concerns of the lesbian community today' as 'one of the most striking and successful aspects of her work' (2008: 83).

Considering that Waters is one of the most acclaimed contemporary literary heavyweights, it is not so surprising that the established cultural gatekeepers such as *The Guardian* and BBC Radio 4 – who represent a (mainly white) middle-class, highbrow, even elitist, culture sector in Britain – rushed to feature interviews with Waters on the theatrical release of *The Handmaiden* in April 2017. For sure, this phenomenon of soliciting the 'original' author's view has now become a common practice. As Simone Murray notes in her book *The Adaptation Industry*, 'the author's role has *not* in fact ceased with the handing over of the book and collecting of money but is, rather, incorporated into the highest profile marketing event for any feature film' (2012: 26). For instance, the appearance of the author at the adapted film's red-carpet premiere is almost a ritual in the contemporary celebrity author culture that became prominent from the 1980s.[5] In such an environment, as Murray goes on to maintain, authors 'function as creative spokespersons and aesthetic guarantors for such trans-format media franchises – reassuring existing and potential audience of an adaptation's artistic bona fides' (26–7).

In these interviews, Sarah Waters duly offers her creative blessings to the film. Appearing on BBC Radio 4's *The Film Programme* (16 April 2017), for example, Waters calls *The Handmaiden* 'a beautiful, beautiful film' and tells its host Francine Stock: 'given that the change of period, change of setting, and change of so much really, nevertheless, it is recognisably my story and my characters, which was wonderful for me' (2017). When questioned about the film's lingering sex scenes and a male gaze, Waters defends the film, as although it portrays 'women trapped by male structures and trapped within the limits of male-authored text', it 'shows them escaping from those things or using them, using bits of them for their own pleasure'. She continues to reflect that the film has 'a paradox at the heart', just like her book, and how 'it knows it and even relishes on its paradoxes and contradictions'. Similarly, in the *Guardian* interview (8 April 2017), she remarks that 'though ironically the film is a story told by a man,[6] it's still very faithful to the idea that the women are appropriating a very male pornographic tradition to find their own way of exploring their desires' (Armitstead 2017). In fact, according to Steve Lewis, head of theatrical distribution at Curzon, 'Sarah Waters' approval' helped to overcome their 'concern that the lesbian storyline when combined with a male director might be an issue' (Gant 2017: 9).

Besides Waters' approval, what stands out the most in these interviews is the fact that she uses the phrase 'faithful to the book' several times. In the aforementioned *The Film Programme*, Waters expresses how astonished she was to find the film being 'really faithful to the book' despite lots of changes. In the

Guardian interview, she mentions that 'the first thing that struck me was how faithful it manages to be to *Fingersmith* even though it's in Korean and Japanese and set in a different period' (Armitstead 2017). This is despite the fact that Waters apparently requested it to be described as 'inspired by' rather than 'based on', having read the early drafts of the film's screenplay (Dale 2015). It is actually rather ironic that Waters uses the idea of faithfulness or fidelity in her discussion of the film, in the respect that the question of fidelity – that is to say, 'when adaptations were being judged in terms of quality by how close or far they were from their "original" or "source" texts' (Hutcheon 2013: xxvi) – is no longer the critical orthodoxy in the field of adaptation studies. As Linda Hutcheon points out in *A Theory of Adaptation*, 'today, if "fidelity" is invoked at all in adaptation studies, it is usually . . . in the context of fan-culture loyalty rather than as a quality of adaptive strategies' (2013: xxvi).

To be sure, Waters is not technically making a judgement on the film based on its faithfulness to her book. In fact, she confesses in *The Film Programme* how she 'could relax and enjoy it more' when the film's narrative starts to depart from hers. Rather, the point is that the film, to her surprise, manages to be faithful to her novel, despite the cultural transportation. Waters reasons that the qualities of excess and madness in the narrative of Park's film – that is 'tittering on the verge of hysteria, as well as transgressive female characters' – lead back to her novel, which is also an excessive narrative full of melodrama and twists and turns, in turn inspired by the Victorian novels of sensation. Certainly, the fidelity criticism is not the concern of this article either. What is of interest is the mediated relationship between the 'source' novel and adaptation, which is articulated by the novel's author Sarah Waters. In many ways, Waters' remarks provide a framework from which to explore the questions as to what has been transformed and yet how it remains 'true' to the novel. In the following sections, questions regarding what exactly has been transferred, reimagined and translated from the novel to the film adaptation will be examined. The 'faithful' transcoding of the novel's sensual expression of lesbian sexuality onto cinematic screen, in particular, will be a pivot of this comparative study.

In Another Time and Place: From Victorian England to Colonial Korea

As noted earlier, *The Handmaiden* transplants the Victorian story of love and deception to 1930s Korea under Japanese colonial rule. In the process of cultural relocation, the film gives prominence to the ethnic identities and hierarchies in colonial Korea, conspicuously presented in the household as the Japanese masters (coloniser) and Korean servants (colonised). Thus, in *The Handmaiden*, a young Korean pickpocket Sook-hee (played by Kim Tae-ri) enters a wealthy Japanese household, pretending to be a maid, in order to help

Count Fujiwara (Ha Jung-woo), a Korean conman impersonating a Japanese nobleman, to seduce and marry Lady Hideko (Kim Min-hee), who lives in lavish imprisonment on a grand country estate owned by her sadistic uncle, Kouzuki (Cho Jin-woong). According to the film's director Park, it is the producer Syd Lim[7] who came up with the idea of moving the setting to 1930s Korea as a solution to Park's predicament of not wanting to follow in the footsteps of the existing BBC miniseries based on *Fingersmith* (Topalovic 2016).[8]

This turns out to be a highly perceptive and effective change, which not only allows the film to deal with the class difference between the characters but also incorporates the colonial aspiration towards the West that was introduced to Korea via Japan. For instance, the mansion within which much of the film's narrative unfolds is built in the hybrid style of Japan and Britain, following the instruction of the owner Kouzuki, Lady Hideko's uncle, who ostensibly admires the two countries[9] (here, the reference to Britain can also be seen as an homage to the original novel). The 1930s was certainly the period of transition when Western-style modernisation and industrial development, such as the extensive transportation infrastructure, took place on the Korean peninsula under the Japanese colonial authorities, as 'part and parcel of Japan's competition with more advanced powers in the world economy' (Cumings 1998: 223). Although it was mainly to facilitate Japan's interests rather than to benefit the Koreans, in accordance with the peninsula's strategic value to the empire, this development of colonial infrastructure, as Bruce Cumings notes, 'put Korea substantially ahead of other developing countries' by the early 1940s (1998: 222).

A more important point of appeal of the period, however, is the colonial condition that provides a compelling tension between Japanese and Korean identities, adding another layer to the class dynamic of *Fingersmith*. In the novel that Waters describes as being all about 'cons and impersonation', people are constantly passing themselves off as someone they are not (Stock 2017): Richard Rivers, a working-class crook, masquerades as a gentleman to infiltrate Briar House, and Sue Trinder poses as a maid to help Gentleman's scheme to cheat Maud Lilly. Lady Maud, in turn, later impersonates her own maid 'Sue Smith' (the name Sue Trinder took when she comes to Briar) in front of the medical staff to ensure that it is Sue who ends up being locked up in the asylum as the delusional Mrs Rivers, instead of her, albeit briefly, being forced by Gentleman.

Such assumed names and identities prevalent in the novel are taken one step further in *The Handmaiden* with the colonial power dynamics between Korean and Japanese identities. In the film, Sook-hee, for instance, takes the role of maid with a Korean name Okju, and is then renamed Tamako, a Japanese name given to her by a Korean housekeeper. The constantly shifting identities are also reflected in the languages the characters use in the film.

Most main characters use both Korean and Japanese languages, and in the theatrical release version, the subtitles of dialogues are colour-coded to show which language is being spoken (Korean in white, and Japanese in yellow).[10] Count Fujiwara, for instance, skilfully uses Japanese to dupe Kouzuki, but when scheming with Sook-hee and/or Lady Hideko, he reverts to Korean. Lady Hideko, who also speaks both languages being brought up in Korea since she was a child, prefers to speak in Korean with Sook-hee because Japanese is the language of the erotic literature that she is forced to recite publically to audiences of men.

Most notably, the character of Uncle Kouzuki, a Korean by birth but now a naturalised Japanese, was once an interpreter who bribed his way into translating for Japanese high officials, as revealed in an inset story told by Count Fujiwara. Aspiring to be an 'authentic' Japanese man of letters, Kouzuki had married a Japanese (noble) woman, and he is planning to marry his Japanese niece Hideko. Explaining the convoluted nature of Kouzuki's identity, the film's director Park describes the character as follows:

> There's a Korean term, *sadaejuui*, that is used to uniquely express this notion, where the people of a smaller nation are so drawn to the power of a larger nation, and become subservient to that power. They internalize it so much that they are not worshiping the bigger power by force, but are doing it voluntarily. Through the character of Uncle Kouzuki, I wanted to paint a portrait of these poor, sad, and pathetic individuals – who are poor, I say – but who become a big threat and a serious danger for the other people of their nation. (Topalovic 2016)

Indeed, Japan's annexation of Korea (1910–45) brought about certain Koreans who not only voluntarily subjugate themselves to the colonial power but who also want to emulate or even 'become' the colonisers. The character of Uncle Kouzuki clearly embodies the confused identity of such individuals. When asked 'why this urge to become Japanese', his answer is unceremonious: 'Because Korea is ugly and Japan is beautiful.' He adds that 'Korea is soft, slow, dull and therefore hopeless'. Ironically, however, Homi Bhabha's notion of 'mimicry', which has come to describe the ambivalent relationship between coloniser and colonised, can be used here to discern the character's potentially threatening aspect that blurs the boundaries of colonial identities. As Bhabha argues, being 'at once resemblance and menace', mimicry destabilises the colonial discourse (1994: 123), including Kouzuki's own blunt assessment of Korea and Japan. As such, the film expands the novel's sense of class and LGBTQ identity politics into the colonial appropriation and blurring of identities in the adaptive process.

Between Literary and Cinematic Sensuality

Despite such changes evident in the transportation, the film retains many aspects of the novel. In both texts, for example, the acts of impersonation are closely associated with the dress code. In nineteenth-century Britain, clothing was an instant signifier of a person's social standing. From the outset, Sue's appearance as a typical borough girl, including her hairstyle and dress, needs to be 'tackled' to convey a neat and proper lady's maid during her hastened training. Similarly, in colonial Korea, different costumes would mark the person's ethnic as well as class identity. In *The Handmaiden*, Sook-hee, for instance, wears her plain Korean dress while working as a maid, whereas Lady Hideko and the count are dressed in either Japanese kimono or Western attire such as dinner jackets and gowns. The rigid dress code of the time and place, however, is being readily appropriated and transgressed in the acts of deception performed by the mistresses, Maud and Hideko, who cultivate and transform their maids' appearances into a Victorian lady and a Japanese lady respectively, through careful feeding and clothing. In short, in exchanging their dresses they are switching their identities. In the process that is akin to a well-orchestrated cosplay, which involves frequent dressing and undressing, both texts manifest their fascination with leather gloves and corsets, and their textures next to bare skin. Sarah Waters aptly comments that 'I was very interested in the texture of Victorian life, and the power dynamics were played out in a material way, and I think [Park has] brought a similar interest in artefacts and fabrics. It's such a crowdedly lush film, with all those shoes and gloves and corsets' (Armitstead 2017).

The film, like the novel, is indeed full of sensuality in the surfaces and textures. A key scene that first displays the physical intimacy between these two women is the bath scene, where Hideko complains about a sharp tooth that is cutting the inside of her mouth. Promptly, Sook-hee files it down with a thimble with a finely serrated surface, but as she works her finger inside the mouth of Hideko, who is naked in the water-filled bathtub, the atmosphere gets distinctly intense. Here, while emphasising their physical proximity to each other, the camera work mainly follows Sook-hee's point of view and shows Hideko's slightly flustered face and bare chest in a rather fetishistic manner. Reviewing for *The Guardian*, Peter Bradshaw calls it a 'quasi-blowjob scene that sounds bizarre in print. On screen, it was so extraordinary that I almost forgot to breathe' (2017). Undoubtedly, this kind of emotive response makes it necessary to note the risks the film carries with its fetishistic and voyeuristic representation of lesbian sexuality, particularly for male audiences.

Notwithstanding such contested issues, however, what is striking about the film's treatment of lesbian sexuality is the way it engages with the source novel.

The bath scene discussed above, for instance, is accounted twice on the pages of the novel. First, Sue describes the moment in Part One as follows:

> I took her to the window and she stood with her face in my hands and let me feel about her gum. I found the pointed tooth almost at once . . . I went to her sewing-box and brought out a thimble . . . I put the thimble on my finger and rubbed at the pointed tooth until the point was taken off . . . Maud stood very still, her pink lips parted, her face put back, her eyes at first, closed then open and gazing at me, her cheek grew *wet*, from the damp of her breaths. I rubbed, then felt with my thumb. She swallowed again. Her eyelids fluttered, and she caught my eye. (Waters 2002: 97, added emphasis)

In Part Two, Maud recounts the same moment:

> She showed me her hand, with the thimble on it . . . it makes for a queer mix of sensations: the grinding of the metal, the pressure of her hand holding my jaw, the softness of her breath. As she studies the tooth she files, I can look nowhere but at her face . . . Her fingers, and my lips, are becoming *wet*. I swallow, then swallow again. My tongue rises and moves against her hand . . . May a lady taste the fingers of her maid? She may, in my uncle's books – The thought makes me colour. (255–6, added emphasis)

Besides the sensual and corporeal aspects, particularly of Maud's description of the taste and sense of touch, what is most palpable in their accounts is the 'wetness' both women feel. In fact, wetness is the eminent textual quality of the novel's eroticism, pronounced in such lines as: 'My mouth was wet, from hers' (141) or 'I am wet, still wet, from the sliding and the pressing of her hand' (284). As Waters comments, 'Maud having sex for the first time is a very moist experience compared with the dry experience of a book' (Armitstead 2017). The film's steamy bath scene, in this sense, is an inventive transcoding of the novel's 'wet' moments onto the cinematic screen.

The Handmaiden's cinematic rendering of such sensuality offers a fitting case study to discuss the notion of 'translation' that Walter Benjamin describes in his essay 'The Task of the Translator' (written in 1932). In the essay, Benjamin 'sees the translation as a strategy that allows texts to survive and adapt to a new cultural milieu' (Kuhiwczak 2012, viii). Although there is a general understanding that adaptations are to a different medium, from novel to film as in this case, many scholars have started to consider adaptation as a form of inter-semiotic translation. Linda Hutcheon, for instance, quotes Benjamin's argument that translation is 'not a rendering of some fixed nontextual meaning to be copied or paraphrased or reproduced; rather, it is an engagement with the original text that makes us see that text in different ways' (2013: 16). Hutcheon regards that this newer sense of translation 'comes closer to defining adaptation . . . [Because] adaptations are to a different medium, they are re-mediations [which is] translation but in a very specific sense: as transmutation or transcoding . . . a recoding into a new set of conventions as well as signs' (16).

Certainly, the ways in which *The Handmaiden* engages with the source novel involve transcoding or translating. In particular, considering that 'the key to a sexuality that is exclusive to women is the exchange of body fluids' (Armitstead 2017), the film offers a visual 'translation' of the novel's sensuality and texture, utilising highly tangible, even affective, materials, ranging from steamy, warm bath water through glittering surface of a deep red lollipop and Sook-hee's glistening face looking up from between Hideko's legs to the oral lubrication of sex toys. In this respect, the film's 'faithfulness' that Waters refers to, is more to do with its 'faithfulness' to the sensation and experience conveyed in the novel rather than a 'literal' cinematic rendering of characters' actions and thoughts.

From One Narrative to Another: Intertextual Dialogues

This section offers a cross-reading of the novel and the film on the level of narrative, focusing mainly on the film's deviation from the original narrative structure. Before delving into the way the film's narrative departs from that of the novel, however, the first thing to say is that the film retains the novel's triptych structure and much of the storyline of Part One, which follows the narration of the pickpocket-turned-maid character. In both texts, at the end of the first act, the maid accompanies her mistress to the asylum to carry out Gentleman's/Count Fujiwara's scheme as planned, despite unfolding feelings for her. In a treacherous double-cross, however, the identities of mistress and maid are switched, and it is the maids – Sue and Sook-hee, not intended ladies – Maud and Hideo – that are incarcerated in the madhouse. The final lines the maids utter convey their shock at the sudden twist of event and realisation of what has been going on. Sue narrates, 'You thought her a pigeon. Pigeon, my arse. That bitch knew everything. She had been in on it from the start' (Waters 2002: 175). In the film, Sook-hee notes: 'I'll tell you that from the start Lady Izmi Hideko had been a rotten bitch.'[11]

While a heavy scent of betrayal still hangs in the air, Part Two begins. In both novel and film, the second act tells the mistresses' story from their perspectives – their traumatic childhood upbringing in their uncles' household and the reasons why they are eager to escape from the clutches of their uncles, even through the devious scheme of the conmen. Indeed, it is revealed here that the uncles' precious book collection is all pornographic material, and that

Maud/Hideko had been made to recite them to the uncles' male guests. Hideko's story in *The Handmaiden*, however, starts to veer away from the novel by the second half of Part Two. The decisive moment is when Hideko attempts to hang herself from the same cherry tree that her aunt had used to commit suicide. She is unable to cope with the pressures of the situation in which Sook-hee carries on encouraging her to accept the count's marriage proposal, in spite of their growing feelings for each other and their intimate lovemaking, albeit done under the pretext of Sook-hee educating Hideko on how to please a man. Before she falls to death, however, Sook-hee appears, holding her by the legs, and confesses her part in the scheme to steal her inheritance. Hideko also reveals the plot to commit Sook-hee in her place. From that moment of revelation, they make plans together to take revenge on both Kouzuki and Count Fujiwara. An important part of their action is for Sook-hee to learn to read and write, which enables her to enlist the help of the woman who raised her, Boksun and her family of thieves later in Part Three. This is indeed a distinct divergence from the novel, in which Sue's illiteracy prevents her from proving her 'real' identity when incarcerated.

As in the novel, the two heroines of the film leave the estate as planned. Notably in the film, however, they go into Kouzuki's library together before their escape. There, deeply offended by what Hideko had been forced to do, Sook-hee wilfully starts to tear the pages of pornographic books. Hideko joins in the spectacular attack on the material, destroying the books, scrolls and tapestries, hurling inks on them and dumping them into the indoor ponds underneath the floorboards. In contrast to this exuberant scene of the film, in the novel, Maud goes to the library alone and does the deed quietly:

> There is only one thing I mean to do, before I go: one deed – one terrible deed . . . as the hour of our flight nears, as the house falls silent, still, unsuspecting, I do it. Sue leaves me . . . I go stealthily from the room . . . I am queasy with fear and anticipation. But time is racing, and I cannot wait. I cross to my uncle's shelves and unfasten the glass before the presses. I begin with *The Curtain Drawn Up*, the book he gave me first: I take it, and open it, and set it upon his desk. Then I lift the razor, grip it tight, and fully unclasp it . . . It is hard . . . to put the metal for the first time to the neat and naked paper . . . [but] my cuts become swifter and more true. (Waters 2002: 288–90)

Cutting up the first pornographic book her uncle gave her, Maud is finally able to express her anger at the very thing that has defined her life – being a secretary to the library of erotica. Using none other than her uncle's razor, Maud here is severing the link with him, breaking off from the life she had been forced to lead. Unlike in the film, however, it is Maud's solo action. In fact, Sue does not even find out what Maud was forced to do until the very end of the book.

By contrast, Sook-hee in *The Handmaiden* is markedly the initiator of the very act of dismantling the library that is full of pornography – male narratives and images about female sexuality. This affords the character of Sook-hee the agency to become a saviour, as Hideko calls her, despite her lowly social status. In some ways, this kind of action counterbalances the film's fetishistic rendering of Hideko's recital scenes that subject her to the gaze of male guests. Indeed, Hideko's performances, which include her spectacular simulation of sex on a wooden mannequin suspended in the air, are all done for male audiences' gratification. Nonetheless, or because of this, Sook-hee's destruction of Kouzuki's insidious library is a highly cathartic as well as transgressive moment in the film. However, it leads distinctly back to the source novel, pointing to an interesting intertextual dialogue between them: when finally figuring out the horrid nature of the books, Sue thinks: 'I gazed across the shelves; and wanted to smash them' (546).

Another striking example of the intertextual dialogue can be found in the following passage from Part Two of the novel, which describes Maud's thoughts soon after she had sex for the first time with Sue:

> *Everything*, I say to myself, is *changed*. I think I was dead, before. Now she has touched the life of me, the quick of me; she has put back my flesh and opened me up. *Everything is changed.* I still feel her, inside me. I still feel her, moving upon my thigh. I imagine her waking, meeting my gaze. I think, 'I will tell her, then. I will say, "I meant to cheat you. I cannot cheat you now. This was Richard's plot. We can make it ours."' – We can make it ours, I think: or else, we can give it up entirely. (283, original emphasis)

The following morning, however, Sue does not meet her gaze. She looks away and tries to pretend nothing has happened. When Maud tells Sue that she was in her (sweet) dream, she dismisses it by saying it must have been Richard who was in her dream, not her. Unbeknownst to Maud, however, Sue had thought the same thing, as narrated in Part One:

> She kept her eyes on mine . . . if I had drawn her to me then, she'd have kissed me. If I had said, *I love you*, she would have said it back; and everything would have changed. I might have saved her. I might have found a way – I don't know what – to keep her from fate. We might have cheated Gentleman. I might have run with her. (143–4, original emphasis)

Sue too thinks of telling Maud the truth, but she is afraid that Maud would 'find [her] out for the villain [she] was' (144). Moreover, Maud was 'too good' for the Borough, the only place she knows and can go back to (144). She just cannot imagine how she would do in the Borough with Maud by her side either. So, Sue 'swallow[s] and [does] nothing' (144–5).

Sue's distant ways make Maud feel confused and dejected, and she also gives up revealing any of the things she thought of. Then, as Sue narrates, 'it was too late to change anything' (145). The film's heroines, unlike their counterparts in the novel, who could not tell the truth to each other, manage to make the conman's plan theirs. This is certainly one of the film's own twists and turns, but it is clear that the above passages have provided the springboard for the film's 'new' narrative: the 'what-could-have-been' moment of the novel is actually realised in the film.

Part Three, the final act of the film, then takes on an overtly different narrative path from the novel. Notably, the film completely foregoes the novel's jaw-dropping twist regarding the secrets of the women's real parentage, virtually writing out the role of Mrs Sucksby, who turns out to be Maud's mother and the person behind Gentleman's plot. Instead, the film shifts its focus on the plight of Count Fujiwara (or the man who pretends to be Count Fujiwara), who, believing that his/their plan has worked, now attempts to seduce Hideko so that they can have a real relationship. Hideko, however, tricks Fujiwara, using the opium he gave her as a wedding gift, and leaves alone to meet with Sook-hee, who has been rescued by her family of thieves in a planned fire heist. Unfortunately for the count, when he wakes up in the hotel room, Kouzuki's henchmen are waiting for him. Taken to Kouzuki's basement, he is tortured and his fingers are cut off. As another body part is to be cut off imminently, he persuades Kouzuki to let him smoke, with a promise to reveal the details of his wedding night with Hideko that he is desperate to hear. As the cigarettes are laced with mercury, however, Fujiwara poisons the air, killing both of them. Just before he dies, Fujiwara quips about his penis being intact at least, which ironically underlines the impotency of the male characters in the film.

In the meantime, the reunited couple board a ferry to Shanghai, with Hideko disguised as a man to evade her uncle's search for any 'two young women travelling together'. The final scene of the film shows the coupling of these two women in their stateroom, safely en route to Shanghai. Here, celebrating their newfound freedom, they are both completely naked, like new-borns in a way. This is in a stark contrast with the dinner-jacketed male guests at the Kouzuki's auctions, who were hiding their perverted and pernicious desires underneath their formal attire. Under the conspicuous full moon, they are indeed luminous. Of the scene, director Park comments that 'with the moon, the ocean, and the clouds, with the colours that I used in the last scene, I wanted to imbue it with that kind of beauty. Even if it's a fairy tale, I wanted to end on a note where we're dreaming about this type of idealized world' (Topalovic 2016).

Evocation of a fairy tale aside, the explicit, yet highly stylised, content of the film's final scene also has recourse to the final pages of the novel. In it, Sue finds Maud back at Briar, the country house where they met and fell in love. Maud finally tells Sue about the pernicious nature of her uncle's book collection and her reciting of them, as well as how she has been making a living since she got back to Briar – by writing pornographic books herself. Sue, who is still illiterate (unlike Sook-hee, who learns to read and write), asks: 'what does it say?' to which Maud replies: 'It is filled with all the words for how I want you . . . Look' (547). The very last paragraph of the novel is Sue's narration:

> She took up the lamp. The room had got darker, the rain still beat against the glass. But she led me to the fire and made me sit, and sat beside me. Her silk skirts rose in a rush, then sank. She put the lamp upon the floor, spread the paper flat; and began to show me the words she had written, one by one. (548)

Here, the passage is brimming with furtive yearning, arrestingly invoked in the 'words' Maud had written. The Sapphic desire portrayed in the film's denouement is a visual 'translation' of the eroticism evident in the novel, albeit rather ironically done in a more 'literal' and prolonged manner.

Furthermore, what is highlighted in the film is that the two women from completely different backgrounds – a Korean thief and a Japanese noble lady – are coming together as equals. Strikingly, the film ends with the two women directly facing each other in the nude, and on the level in every possible way. Through such coupling, intertwined with the fraught and compelling historical setting, *The Handmaiden* offers, as Sarah Waters puts it, a 'transgressive and exciting story' (Armitstead 2017), despite the lingering issues around the film's jarring fascination with the pornography itself, along with Park's identity as a male director. According to Waters, *Fingersmith* 'was about finding space for women to be with each other away from prying eyes' (Armitstead 2017). In recounting the same lesbian love story, the film carries over the transgressive allure of the original, and in turn provides a captivating example of transnational and cross-cultural adaptation that is in a constant intertextual dialogue with the original novel on the big screen.

Notes

1. The Korean title of the film, *Ah-ga-ssi*/아가씨, translates as 'Lady' or 'Miss'. English title *The Handmaiden* counterbalances its Korean title, as well as underlining the fact that the two characters are equal. Interestingly, it was released in France under the title of *Mademoiselle*.
2. Gant points out other factors that helped the surprising success of *The Handmaiden* in the UK such as the BFI Distribution Fund, which contributed £150,000

to release costs and the immersive film event organizer Secret Cinema. For more details, see Gant's *Sight & Sound* report (2017: 9).
3. *Fingersmith* especially shares kinship with Wilkie Collins's *The Woman in White* (1860), in which a young drawing master is drawn into a conspiracy when he is hired to tutor two women (half-sisters) who live in a country house, owned by their hypochondriac uncle who lives mostly in his library. The novel is widely considered to be one of the first mystery novels as well as a first in the genre of 'sensation' novel.
4. For instance, her 2006 *The Night Watch* is set in post-war Britain, while the 2014 novel *The Paying Guests* has the 1920s as its backdrop.
5. Sarah Waters attended the film's Gala screening during the sixtieth BFI London Film Festival at Embankment Garden Cinema on 7 October 2016, and was photographed with the director Park Chan-wook.
6. Incidentally, Park's screenplay is co-written with his long-time collaborator (since *Lady Vengeance*, 2005) Chung Seo-kyung, who is a woman writer, a fact that is often overlooked.
7. It is apparently Syd Lim's wife who read *Fingersmith* and thought that it would make for a great movie. See Topalovic 2017.
8. In *The Film Programme* (Stock 2017), Waters describes the TV miniseries as 'done in the tradition of good-quality BBC TV adaptation with high-production values with great acting'.
9. The hybrid character of the mansion's exterior was achieved through CGI (computer generated imagery) by a Korean visual effects studio (4th Creative Party) that previously worked for many notable Korean features, including Park's *Oldboy*. The film's production designer, Ryu Seong-hee, won the Vulcan Award of the Technical Artist at the 2016 Cannes Film Festival for her art direction.
10. For Japanese audiences, the Korean cast's apparent struggle to deliver sophisticated old-world Japanese dialogue reportedly hampered the enjoyment of viewing. Reviewing for *The Japan Times*, James Hadfield, for instance, advises that 'viewers who wince at clumsy Japanese dialogue may want to give this a miss' (2017).
11. In Korean: '우리 아가씨 이즈미 히데코로 말씀드릴것 같으면, 그분은 원래부터 나쁜 년이다.'

References

Armitstead, C. (2017), 'Interview: Sarah Waters: "The Handmaiden turns pornography into a spectacle – but it's true to my novel"', *The Guardian*, 8 April, <https://www.theguardian.com/film/2017/apr/08/sarah-waters-the-handmaiden-turns-pornography-into-a-spectacle-but-its-true-to-my-novel> (accessed 12 April 2018)

Bhabha, H. K. (1994), *The Location of Culture*, London: Routledge.

Bradshaw, Peter (2017), '*The Handmaiden Review*: outrageous thriller drenched with eroticism', *The Guardian*, 13 April.

Cumings, B. (1998), 'The legacy of Japanese colonialism in Korea', in S. S. Large (ed.), *Shōwa Japan: Political, Economic and Social History 1926–1989, Volume II, 1941–1952*, London: Routledge, pp. 222–30.

Dale, M. (2015), 'Park Chan-wook talks about next pic "The Handmaiden"', *Variety*, 10 December, <https://variety.com/2015/film/global/park-chan-wook-next-pic-the-hand-maiden-1201658129/?> (accessed 20 February 2018).

Gant, C. (2017), 'The numbers: *The Handmaiden*', *Sight & Sound*, 27: 7, 9.

Hadfield, J. (2017), '*The Handmaiden*: a sinfully silly Gothic psychodrama', *The Japan Times*, 1 March, <https://www.japantimes.co.jp/culture/2017/03/01/films/film-reviews/the-handmaiden/> (accessed 10 April 2018).

Hutcheon, L. (2013), *A Theory of Adaptation*, 2nd edn, Abingdon: Routledge.

Kuhiwczak, P. (2012), 'Preface', in L. Raw (ed.), *Translation, Adaptation and Transformation*, London: Continuum, pp. viii–ix.

Lo, M. (2006), 'Interview with Sarah Waters – Beyond Any Label', *AfterEllen.com*, 6 April, <www.afterellen.com/more/4238-interview-with-sarah-waters-2/4> (accessed 5 April 2018)

Murray, S. (2012), *The Adaptation Industry: The Cultural Economy of Contemporary Literary Adaptation*, Abingdon: Routledge.

Palmer, P. (2008), '"She began to show me the words she had written, one by one": lesbian reading and writing practices in the fiction of Sarah Waters', *Women: A Cultural Review* 19: 1, 69–86.

Paquet, D. (2016), 'Review of Korean films: year to remember', *Korean Cinema 2016*, Korean Film Council (KOFIC), pp. 7–14, <https://www.koreanfilm.or.kr/eng/publications/books.jsp> (accessed 20 April 2018).

Stock, F. (2017), 'Interview with Sarah Waters', *The Film Programme*, BBC Radio 4, 13 April.

Topalovic, G. (2016), 'Interview: Park Chan-wook', *Film Comment*, 28 October.

Waters, Sarah (2002), *Fingersmith*, London: Virago Press.

12. CHAINS OF ADAPTATION: FROM *D'ENTRE LES MORTS* TO *VERTIGO*, *LA JETÉE* AND *TWELVE MONKEYS*

Jonathan Evans

The aim of this chapter is to explore what happens when the study of adaptations goes beyond the common binary pairing of a text and its filmic or televisual adaptation. The combination of literary/written text and filmed version, common in adaptation studies since George Bluestone's *Novels into Film* (2003, first published 1957), is decentred in Linda Hutcheon's *A Theory of Adaptation* (2006), which demonstrates how adaptation works across a range of media and in different directions, such as the novelisation of films or the adaptation of video games into films and films into video games. However, the notion of adaptation consisting of a pair of texts, one source and one target,[1] remains common in the practice of writing about adaptations. The case study method in adaptation studies somewhat encourages this practice, as it structures analyses around close readings of the adaptation in relation to its source. Indeed, Hutcheon (2006: 120) argues that to experience a text as an adaptation (rather than as any other form of text), we must know the source text and be able to compare the two texts. Her point is echoed by Daniel Herbert (2017: 124), who notes that some forms of adaptation, such as the remake, encourage viewers to compare the adaptation with its source.

The connections between texts are seldom so simple. There are various layers of mediation between them: paratextual features (Genette 1987, Gray 2010) such as posters, covers, blurbs, tag-lines and even merchandise, can and do affect how texts are read and experienced and complicate the notion of smooth adaptation from one text to another. Translation, too, is often required for adaptation across languages: either there needs to be a translation of the source text, for example the novel being adapted will be translated into the language of the adapters, or there may be other processes of interlingual translation used in the process of adapting a text across languages. These paratexts and translational practices are often overlooked in analyses of cross-cultural adaptations, despite the effect they have on the perception of a text. Some of this may be related to the way in which translation tends to be made invisible in the West (Venuti 1995), or it may be due to the fact that paratexts and translations have lower cultural capital than novels and films.

Furthermore, adaptations are themselves texts that are subject to adaptation and creative interpretation in various forms. Not only do they generate their own paratexts and translations, as adaptations need to be marketed for various national and international audiences, they also generate reviews and commentary, as well as other forms of textual interaction that could include fan fiction, adaptation in another medium, further adaptations in the same medium, or other forms of rewriting. While there has been some critical analysis of remakes as readaptations (e.g. Evans 2014, Mazdon 2017, Palmer 2017, Verevis 2017), this idea of a chain of adaptations remains largely underexplored in adaptation studies.[2] Remakes attract more attention in this sense as they have long been understood as having a triangular frame of reference (Leitch 2002: 39): the source text for both the first film and its remake is another written text, sometimes a literary text, but always some form of written property (e.g. a story, a pitch, a script, etc). Yet the concept of a chain of adaptations goes beyond this to include adaptations of adaptations, as I shall demonstrate here. This focus on adaptations of adaptations also makes it different from the one-to-many adaptations discussed by Thomas Leitch (2007: 207–35) and Iain Robert Smith (2017), where multiple adaptations stem from the same source text but do not necessarily adapt each other.

This chapter will focus on the chain of adaptations from Boileau-Narcejac's novel *D'entre les morts* (*Among the Dead*),[3] first published in 1954, to the film *Vertigo*, directed by Alfred Hitchcock and released in 1958, which is then adapted, quite freely, by Chris Marker's short film *La Jetée*, which itself was remade by Terry Gilliam's *Twelve Monkeys* (1995).[4] It asks how these texts relate to each other, but also, how they relate to their contexts of production, particularly in relation to the concepts of nation and colonialism. This corpus has been chosen partly as there is a clear connection between the texts, but also because of the transnational 'conversation' here: a French book is adapted by an American movie, which is adapted by a French short film, which is then adapted by another American movie. And while the relationship between *Vertigo* and *La Jetée* may not be one of close adaptation – there are significant alterations of plot between the two films, among other things – it is understood in the literature on *La Jetée* that it is a remake of *Vertigo*, as Marker himself suggests (see Harbord 2009: 5, n. 5)[5] and there are certainly a number of elements that make the category of adaptation apply.

The sequence of the three films here has been written about by other scholars (e.g. Cohen 2003, Varndell 2014: 161–8, Martins 2015), but none extends their analysis beyond the cinematic versions. Indeed, Alain J.-J. Cohen avoids describing the films as adaptations of each other, preferring to focus on the term 'inspired by'. This seems to me to underplay the connections, both textual and paratextual, between the movies and, moving beyond Cohen's analysis, their other adaptational forms. Daniel Varndell (2014: 168) avoids seeing any of the films as a source for the others, which seems more reasonable for the relationship between *Vertigo* and *La Jetée* than for *La Jetée* and *Twelve Monkeys*, given the paratextual statement that *Twelve Monkeys* was inspired by *La Jetée* in the film's posters and in the credit sequence. Varndell's argument is based on Deleuze's discussion of series (see Deleuze 1969) and within that context may be reasonable, but approaching the texts from the point of view of adaptation, which necessarily faces a question of which text came first but does not see adaptations as repetitions of the first ('source') text, as Varndell (2014: 2) argues remakes are, then it is arguable that a text forms the source for its adaptation. However, they also spawn other adaptations and other possible readings.

The space allowed for this chapter and the necessity of a cohesive analysis has influenced my choice to limit myself to the three film texts and the novel, as there are other adaptations of the texts in existence. There are too many to list all of them, but categories would include translations, rewritings, further adaptation and even fan fiction. I am intentionally excluding critical writing from the category of adaptation here, even though one could argue, following André Lefevere's (1992) work on rewriting and translation, that critical work does extend understandings of a text and acts as a form of rewriting. However, to include it would make the concept of adaptation too vague and too all-encompassing. I am sticking to an idea of adaptation of an artistic reimagining of a text, sometimes but not exclusively in another medium, as it has generally been understood by adaptation studies.[6]

To help structure my analysis of my corpus, I will be referring to Ian Bogost's concept of 'unit analysis' (2006: 3–19). Bogost elaborates this concept as a way of comparing across different forms of media, specifically video games and literary forms. He explains: '[unit] operations are modes of meaning-making that privilege discrete, disconnected actions over deterministic, progressive systems' (Bogost 2006: 3). Using unit operations, then, in adaptation studies would meaning looking at discrete moments, units of narrative or other isolatable features of the texts, rather than trying to compare the entirety of the texts. Bogost's own example is a reading of the film *The Terminal*, about a man trapped in an airport after a diplomatic coup renders his passport void and he cannot enter the country or return to his previous one. In Bogost's unit analysis, the unit that film stages repeatedly is the act of waiting: the central character must wait in different ways until the narrative is resolved (Bogost 2006: 15–19). The contours of what form a unit are somewhat vague, and Bogost later offers the 'chance encounter' as the unit he analyses across literary, cinematic and video game texts (2006: 73–89). However, this vagueness offers the possibility of adaptation to various situations and media, allowing the reader to define the unit under analysis and then use it as a point of departure for their investigation. In this way, what seem to be disparate narratives can be seen to consist of similar units, and points of comparison can be drawn between them.

D'ENTRE LES MORTS AND VERTIGO

The story of *D'entre les morts* will be familiar to all those who have seen *Vertigo*, or even those who have heard it discussed: Flavières is hired to watch his old school friend Gévigne's wife, Madeleine, who is suffering from 'quelque peur irraisonée provoquée par la guerre' [some irrational fear caused by the war] (Boileau-Narcejac 1999: 12).[7] She has apparently become obsessed with Pauline Lagerlac, her great-grandmother who committed suicide. Flavières follows Madeleine, saves her from drowning (49) and befriends her. Flavière's feelings grow for her and he falls in love. On one of their trips together, she drives them out into the countryside around Paris, where she falls from the tower of a church (84). Following the intensification of the Second World War, Flavières leaves Paris, to return four years later, after having lived in Senegal for most of the war and set up a lawyer's practice there (103). His alcoholism has increased notably. He continues to be obsessed with Madeleine and revisits the scene of her death. He thinks he sees her in a newsreel (118) and travels to Marseille hoping to see her. He then encounters her in the hotel, though she seems different and less refined (130), and it turns out her name is Renée Sourange (131). The pair start an affair and Flavières begins to call Renée Madeleine and refer to his life with Madeleine to her. He buys her a grey suit (138) and puts up her hair in the same style as Madeleine's (160). Eventually, she confesses the plot (181) and he strangles her.

I recount the plot here as it differs in a number of interesting ways from *Vertigo* and some of the elements of setting – Paris in the early years of the Second World War and then Marseille immediately after it – anchor the novel in a way that is pertinent for the discussion of nation in these texts. Any discussion of plot alone, especially a rather short summary as I have just given, simplifies the texture of the novel. For example, the novel keeps stressing how Flavières is tormented by his memories, first of his colleague Leriche, who fell from a roof, and then of Madeleine.

The plot of *Vertigo* follows quite closely the actions of *D'entre les morts*, but with a number of narrative divergences in addition to the differences already mentioned. The 'unit', to follow Bogost's terminology introduced earlier, is returning to look for a woman: both texts feature this obsessive seeking for the lost Madeleine and her recreation. Scottie is hired by his college buddy Gavin Elster to watch his wife Madeleine in San Francisco. In a museum, he watches her stare at a picture of Carlotta Valdes, who bears some similarities to her, and whose name she uses to book into a hotel (echoing the Pauline Lagerlac narrative in the novel). Scottie saves Madeleine from drowning at Golden Gate Park and takes her home to dry off. They next drive out into the forest and look at sequoia trees, with Madeleine showing Scottie on the cross-section of a log when she (Madeleine/Carlotta) was born and when she died. After they kiss, Madeleine visits Scottie's house and they go to visit the old Spanish mission where Valdes lived. Once again Madeleine seems to act like Valdes, before kissing Scottie again and disappearing to climb the bell tower, from which she apparently falls to her death.

Scottie is exonerated but has some sort of breakdown. An uncertain amount of time passes, somewhat like the caesura in the narrative of the novel though less specific in its term, and we then see Scottie searching the places where he met Madeleine, showing his obsession with her that echoes Flavière's. He follows a woman who looks like Madeleine to her hotel and asks to be let in, frightening her. She agrees to go to dinner with Scottie after much persuasion. A flashback reveals the truth of 'Madeleine's' death and Judy (the woman) writes a confession to Scottie, which she then rips up. Scottie buys Judy a grey suit and, later, has her hair done in the same style as Madeleine (and Valdes). They drive to the mission where Scottie forces Judy up the bell tower and tells her he has worked out what happened. A nun surprises Judy, who falls to her death.

The film and novel have many details in common – sometimes surprisingly, as the details themselves, such as the new grey suit that Flavières and Scottie buy for Renée and Judy, are not all that important for the development of the story or the characters. These might be conceived of as 'units' in Bogost's sense, as they function as independent narrative events, but they are not as central as the 'return' unit. Narratively, the plots of the texts are very similar, with the key change that Judy's death echoes Madeleine's, as well as the revelation of the story to the viewer earlier on. These differences give the film a more easily accessible narrative shape, as the ambiguity of the novel is downplayed: it is clearer earlier on what has happened and that Judy is the same person as the 'Madeleine' that Scottie knew. The repetition of the death scene gives the two halves of the film a closer repetitive shape, allowing the second to echo the first. This gives the film a more formal quality but also feels like a more fitting narrative closure that is more in line with the various repetitions in the film.

Where the divergences become more interesting is in the settings of these texts and their sense of connection to a nation. *D'entre les morts* is a French novel, and *Vertigo* is an American – more specifically a Californian – film. This seems almost too obvious: the place of production of a text and the language it is written in are not enough to make a text belong to that nation. Both of these texts are more intimately connected to their locales than just coming from them, as I shall discuss, but at the same time their reception suggests that they are also more than just French or American. *Vertigo*, as the better known of the two texts, has had a massive influence around the world, topping the *Sight & Sound* critics' poll in 2012. French film critics, especially those connected to *Cahiers du Cinéma* in the 1960s such as François Truffaut and Jean-Luc Godard, helped to cement Hitchcock's reception as a serious director (see, for instance, Truffaut's interviews with Hitchcock, 1966). While Hitchcock's adaptation of *D'entre les morts* may have brought it more attention, it was also translated in 1956 as *The Living and the Dead* (Boileau-Narcejac 1956), although later editions took the title *Vertigo* (Boileau-Narcejac 2015). It is more likely that Hitchcock read it in English than in the French original, even though the credits to *Vertigo* cite the French title. Henri-George's Clouzot's *Les diaboliques* from 1955, based on another novel by Boileau-Narcejac, would have made its authors well-known internationally at that time as thriller writers. While the authors may have been French and wrote in French, their texts circulated beyond France and French speakers, just as Hitchcock's circulated beyond America and English speakers. This fact in no way erases their national origin but suggests that to think of a text solely in its national setting elides its international (after-) lives and ignores the fact that cultural products circulate relatively freely internationally.

The two texts do, however, locate themselves firmly in their contexts of production and ask to be read as texts about France and California through their references to the immediate present and the recent past. The viewer cannot avoid noticing San Francisco in *Vertigo*: it is always there, as background and as environment. The view from Scottie's confidante Midge's window could be an advert for the city or, with the passing of time, a reminder of what it once was.[8] Paris plays a similar role in the first half of *D'entre les morts*, where Flavières and Madeleine wander (*flâner* in French) the centre of Paris, with street names serving as an index of their location. But I'm less interested in this rather obvious use of setting than reading the two texts in relation to the Second World War and colonialism, both of which play a part in each of the texts, and both of which are reflected in various ways in *La Jetée* and *Twelve Monkeys*.

The Second World War is unavoidable in *D'entre les morts*. It is there from the first moments of the book, where Madeleine's condition is blamed on it (13). The first part of the novel takes places in Paris before the German invasion in June 1940, but the threat of war is constant. To readers in the 1950s, this atmosphere would have been of the recent past and no doubt still memorable. Flavières likes both the quiet of the evening, where the streets are empty (30), and at the same time the fact that he is not in uniform has made him feel that people look at him with hostility (32). This atmosphere at the beginning of the war gives the first half of the novel a sense of exceptionality – the situation that all the characters find themselves is one where there could be a rupture at any time and this gives the relationship between Flavières and Madeleine the sense of something exceptional. Flavières feels relief ('soulagement', 78) when he hears that the German offensive has begun, signalling the beginning of the war in earnest for him. This news comes just before his and Madeleine's last trip that leads to her death. The war, then, serves as both a background and a structuring device for *D'entre les morts*. Indeed, it is due to the war that Flavière leaves Paris for four years, as echoed in the lacuna in the narrative between the first and second part of the novel.

The war is present in *Vertigo*, too, but as something more distanced. The film takes place after the war, which is one reason why it moves into the background, but San Francisco was also less directly affected by the Second World War than Paris. While there may have been effects on demographics in the city due to the relocation and internment of Americans of Japanese heritage (who are more or less absent from *Vertigo*),[9] the city was neither physically threatened nor occupied by invading forces. This is reflected in the film, where the war is mentioned, but as something in the past. It is one of the reasons why Scottie and Elster lost touch. Elster survived the war, unlike Gévigne, whose car was machine-gunned on the road near Le Mans (108). Each narrative is affected by the Second World War, but in ways that are connected to their settings: in *D'entre les morts*, it is experienced as a traumatic rupture, whereas in *Vertigo*, while it also serves as a rupture, it is far less traumatic.

Just as the war is present in each text, colonialism also haunts them. Flavières spends the war in Senegal, where he sets up a lawyer's practice (103). France's African colonies are an absent presence in the novel, much like the war is in *Vertigo*. They are acknowledged and present in the background, but the novel itself does not question or engage with them. The Spanish colonial presence is more complex in *Vertigo*. As Roland Greene (2012: 28) notes, the film's presentation of San Francisco obscures this Hispanic past by focusing on the post-Gold Rush white population (as one might expect from a Hollywood film from the 1950s aimed at white viewers, the presence of other ethnicities is minimal). However, as Greene goes on to argue, the story is situated in the longer history of California through the figure of Carlotta Valdes and the Mission San Juan Bautista, where Madeleine and Judy fall to their deaths. In a sense, then, the Spanish history is acknowledged, but it remains in a repressed form, associated with madness and death. There are different colonial moments here: the original Spanish missions, and the movement to the Bay area following the nineteenth-century Gold Rush, which altered the demographics of the area dramatically. This is not just a case of European colonialism in Africa, as in *D'entre les morts*, but a history of colonialism that features European colonialism as well as internal migration and the displacement of Hispanic settlers.

What comes through each text is far more than a simple man-obsessed-with-woman trope: in the margins of each there are complex relations with the nation, both in its present form and its history. *D'entre les morts* in that sense reflects its status as a French text, drawing on and staging the French experience of the Second World War while also acknowledging, albeit obliquely, the French colonial presence. For *Vertigo*, the colonial history of California intrudes on the story and becomes part of the narrative, but as a return of the repressed, connected to madness and death. Reading these texts as a pair, then, highlights the national aspect of each in the contrast between them.

Vertigo and La Jetée

In the next link on the chain, *La Jetée* takes on some of the units of *Vertigo*, and arguably some from *D'entre les morts*, but offers quite a different narrative. Catherine Lupton notes that 'allusions to *Vertigo* are legion' (2005: 95) and highlights a range of details that are present in both films: the giant sequoia, the woman's hairstyle, the flowers in the department store where he first sees her that reference the florists in *Vertigo* (ibid.). Indeed, like the adaptation of *D'entre les morts* by *Vertigo*, a surprising number of details are carried over in the adaptation; details that are not themselves significant in the plot of the film, but serve to index the text being adapted,[10] suggesting connections to knowing viewers (i.e. those who are familiar with that text) and who can therefore read the adapted text precisely as an adaptation (Hutcheon 2006: 120). In other words, these points of reference between the texts highlight the links in the chain of adaptation.

La Jetée is also a man who is haunted by an image from his past, as the narrator tells us at the beginning of the film. It is not clear whether the image this refers to is the image of the woman's face, seen on the observation pier at Orly airport, or it's the image-sequence of a man's death that he witnesses there, at which the woman (played by Hélène Chatelain) is also present. This image, we are told, sustains him through the war. Such a strong mental image is why he is chosen to be sent back in time as part of the scheme to be able to travel in time and find ways out of humanity's post-war predicament.

Before mentioning the rest of the plot of *La Jetée*, I want to argue that the plot of the film literalises the metaphorical return to the past in *D'entre les morts* and *Vertigo*. The holding of a woman's image through the war and returning to it afterward evokes the narrative of *D'entre les morts*, which Marker was likely familiar with.[11] This is the shared unit of narrative between the texts, the return to look for a woman, but it is played out in slightly different ways in each text, and in *La Jetée* it has become literal time travelling. As the rest of the plot plays out differently, this repeated narrative unit, as well as the indexical connections to *Vertigo*, place the film in the chain of adaptations that I am discussing here, but it is clear that this is not a straightforward adaptation. The rest of the film, once the central character has become adept at travelling to the past, shows him travelling to the future to look for ways of surviving the post-war moment. A power source is given to him, and he realises the experimenters plan to kill him. The people from the future offer to take him to the future, but he chooses to go back to the pier at Orly and the moment he remembers so clearly, only to be killed there by one of the camp doctors.[12]

Nation and colonialism intertwine in *La Jetée*. The film clearly draws from memories of the Second World War and its effects on Paris, but it was made and released around the end of the Algerian war of independence (1954–62).[13] There was in effect censorship regarding this war (Hilliker 2000: 2), yet it would be one of the reference points that original viewers would have thought of when regarding the film, as well as the less recent Second World War. Marker had also worked with Alain Resnais, director of one of the first Holocaust films, *Nuit et brouillard* (*Night and Fog*, 1956), and the camp sequences of *La Jetée* would also bring to mind images of concentration camps. The relation to war and colonialism is far more complex, then, than in *D'entre les morts* and *Vertigo*. Lee Hilliker (2000: 3) argues that the film is critical of the contemporary political situation in France, and it would seem that all these possible indices of recent and ongoing colonialism, which are at the same time ambiguous in what they refer to, bear that out. *La Jetée*'s pessimistic, post-war dystopia is an invitation to reconsider the French nation and its relationship to war.

Yet at the same time *La Jetée* visually celebrates France. The film's title comes from the viewing pier at the Orly airport that serves Paris. Watching planes taxi, take off and land as an activity, the sort of thing one might take a young child to do, reveals a pride in modernity that seems somewhat out of place nowadays when air travel is much more common and less of a novelty. The film may begin with the Third World War and the destruction of Paris, but how it shows this is through shots of the skyline of Paris, including iconic buildings such as the Eiffel tower. Visually, then, the film highlights Paris even as it critiques France in other ways. The fact that the survivors gather under the Palais de Chaillot – located across the Seine from the Eiffel tower – should also give pause for thought: this was where the Declaration of Human Rights was signed in 1948 and was also home to the *Musée de l'homme*, an anthropological museum. While the later street scenes (when the man is visiting the past) are also Parisian, they are less obviously images of Paris that would be recognised as such (unlike the earlier iconic scenes and the shots of Scottie in San Francisco in *Vertigo*). These images of Paris are also tainted by the fact that Paris is destroyed in the narrative; the film presents bombed-out and collapsing buildings to demonstrate this. The celebration of Paris, then, is never unambiguous.

La Jetée takes a more nuanced approach to nation and colonialism than *D'entre les morts* and *Vertigo*, which might be explained by its status as an independent film[14] and by Marker's left-wing sensibilities, but also by its later context of production at the end of the Algerian war of independence. Read in parallel with the earlier links in the chain of adaptation, it serves to highlight their approaches to nation and colonialism through comparison.

LA JETÉE AND TWELVE MONKEYS

The last link in the chain that I want to discuss here is *Twelve Monkeys*. It claims *La Jetée* as an inspiration and also cites *Vertigo*, suggesting that Gilliam was aware of the links between *La Jetée* and *Vertigo*, even when he claims, in an interview that accompanies the British DVD version of *La Jetée*, to have only ever seen the film in French and not necessarily needed to understand the narration. The overall lines of the narratives are indeed similar, with *Twelve Monkeys* also revolving around a time travel plot: Cole (Bruce Willis) is sent back in time to solve the mystery of the Twelve Monkeys, which led, within the narrative, to the near death of humanity. Cole has a strong memory from his childhood of a man being shot in an airport, which, the film reveals, is actually his own death.

Twelve Monkeys differs from the earlier film not only formally – it uses moving images, is in colour and does not use a narrator – but also in the way it approaches the various units of narrative that I have been discussing throughout this chapter. Most importantly, while Cole does go into the past and meets a woman, the psychiatrist Kathryn Railly (Madeleine Stowe), their meeting is accidental. She becomes his psychiatrist, then kidnap victim and later his accomplice. His journey into the past is not motivated by his obsession with this woman, as was the case of the central character in *La Jetée* and metaphorically for Flavières and Scottie. He is sent back into the past in order to gather information that can stop the plague that nearly annihilates humanity in the film's narrative. This change in motivation is indicative of the alterations taking place from text to text in adaptation (and particularly in a chain of adaptations like this one). This changing motivation can be seen also in the changing representation of time travel: no longer is Cole's strength his obsessive memory of a moment in the past – while he does have a recurring dream of a moment in the past that parallels that of *La Jetée*, his interlocutors appear to have no interest in it – but rather that he is a good observer. This is a more easily understandable motive for choosing him than in *La Jetée*. The reason for sending him to the past is also more explicit. Rather than travelling to the past in order to be able to travel to the future to ask for help, it is to find information that can lead to curing the plague. This shift towards more explicit motivation is common in American remakes (Vincendeau 1993: 23; Harney 2002: 73–5) and parallels the movement towards making texts more explicit at a syntactical level in translation (Evans 2019: 164–5). The movement towards a more mainstream (Hollywood) form of cinema can be seen at multiple levels here: the reduction of formal innovation, the clearer motivations of the protagonists, and what Elena Del Rio (2001) analyses as a rhetoric of visibility in *Twelve Monkeys*, that is, the tendency to focus on the visual and making visual of aspects of the narrative that are not clearly shown in *La Jetée*. For instance, the movement of time travel appears physical in *Twelve Monkeys*, with Cole being shot into some sort of tunnel, but relies 'on the traveler's mental and emotional facilities' (Del Rio 2001: 338) in *La Jetée*, where time travel is shown through the protagonist's awareness of and presence in the past, and later in the future. Importantly, in *La Jetée*, time travel is a solitary pursuit, whereas Cole is only one of many 'volunteers' sent into the past in *Twelve Monkeys*, reducing, once again, the importance of his memory from before the catastrophe.

There do remain, as in the other cases I've analysed in the chapter, the same sorts of indexical links between the two films: the image of a blonde woman, travelling back in time, the refuge of humanity underground following a catastrophe. These aspects make clear textual connections between the two films, but they have different diegetic and textual meanings and they are recontextualised in the new film. I would argue that this is typical of the process of adaptation as all adaptations differ from, build on, explore and otherwise rework the narratives of their sources. Over this chain of adaptations, the process is magnified through repetition as features and narrative units from *D'entre les morts* are adapted and altered in *Vertigo*, and then again in *La Jetée* and once more in *Twelve Monkeys*, which bears little resemblance to *D'entre les morts* even if it can trace a lineage from it.

These divergences can also be seen in the way in which the film deals with nation. The two cities in which *Twelve Monkeys* takes place are Baltimore and Philadelphia, with more focus on the homeless and the slum areas than in another of the other texts discussed in this chapter. There are very few establishing shots that give an impression of either city's skyline or downtown, though we do see, as Cole and Railly head towards the airport, Philadelphia overrun by animals from the zoo, which has been prefigured by the rewilded city of the future at the beginning of the film. Indeed, *Twelve Monkeys* shows a post-apocalyptic United States early in the film that looks very similar to the present-day one that Cole visits. When Railly and Cole are driving through the countryside, the film tends to use medium shots, focusing on the inside of the car and not on any of the countryside that can be seen from the road. The film therefore backgrounds its setting and allows it to stand in for any advanced capitalist country.

Parallels between the totalitarian government that rules after the spread of the virus and the government in the 1990s are shown by repetition of Cole being washed (once when he returns from the surface in the future, once when he is taken into the psychiatric hospital in the present) and also by the parallels between his interviews with the future scientists and the present-day authorities. Some criticisms of the ideology of capitalism, which draw on countercultural criticisms of consumer culture, are also mouthed by Jeffrey Goines (Brad Pitt) in the psychiatric ward, but this placement of them posits them as fringe opinions. The critique of the United States here is therefore both present and somewhat diffused; no alternative is offered, beyond the annihilation of the human race (where *La Jetée* shows a possible future). Instead, the film shows a form of internal colonialism, based on mass incarceration and forced labour, in the sections of the narrative set in the future. But this need not just be a future for America; it could be anywhere.

Chains of adaptation

It should be clear, then, that looking at chains of adaptation shifts the perspective from the comparison of two texts to tracking the alterations and evolutions of narrative structure and tropes across a corpus of works. What are shared features of some of the narratives disappear in other narratives; here, the return to an object of obsession, which is present in the first three texts, disappears in *Twelve Monkeys*. Across these adaptations, various details are repeated and recontextualised in the new texts. The details serve to link them indexically to the texts they adapt, but they may not be important within the narrative (e.g. the grey suit Madeleine wears, the sequoia tree that appears in all the films here). As such, Wittgenstein's (1968: §66–71) notion of 'family resemblances', where members of a family resemble each other but not all family members share the same traits, could be a fruitful way of characterising the relationships between the members of the chain. This notion of 'family resemblance' continues the work of decentring the original (source) by making it one in a sequence of texts that all can be placed in a position of source and target, and are connected through a number of traits. In addition, 'family resemblance' also encourages the exploration of less canonical adaptations, moving away from the comparison of two texts that has traditionally been the focus of adaptation studies. In relation to the corpus examined in this article, it would mean exploring the network of links, affinities and divergences across texts such as the TV series of *12 Monkeys* (2015–current) and a rewriting of *Vertigo* included in Rebecca Solnit's *A Field Guide to Getting Lost* (2006: 138–49). These texts further extend readings of the existing network of texts by exploring further narrative possibilities or, in Solnit's case, minor characters that have been given insufficient attention elsewhere. Understanding adaptations as 'families' of texts, then, recasts adaptation not as a process of creating a text based on another one but as an ongoing, generative process that incorporates multiple texts with many different relationships between them.

Exploring adaptation beyond dyadic structures also encourages the exploration of intercultural relations between texts. In this chapter, the corpus forms a sort of conversation between French and American cultural products that highlights contextual elements and the differing cultural relationships with the past, especially, in this case, the Second World War and colonial histories, which may otherwise be overlooked when addressing the texts as adaptations. Using Bogost's 'unit' analysis, as I have here, can also open up readings of the texts beyond their surface narrative features to explore repeated details (e.g. the grey suit) or other aspects of the texts. Expanding beyond the texts analysed in this chapter, the notion of chains of adaptation would also suggest more nuanced ways of approaching the relationships between texts from different locations across time without reducing them to simple iterations of a source text, but rather allowing them to be read as both independent texts and part of a larger group (as the analysis above read its corpus). In addition, tracing these chains would further develop understanding of the flows of global media and how texts can be revalued by their adaptations elsewhere, as *D'entre les morts* was by *Vertigo* and as *Vertigo* was by *La Jetée* – these adaptations change how we approach the source text and forever alter how it is read.

Finally, it is important to differentiate what I am calling a chain of adaptations from the notion of 'franchise', which may include a huge range of texts across multiple media that refer to, extend and otherwise interact with a source text: something like *Star Wars* consists of the franchise of films and TV series, as well as an enormous range of merchandise including toys, clothing, video games, novels, Lego and so on. All of the texts following the first film can be considered forms of adaptation. Where the notion of chain that I am elaborating differs is that there is little or no 'shared world' (Herbert 2017: 85) between the texts. All of the instances of Star Wars, from the original film to a Lego set, create and maintain the Star Wars universe in some way. The links between these texts are 'made by industrial design' (Herbert 2017: 86), that is, the intellectual property owners have tried to maintain control over the different elements and created them in order to exploit viewers'/consumers' interest in that world. The corpus of texts I have analysed is less homogeneous and, despite similarities of plot and detail, individual texts narrate different worlds. However, the notions of franchise and chain of adaptation begin to blur into each other once one considers the varieties of unofficial and non-canonical sequels and products. In each case, importantly, adaptation connects more than two texts and so new approaches to adaptation and comparison are needed.

Notes

1. Using the common translation studies terminology, 'source' refers to the text that is being adapted, 'target' to the adaptation.

2. Jan Baetens (2018: 32) also notes that the process of adaptation is a 'chain', but does not discuss what happens to adaptations of adaptations as I do in this chapter.
3. Following the French title of Hitchcock's film, the book is now published as *Sueurs froides* (*Cold Sweat*) in French (Goodkin 1987: 1171). The copy I am using has this title but is, as far as I am aware, the same as the original publication in terms of the text.
4. A further remake of *La Jetée* was made by Sam Brooks as a student film in 2016 and is available on his youtube channel: <https://www.youtube.com/watch?v=rer6of654a4> (accessed 17 August 2018). However, it reduces the length of the film to five minutes and uses live action rather than *La Jetée*'s use of still photographs. There are other narrative developments too, but to discuss these in detail would require more space than currently available. Catherine Lupton (2005: 83) lists further texts that cite or adapt *La Jetée*.
5. Marker's statement is, as one might expect from Marker, not quite as straightforward as this. He refers to *Vertigo*'s 'remake in Paris' in an essay on Hitchcock first published in *Positif* in 1994 and now available in English translation online (Marker n.d.). This statement has been taken to refer to *La Jetée*. Friedlander (2013: 184) also calls *La Jetée* an 'homage' to *Vertigo*.
6. I would also include translation as form of adaptation, following on from work by Lefevere (1992), Hutcheon (2006) and Laurence Raw (2013), all of whom have connected translation to other forms of adaptation (see also my discussion in Evans 2016: 126–48).
7. Further references to this novel are given parenthetically in the text. Unless otherwise noted, translations from the novel are my own.
8. Here I draw on Roland Barthes' argument that photographs show evidence of the past in *Cameria Lucida* (1984, especially p. 115) and Laura Mulvey's extension of this hypothesis in her *Death 24× a Second* (2006) to include cinema.
9. On the post-war experience of Japanese Americans, see Robinson 2012.
10. On C. S. Peirce's notions of icon, index and symbol, especially in relation to film, see Silverman 1983: 19–24.
11. As a fan of *Vertigo*, a film he discusses again and revisits scenes from in his *Sans soleil* (1983), it seems likely that Marker would have read the novel it was based on in French.
12. For a philosophical reading of the time loop in *La Jetée* see Zupančič 2003: 19–22.
13. Lupton (2005: 86–7) discusses the production of the film.
14. *La Jetée*'s independent status is reinforced by the fact that Parker Tyler (1995: 204–5) discusses it in his *Underground Film: A Critical History*, first published in 1969.

References

Baetens, J. (2018), 'Adaptation: a writerly strategy', in Benoît Mitaine, David Roche and Isabelle Schmitt-Pitiot (eds), *Comics and Adaptation*, trans. Aarnoud Rommens and David Roche, Jackson: University Press of Mississippi, pp. 31–46.

Barthes, R. (1984), *Camera Lucida*, trans. by Richard Howard, London: Flamingo. First published in French 1980.

Bluestone, G. (2003), *Novels into Film*, Baltimore, MD: Johns Hopkins University Press.

Bogost, I. (2006), *Unit Operations: An Approach to Video Game Criticism*, Cambridge, MA: MIT Press.

Boileau-Narcejac (1956), *The Living and the Dead*, trans. Geoffrey Sainsbury, London: Hutchinson.

Boileau-Narcejac (1999), *Sueurs froides*, Paris: Folio Policier. First published as *D'entre les morts* in 1954.

Boileau-Narcejac (2015), *Vertigo*, trans. Geoffrey Sainsbury, London: Pushkin.

Cohen, A. J.-J. (2003), '*12 Monkeys*, *Vertigo* and *La Jetée*: Postmodern Mythologies and Cult Films', *New Review of Film and Television*, 1: 1, 149–64.

Deleuze, G. (1969), *Logique du sens*, Paris: Minuit.

Del Rio, E. (2001), 'The remaking of *La Jetée*'s time-travel narrative: *Twelve Monkeys* and the rhetoric of absolute visibility', *Science Fiction Studies*, 28: 3, 383–98.

Evans, J. (2014), 'Film remakes, the black sheep of translation', *Translation Studies*, 7: 3, 300–14.

Evans, J. (2016), *The Many Voices of Lydia Davis: Translation, Rewriting, Intertextuality*, Edinburgh: Edinburgh University Press.

Evans, J. (2019), 'Film remakes as a form of translation', in L. Pérez-González (ed.), *The Routledge Handbook of Audiovisual Translation*, Abingdon: Routledge, pp. 160–74.

Friedlander, E. (2013), 'Being-in-(techni)color', in Katalin Makkai (ed.), *Vertigo*, Abingdon: Routledge, pp. 174–93.

Genette, G. (1987), *Seuils*, Paris: Seuil.

Goodkin, R. E. (1987), 'Fiction and film: Hitchcock's *Vertigo* and Proust's "Vertigo"', *Comparative Literature* 102: 5, 1171–81.

Gray, J. (2010), *Show Sold Separately: Promos, Spoilers and Other Media Paratexts*, New York: New York University Press.

Greene, R. (2012), 'Baroque Vertigo', in Douglas A. Cunningham (ed.), *The San Francisco of Alfred Hitchcock's Vertigo: Place, Pilgrimage and Commemoration*, Lanham: Scarecrow Press, pp. 27–40.

Harbord, J. (2009), *Chris Marker: La Jetée*, London: Afterall Books.

Harney, M. (2002), 'Economy and aesthetics in American remakes of French films', in Jennifer Forrest and Leonard R. Koos (eds), *Dead Ringers: The Remake in Theory and Practice*, Albany: State University of New York Press, pp. 63–87.

Herbert, D. (2017), *Film Remakes and Franchises*, New Brunswick, NJ: Rutgers University Press.

Hilliker, L. (2000), 'The history of the future in Paris: Chris Marker and Jean-Luc Godard in the 1960s', *Film Criticism* 24: 3, 1–22.

Hutcheon, L. (2006), *A Theory of Adaptation*, London: Routledge.

Leitch, T. (2002), 'Twice told tales: disavowal and the rhetoric of the remake', in J. Forrest and L. R. Koos (eds), *Dead Ringers: The Remake in Theory and Practice*, Albany: State University of New York Press, pp. 37–62.

Leitch, T. (2007), *Film Adaptation and Its Discontents: From* Gone with the Wind *to* Passion of the Christ, Baltimore, MD: Johns Hopkins University Press.

Lefevere, A. (1992), *Translation, Rewriting and the Manipulation of Literary Fame*, London: Routledge.

Lupton, C. (2005), *Chris Marker: Memories of the Future*, London: Reaktion.

Marker, C. (n.d). 'A free replay (notes on *Vertigo*)', <https://chrismarker.org/chris-marker/a-free-replay-notes-on-vertigo/> (accessed 23 July 2018).
Martins, A. (2015), 'Theorizing *La Jetée* and *Twelve Monkeys*, but also *Vertigo*', in M. Medeiros, T. M. Flores and J. C. Leal (eds), *Photography and Cinema: 50 Years of Chris Marker's La Jetée*, Newcastle: Cambridge Scholars Press, pp. 285–95.
Mazdon, L. (2017), 'Disrupting the remake: *The Girl with the Dragon Tattoo*', in I. R. Smith and C. Verevis (eds), *Transnational Film Remakes*, Edinburgh: Edinburgh University Press, pp. 21–35.
Mulvey, L. (2006), *Death 24× a Second: Stillness and the Moving Image*, London: Reaktion.
Palmer, R. Barton (2017), 'Fritz Lang remakes Jean Renoir: film noir in three national voices', in I. R. Smith and C. Verevis (eds), *Transnational Film Remakes*, Edinburgh: Edinburgh University Press, pp. 36–53.
Raw, L. (ed.) (2013), *Translation, Adaptation and Transformation*, London: Bloomsbury.
Robinson, G. (2012), *After Camp: Portraits of Midcentury Japanese American Life and Politics*, Berkeley: University of California Press.
Silverman, K. (1983), *The Subject of Semiotics*, Oxford: Oxford University Press.
Smith, I. R. (2017), *The Hollywood Meme: Transnational Adaptations in World Cinema*, Edinburgh: Edinburgh University Press.
Solnit, R. (2006), *A Field Guide to Getting Lost*, Edinburgh: Canongate.
Tyler, P. (1995), *Underground Film: A Critical History*, New York: Da Capo.
Truffaut, F. (1966), *Le Cinéma selon Hitchcock*, Paris: Robert Laffont.
Varndell, D. (2014), *Hollywood Remakes, Deleuze and the Grandfather Paradox*, Basingstoke: Palgrave Macmillan.
Venuti, L. (1995), *The Translator's Invisibility*, London: Routledge.
Verevis, C. (2017), 'Trading places: *Das dobbelte Lotchen* and *The Parent Trap*', in I. R. Smith and C. Verevis (eds), *Transnational Film Remakes*, Edinburgh: Edinburgh University Press, pp. 130–43.
Vincendeau, G. (1993), 'Hijacked', *Sight & Sound* NS3 (7), 22–5.
Wittgenstein, L. (1968), *Philosophical Investigations*, trans. by G. E. M. Anscombe, Oxford: Blackwell.
Zupančič, A. (2003), *The Shortest Shadow: Nietzsche's Philosophy of the Two*, Cambridge, MA: MIT Press.

Filmography

Clouzot, H. (1955), *Les diaboliques*. Paris: Filmsonor.
Fickett, T. and Matalas, T. (2015–), *12 Monkeys*. Los Angeles, CA: Atlas Entertainment.
Gilliam, T. (1995), *Twelve Monkeys*. Hollywood, CA: Universal Pictures.
Hitchcock, A. (1958), *Vertigo*. Hollywood, CA: Alfred J. Hitchcock Productions.
Marker, C. (1962), *La Jetée*. Paris: Argos Films.
Marker, C. (1983), *Sans soleil*. Paris: Argos Films.
Resnais, A. (1956), *Nuit et brouillard*. Paris: Argos Films.
Spielberg, S. (2004), *The Terminal*. Hollywood, CA: Dreamworks.

13. A 'DOUBLE TAKE' ON THE NATION(AL) IN THE DUTCH-FLEMISH MONOLINGUAL FILM REMAKE

Eduard Cuelenaere

Introduction

Known for its fragmentation and diverse languages and cultures, the European film industry still experiences difficulties in competing with the dominance of Hollywood. While roughly 1.9 million cinema tickets are sold annually for American films – both studio and independent – in Europe, non-national European (NNE) films[1] only sell an average of 185,000. NNE films account for 12 per cent of total European cinema admissions, while national films (those made for a domestic audience) account for 21 per cent of admissions. This is in stark contrast to the figure for American films, which stands at 65 per cent (Jones 2020). What is clear from these figures is that, from an audience standpoint, Hollywood is still at the heart of European film culture, and European films still encounter major obstacles in crossing their national borders (Higson 2015: 138). When European audiences are drawn to NNE films, it is because they offer an alternative (in terms of narrative, genre, casting, etc.) to popular Hollywood cinema, not (necessarily) because of their (foreign) nationality or opportunity to encounter a different culture or place (Jones 2017: 479). In sum, European films are unlikely to travel in Europe unless they are:

> (a) a big-budget Hollywood-style action/adventure blockbuster or animation; (b) a medium-budget middlebrow quality drama based on a best-selling book and an Oscar-winning Hollywood star attached; or (c) a low-budget MEDIA-supported art-house film made by a Palme-d'Or-winning auteur. (Jones 2020)

Looking at recent developments, one could also add 'or a remake of a popular, commercial European film' to the above enumeration. In Europe, nationally produced films supply increasingly universal themes and subject matter for border-crossing (translation) purposes (Verevis 2017: 153). Because of these opportunities, several pan-European enterprises have been formed in the past two decades. These enterprises simultaneously distribute films in European and international areas, with remakes and re-adaptations 'at the heart of [their] creative strategies' (Meir 2018: 4). Looking at box-office revenues, such intra-European remakes generally turn out to be quite successful. Moreover, and perhaps more importantly, the practice might present a potential solution to the inability of popular European films to cross borders. Even European film industries that are part of the same geo-linguistic region (e.g. Scandinavia) are dealing with these barriers. It therefore seems that alongside strategies such as transnational co-production, remaking films might offer a new and viable way to circumvent the aforementioned issues.

The film industries of Flanders (the Dutch-speaking region of northern Belgium) and the Netherlands – together forming the Low Countries – deal with the aforementioned issues. Indeed, both film industries have always experienced problems in releasing their films across their mutual border. Besides obvious commercial reasons – think of the shortcomings in distribution and promotional strategies – this lack of interest in their respective film culture and products is indicative of a bigger intercultural context between both regions. Cajot (2012: 53) argues that since the 1990s, the intercultural contact between the Netherlands and Flanders has sharply deteriorated, which is reflected in a reduction in the exchange of various cultural products – not only cinema but also newspapers, literature, radio and television. However, the new millennium marked an essential shift in the Low Countries when a new film practice was established: Instead of (unsuccessfully) releasing each other's films, multiple Flemish filmmakers began to remake Dutch films domestically, and vice versa (Cuelenaere et al. 2016). In the context of European cinema (and even within a broader global context), the case of Dutch-Flemish film remakes is quite exceptional when one considers that the 23 million inhabitants of both regions essentially speak the same language (with some minor differences in accent and vocabulary), have a partly shared history, are neighbouring regions and could be considered culturally proximate. Paradoxically, it is also because of these elements that both film industries show a mutual interest in producing remakes of each other's films. Dealing with the same issues – having a small domestic market and experiencing difficulties in finding broader audiences, while enjoying more substantial revenues for their domestically produced films – several filmmakers saw opportunities in remaking already existing and commercially viable films and scripts.

Considering the above, this chapter will explore the Dutch-Flemish remake phenomenon, which generated no less than eleven film remakes in a period of eighteen years (see Table 13.1), as a relatively new, yet highly significant

Table 13.1 Complete list of Dutch-Flemish source films and subsequent remakes

Source film	Film remake
All Stars (1997, van de Velde, NL)	*Team Spirit* (2000, Verheyen, BE)
In Orange (*In Oranje*, 2004, Lürsen, NL)	*Gilles* (*Buitenspel*, 2005, Verheyen, BE)
Love Is All (*Alles is Liefde*, 2007, Lürsen, NL)	*Crazy About Ya* (*Zot van A.*, 2010, Verheyen, BE)
Loft (2008, Van Looy, BE)	*Loft* (2010, Beumer, NL)
Madly in Love (*Smoorverliefd*, 2010, Van Mieghem, BE)	*Madly in Love* (*Smoorverliefd*, 2013, Van Mieghem, NL)
Come as You Are (*Hasta La Vista*, 2011, Enthoven, BE)	*Adios Amigos* (2016, van Rees, NL)
Brasserie Romantique (*Brasserie Romantiek*, 2012, Vanhoebrouck, BE)	*Brasserie Valentine* (*Brasserie Valentijn*, 2016, Vogel, NL)
Family Way (*Alles is Familie*, 2012, Lürsen, NL)	*The Family Way* (*Allemaal Familie*, 2017, Vos, BE)
Men's Hearts[a] (*Mannenharten*, 2013, de Cloe, NL)	*What Men Want* (*Wat Mannen Willen*, 2015, Peeters, BE)
Homies (2015, Karthaus, NL)	*Bad Trip* (2017, Vos, BE)
The Longing (*Het Verlangen*, 2017, Lürsen, NL)	*Hidden Desire* (*Verborgen Verlangen*, 2018, Moerkerke, BE)

[a] It should, however, be noted that this film is actually already a remake of a German source film entitled Männerherzen (Verhoeven 2009).

industrial practice in the Low Countries' film industries, and in a broader sense, those of Europe. Beginning with the particular nature of this unique remake phenomenon, the tensions between sameness and difference, universalism and particularity, and the transnational and national will be explored, as well as the strategies that filmmakers apply to bypass theses tensions. This chapter criticises the clear-cut demarcation between these tensions and argues for a more interactive and interwoven take on the film remake. Adopting both macro and micro perspectives, it will first consider the Dutch-Flemish film remake practice from a broader industrial perspective and will then address the textual properties of the films under consideration. In doing so, this chapter asserts that the remake cycle in the Low Countries is both a nationally and transnationally oriented phenomenon. Moreover, it provides new insights into the ways film and cinema are connected to or are part of – or rather, are made part of – a specific local, national or transnational context.

The (Trans)national Cinema Debate: Enter the Film Remake

Notwithstanding the varying perspectives of scholars working in the fields of remake, adaptation, translation or intercultural studies, most seem to agree that the film remake is characterised by an inherently hybrid status. Whether or not one is convinced that every text is *in se* an intertext, it is clear that film remakes are directly linked to one or more preceding (film) texts – rendering their status inherently hybrid. This relationship complicates assumptions of originality, imitation, imperialism, ownership, high versus low culture, and identity. Indeed, the film remake, both as process and product, impedes fixed or essential notions of identity, not only on the level of on-screen identities (characters' ethnicities, genders, cultures, etc.), but also on the level of the film *an sich*. Connecting this to the concept of nation and national identity, one might think of Homi K. Bhabha, who coined the concept of hybrid nation, arguing that:

> What is at issue is the performative nature of differential identities: the regulation and negotiation of those spaces that are continually, *contingently*, 'opening out', remaking the boundaries, exposing the limits of any claim to a singular or autonomous sign of difference. (1994: 219, original emphasis)

Thus, the film remake's inherent hybridity mirrors the performative, negotiating and contingent nature of nations and their subsequent national identities. In the context of Hollywood remakes of French films in the 1980s, Lucy Mazdon states that the 'very act of moving a film across cultures calls into question its own identity as "national" product' (2000: 65). Here, she raises the critical question of whether these Hollywood remakes of French films are by definition less (or not) French when compared to their source texts. If yes, then what are the constitutive elements that make us believe they carry a (different) national label? By pointing out this ambiguity, Mazdon touches on debates in film studies, where the idea of national cinema, and more recently of transnational cinema, is challenged.

Keeping recent political events in mind – think of Brexit or the sustained wave of nationalist and protectionist movements throughout Europe – it seems that since the beginning of the twenty-first century, the nation as an imagined community (cf. infra) has grown in significance. Symptomatic of this trend are the statistics of the Eurobarometer, which show that up to the present day, most Europeans still feel principally national and less European (Standard Eurobarometer 2018). In an era 'of mounting tensions and increasing hostilities to difference, understanding the ways in which cultural artefacts and artistic texts respond will provide a vital perspective on the contemporary moment' (Harvey 2018: 2). This growing antipathy to, or at least disinterest in, difference, the unknown, the foreign or the exotic could also be linked to the practice of Dutch-Flemish film remakes, which – coincidentally or not – also originated in the new millennium. Indeed, although possibly far-fetched, one could interpret the practice as a form of unwillingness to watch films of other cultures – even those that are very closely related, as in the case of Flanders and the Netherlands. In that sense, the remake phenomenon in the Low Countries reads as a confirmation of the prominence of nationalist sentiments. Explained by concepts such as cultural proximity (Straubhaar 2007), in the age of globalisation, audiences apparently continue to prefer cultural products that feel familiar or are at least as close as possible to their own cultural, local or national background. Looking specifically at the context of television in Europe, Milly Buonanno (2002) asserts that most European nations generate an increasing amount of domestically produced prime-time programmes (such as drama) whereby (national) cultural proximity appears to be a crucial factor. This should, however, also be nuanced. According to Buonanno, it is true that people are prone to watch their own national culture on television – and, as Jones's statistics show, albeit to a lesser extent, at the cinema as well – but they are also highly familiarised with (and seem to heavily enjoy) cultural artefacts from the US.

If one wants to theorise the nation in film studies today, it seems necessary to adopt a dialectical approach, whereby both the notion of transnational cinema and the more traditional frame of national cinema are taken into account (Harvey 2018: 8). Although it is undoubtedly important to acknowledge that the transnational notion is essential to understand cinema's history, current status, and future, one should not neglect the still-significant notion of the nation(al). In this context, Berry (2006) calls for a paradigm shift, wherein the various relationships between national and transnational concepts are studied. As a way of combining both the national and transnational lenses to study the remake phenomenon in the Low Countries, it might be elucidatory to approach the subject by employing Mette Hjort and Duncan Petrie's (2007) concept of 'small nations'. They believe that an analysis of the relations between film and various national elements should be part of present and future film studies, claiming that research on cinema can benefit from a consideration of small national cinemas and industries, provided that these are seen as small but permeable aspects of a transnational network. According to both authors, in the context of such interconnected networks, small nations often choose to emphasise the uniqueness of their national identity in order to sustain their existence. By examining the relations between cinema and the nation, one can understand 'the specificity of various contemporary and historical conjunctures' (Hjort and Petrie 2007: 13). Moreover, analysing small nations can uncover 'the emergence of regional networks and alliances that are providing transnational alternatives to the neo-liberal model of globalisation driving contemporary Hollywood' (Hjort and Petrie 2007: 17). The Dutch-Flemish remake practice could indeed be regarded as such: a commercially driven international collaboration, whereby scripts and films are shared for remake purposes, with the ultimate goal of countering Hollywood's dominance and bringing audiences back to domestic cinema. This adds an important nuance to the seemingly pure national status of the phenomenon, suggesting the involvement of a broader perspective that includes a transnational aspect.

Understanding the Film Remake: Transnational Localisation or National Echo Chamber?

These allegedly – or indeed, false – oppositional stances between the national and transnational are illustrative of the paradox of film remakes. Although many of these films are inherently hybrid (both textually and contextually), their reason for existence is often the need for localisation and the staging of distinct national elements. Localisation is then used as a way to sidestep the aforementioned tension between the particular and the universal. When, for instance, European movies are remade in Hollywood, different formal, narrative, and cultural elements are localised – the 'different' can be transformed into the 'universally applicable' – and they then have to 'undergo considerable change as they cross the Atlantic – despite a seeming similarity of plot' (Vincendeau 1993: 23). When considering its production context, the practice of remaking films in the Low Countries could almost be perceived as a purely national affair. First, the directors of the remakes originate from the country of production in almost all cases, except for one.[2] This is also true for the main actors who have a part in the films. Then, on the level of promotion and distribution, it quickly becomes clear that these Dutch-Flemish film remakes only aim for their domestic markets and are, therefore, released exclusively in the country of production, again, except for one.[3] Lastly, interestingly enough, it appears that almost all of the remakes are co-productions between Flanders and the Netherlands. Therefore, even though the practice of Dutch-Flemish remakes appears to be predominantly national at first sight, on a production level, the phenomenon appears to transcend national borders. Moreover, both these Dutch and Flemish filmmakers constantly decide to remake Flemish and Dutch films, and not, for instance, Italian, Korean or Mexican films. Therefore, on a more structural level, there seems to be an incentive that motivates filmmakers from both sides of the border to remake each other's films – pointing again to the aforementioned paradox of the practice. In this context, Daniel Herbert argues the following:

> for all that it is clear that 'transnational remakes' constitute an important aspect of transnational cinema, we need to attend always to the multiple ways in which any given remake, like any other film or collection of films, is 'transnational'. (2017: 221)

When applied to Dutch-Flemish remakes, a combination of what Hjort (2009) calls affinitive, milieu-building and opportunistic transnationalism seems most suitable. Affinitive transnationalism centres on the inclination of people (in this case, filmmakers) to connect with those who are similar to them, 'typically being understood in terms of ethnicity, partially overlapping or mutually intelligible languages, and a history of interaction giving rise to shared core values, common practices, and comparable institutions' (Hjort 2009: 17). Next to cultural affinity, this type of transnationalism can also 'arise in connection with shared problems or commitments in a punctual now, or with the discovery of features of other national contexts that are deemed to be potentially relevant to key problems experienced within a home context' (Hjort 2009: 17). Indeed, the decision to remake films from across the border in the Low Countries can be seen to be driven by a sort of transcultural affinity and shared problems that both industries are dealing with. Milieu-building transnationalism points to 'a model of transnational collaboration aimed at jointly developing solutions to particular problems that hamper the development of thriving film milieus' (Hjort 2009: 19). This form of transnationalism is closely related to the former, although its goal is partially different – and possibly more far-reaching and radical – namely, the development of a transnational model of cooperation that proposes a solution to the aforementioned obstacles that European productions have to deal with. Lastly, opportunistic transnationalism 'involves giving priority to economic issues to the point where monetary factors actually dictate the selection of partners beyond national borders' (Hjort 2009: 19). This type of transnationalism focuses on the often-commercial incentives behind transnationalism. Illustrative of the latter are production companies such as the Ghent-based Marmalade – which focuses mainly on producing commercial, mainstream films and uses the process of remaking films as one of their principal strategies – and the Amsterdam-based Fabiola – a venture of three independent production companies based in Belgium that work together to sell their formats to the Dutch television market.

In light of commercially motivated transnationalism, one might also think of the production and distribution of television formats. Indeed, one of the crucial components of the European transnational television industry is the use of such television formats (Bondebjerg *et al.* 2017: 6), of which the aforementioned Fabiola is an exponent. This use is also relevant to the context of the Low Countries, where many television programmes are remade or formats exchanged. Even though such television formats offer novel ways of exchanging media products, it is claimed that the process of localisation in format trading in Europe (indirectly) complicates or impairs 'real transnational encounters' (Bondebjerg *et al.* 2017: 6). As film remakes generally localise the foreign, the same could be said of intra-European (and, thus, Dutch-Flemish) film remakes, which indirectly complicate the creation of a shared and strong pan-European (cinema) culture. In other words, remaking films in Europe could equally be regarded as a process that prevents mediated cultural encounters in a kind of national echo chamber. These encounters might result in a scenario wherein European audiences mainly perceive their culture as being national or local, 'despite its obvious global and European dimensions' (Bondebjerg *et al.* 2017: 4). However, one should be cautious in equating the process of remaking with localisation. Think, for example, of the Swedish film adaptation of the Millennium book trilogy by Stieg Larsson. Analysing the film trilogy, Mazdon writes:

> In their mobilisation of elements of the action/crime thriller genres[,] the films are arguably far more 'American' than the slow-paced, broody dramas stereotypically associated with Scandinavian production by Anglophone audiences. The films were marketed in the English-speaking market so as to deliberately disguise their 'foreign' origins and position them as a Hollywood-style product. (2017: 22)

The first film of the trilogy, *The Girl with the Dragon Tattoo* (Oplev 2009), a Swedish/Danish co-production, wanted to circumvent the problems associated with cultural discount by disguising its 'foreign' status and opting for the opposite of localisation by delocalising its content. However, the film proved unpopular and 'was faced with the usual resistance of the mainstream audience' (Mazdon 2017: 24). This is probably in part related to the fact that the language of the film was not English. Two years later, in 2011, an English-spoken Hollywood remake, directed by David Fincher, was released. Wanting the film to be as authentic as possible, the American director found it of essential importance to work with a Swedish crew and included textual elements that are typical of Scandinavia and its Nordic Noir genre. Aware of its European embedment, Fincher did the exact opposite with his remake when he opted to 'foreignise' the Hollywood-inspired source film. Thus, this example shows that a Hollywood remake of a European source text may be more 'European' than the preceding film that was produced in Europe. This, in turn, although being an American remake, may facilitate a mediated cultural encounter with European culture.

Making Sense of National Themes and Sentiments in the Film Remake

Central to the above discussion is how the relationship between cinema and culture (or nation) should be understood. Although cinema is never a mirror of 'an already fully formed and homogeneous national culture and identity' (Higson 2002: 63), in most cases, it does privilege specific subject positions of the national subject. According to Higson, these subject positions are consequently reproduced, making it increasingly difficult to leave open the possibility of alternative positions. This idea is reminiscent of Benedict Anderson's (1983) well-known concept of 'imagined community', which argues that the nation (and, therefore, also a supra-nation like Europe) only exists in the minds of people. Although the social construction of notions such as nation and national identity is agreed upon by many scholars, one should not underestimate the materialised outcomes of such imaginations. Like many other cultural artefacts, cinema can convey political or even nationalist messages, and 'if we are to understand the relationship between cinema and nationalism, we must engage with its capacity both to represent and construct a people' (Harvey 2018: 8).

In the context of the Low Countries, Jaap Verheul explores the growing success of Flemish cinema since the 2000s and articulates that 'a certain notion of Flemishness should . . . be seen as a political barometer for the intensified assertion of Flemish sovereignty' (2016: 327–8). He also expresses (implicitly) that the Flemish nationalist movement was an important matrix for the development of the Dutch-Flemish remake cycle, and it should, therefore, be considered when analysing the phenomenon. If these Flemish film remakes express a clear sentiment of Flemishness, it seems quite manageable to perceive these film remakes as national echo chambers (i.e. archetypical examples of quasi-all-encompassing localised products that previously emanated a certain amount of Dutchness). Consequently, such a stance presumes that their source films were clearly national or that the filmmakers of the remake added new nation-specific traits to the film. However, how can one make sense of or describe national cinemas and their defining content(s) in a textual manner? Hjort (2000: 95) argues that, in academic literature, national cinemas are often characterised as dealing with national theme(s) but little research has been done on what specifically establishes the themes of a nation. Building on Peter Lamarque and Stein H. Olsen's (1994) theory, Hjort differentiates between topical themes on one hand – namely, those that 'involve only concepts that arise within, and remain relevant to, a highly specific historical or cultural formation' (2000: 97), and perennial themes on the other hand – namely, those that 'bring into focus subject matter that resonates across historical and cultural boundaries' which is why they 'are universal or quasi-universal in their thrust' (2000: 97). A theme implies thematisation and can therefore only arise when, during the viewing of the film, the audience's attention is drawn to the features that signify the theme(s) by flagging, foregrounding or focusing on specific elements. Hjort advances that naturally, thematic hybridity (e.g. combining perennial with topical themes) can also occur, and a topical theme may often function as a secondary background, providing 'the necessary means of anchoring perennial themes within specific cultural formations' (2002: 309).

Since the notion of nation indicates the particularity of a community and its cultural context, 'the theme of nation is a likely candidate for topical theme par excellence' (Hjort 2000: 98). Starting from such a rigid description of the theme of nation, Hjort (2002: 308) contends that not many filmmakers would agree that their films have the nation as a primary theme. However, many would concur that their films are about a specific reality in which they (and their audiences) find themselves (e.g. Flanders). To explain the latter, she puts forward the concept of 'banal aboutness', arguing that:

> all films that make use, for example, of recognisably Danish locations, the Danish language, Danish actors and props that mirror the material culture of Danes, qualify as being about Denmark [and] that such elements can provide the basis for a given film's national quality, but that they cannot, in and of themselves, constitute a theme. (Hjort 2000: 99).

Hjort's concept is, of course, inspired by Michael Billig's notion of 'banal nationalism' (1995), whereby it is illustrated that one should be wary of reducing nationalism to only obvious or explicit utterances, as in propagandist cinema. Billig's notion of banal nationalism refers to those banal – but ideological – messages that 'enable the established nations of the West to be reproduced' (1995: 6). Applying this to cinema and the national cinema debate, Hjort argues that the most important characteristic that differentiates banal or habitual (in a Bourdieusian sense) instances of aboutness and 'the kind of aboutness that is constitutive of full-blown themes of nation' (2000: 101) is focal attention and the degree to which it is constitutive of (or of elementary importance to) the story.

Banal Aboutness in Dutch-Flemish Film Remakes

As the narratives of Dutch-Flemish film remakes and their source films are very similar, small, quasi-invisible, or often banal, textual changes are magnified when compared; potentially added or changed themes also become more apparent. Indeed, when textually comparing a source text with its remake, a prism is conceived that aids us in pinpointing the perennial and topical themes of the two versions, or the transformations that occurred during the remake process. Moreover, the prism of the remake makes it easier to trace instances of banal aboutness, as such habitual elements are defamiliarised through the remake process and become highly legible when juxtaposing two similar texts (Cuelenaere *et al.* 2019a: 14). It is, however, important to note that such a textual analysis does not (and cannot) disclose the essential properties of a particular nation, nor does it wish to claim that national sentiment is the constitutional element of people's multi-layered identity – two known pitfalls of dogmatic essentialism and rigid constructivism.

Examining the entire sample of Dutch-Flemish film remakes and their source films (see Table 13.1), it becomes clear that they are all commercial genre films intended for mainstream domestic audiences. In total, fourteen out of the twenty-two films are romantic comedies; two are tragicomedies; two are family films; two are of the thriller genre; and one film couple switches during the remake process – *Brasserie Romantique* can be considered a drama (with comedy accents), while its remake, *Brasserie Valentine*, is more of a romantic comedy. The fact that the majority of films being remade in the Low Countries are comedies is indicative of the 'apparent inability of much comedy to transcend national boundaries [which] explain[s] the frequency of the comic remake' (Mazdon 2000: 92) – which is why they are in need of a remake. This confirms that, compared to other genres, comedy is generally defined more by its surrounding culture (i.e. its specific sense of humour).[4] Here, the notion of banal aboutness seems elucidatory. Although the perennial comedic aspect is maintained in the different Flemish and Dutch versions, the specific humour (i.e. gags and jokes) is transformed in order to create a feeling of proximity, taking into account the different socio-cultural contexts (Cuelenaere *et al.* 2019b). In addition, the (often small) adjustments made to humorous aspects in both Dutch and Flemish versions certainly do not constitute the theme of a specific nation; at most, they could be perceived as banal re-enactments of real-life situations. Hence, although these changes made during the remake process tell us how these films wish to create a feeling of (national) familiarity, it is unlikely audiences perceive them in this way.

The exact same procedure (i.e. banal aboutness) can be found in many other elements of these twenty-two films. As argued in earlier work (Cuelenaere *et al.* 2018; 2019a; 2019b), the use of space (i.e. rural space versus urban landscape) was not generally transformed during the remake process, but the locations were (almost always) changed, which, again, adds a national quality to these films. Think also of the dialogue: the structure and purpose of the dialogue between the films' characters are generally not altered substantially. However, the speech itself (i.e. jokes, tone and cultural references in the dialogue, as well as the actors' accents) is transformed in consideration of the different linguistic and cultural contexts. The same counts for the characters (and their role in the overarching narrative) in these films, as they are generally kept the same after being remade. Nevertheless, small adjustments are made to their personalities and names, and, of course, the actors playing them are also changed. In terms of representation, one can also find compelling differences in relation to the portrayal of, for instance, nudity, sexuality, gender and ethnicity. To a certain extent, these are all changed because of various differences in the socio-cultural contexts, or, more rightly, because of perceived differences in these contexts (Cuelenaere *et al.* 2018). Therefore, if one looks from a distance, patterns of universality versus locality keep returning in every pair (i.e. source film and remake), proving that there might be some kind of dialectic balancing mechanism between the universal and the particular – or between transnational aspects and banal national recognisability – at play in these films. Even though all of the remakes that came out of this practice seem to present themselves as unique and 'new' Dutch or Flemish films, they all share the same mechanisms and underlying frameworks – regardless of the small and banal changes made to them, aiming to recreate a Dutch or Flemish aboutness.

Looking at all of the Dutch-Flemish film remakes and their previous source films, none can be regarded as positing the nation as a primary theme. Indeed, the primary themes of these films are clearly perennial, including friendship, love, sexuality, adultery, growing up, death and murder. Given that the films under consideration are produced only for national domestic audiences, these themes show that there are indeed many shared dimensions and 'commonalities behind what often seem to be strong national, cultural identities' (Bondebjerg *et al.* 2017: 27). As mentioned above, Hjort contends that thematic hybridity might occur, giving the example of the Danish *Let's Get Lost* (Jonas Elmer 1997). According to Hjort, this is an apt example of a film that uses the theme of nation, albeit in a less foregrounded way (2002: 309). In this light, the following section will delve deeper into the dynamics between primary and secondary themes on the one hand, perennial and topical themes on the other, and how these relate to the nation(al), by building on an illuminating case study that came out of the Dutch-Flemish remake practice.

Textually Dissecting the National in Film Remakes: A Case Study

The case study that will be used to further elucidate the aforementioned theoretical statements is the Dutch source film *In Orange* and its Belgian remake *Gilles*. Both are about a young boy who wants to become a professional player in the national football teams of respectively the Netherlands (the Dutch Eleven) and Belgium (the Belgian Red Devils). This case is particularly characteristic of most of the other films that are included in the sample because, on many different levels, it shares those features – inter alia, of domestically oriented and recognisable popular genre films directed by famous national directors including famous national actors – that almost all films in the Dutch-Flemish remake practice use. Another reason for focusing on this case is because, at first sight, *In Orange* and *Gilles* seem to clearly concentrate on the nation – for instance, by focusing on the national sport of football – which appears to be more explicitised than in the other films in the sample. This is obvious from the first sequence of both films, which is symptomatic of the rest of the films: When the young boy appears on screen for the first time, we can see that his room is filled with posters of the national football team and covered in the national colour (i.e. orange in the Dutch version and red in the Belgian version). This focus on the nation becomes even more apparent when the boy starts to sing the national anthem, with the music of the 'Wilhelmus' (in the Dutch version) and the 'Brabançonne' (in the Belgian version) playing in the background. Although of secondary importance to the story, this hyper-saturation of national elements appears to point towards the existence of the theme of nation in both films. The principal themes of both versions are, however, the difficulties that arise when having to say farewell to one's childhood (closely related to coming-of-age narratives); the emotional suffering and mourning of the main character brought on by the death of his father; and the oftentimes harsh differences between people's dreams, hopes, expectations and reality.

Another argument, which at first glance may speak in favour of the theme of nation in both versions, is that the young boy, Remco van Leeuwen (the main protagonist in the Dutch version), is clearly inspired by two Dutch football legends: Marco van Basten and Johan Cruijff. In the first sequence of the Dutch source film, the camera sweeps across Remco's bed, which shows a leaky football at its head. Remco is such a fanatic that he prefers to sleep on a leaky ball instead of a soft pillow. However, this striking detail is not coincidental: It is actually a cultural reference to Marco Van Basten, who used a deflated ball as a cushion when he was a teenager. Moreover, Remco's stubborn and wilful personality, which becomes apparent when he refuses to accept the doctor's advice to rest (and stop playing football) after being tackled during a match, is also based on Van Basten, who is known to be a stickler and, similarly, did not listen to his doctor as a young boy. Moreover, in *In Orange*, the father of the twelve-year-old Remco is a greengrocer who owns a small grocery in town. Quite early in the film, he dies of a heart attack. Both these elements show striking similarities with the life of Johan Cruijff, whose father was also a greengrocer and died young because of cardiac arrest. One might contend that both these elements are only small details in a much bigger story. But looking at the press articles that circulated during the film's release, many do mention that the character of Remco, played by Yannick van de Velde, is based on the two Dutch football legends. This finding suggests that the use of van Basten and Cruijff's biographies as a frame of reference plays a significant role in understanding and interpreting the film's main protagonist.

Conceptualising the theme of nation, Hjort argues that '[t]hematisations of nation, particularly in the case of hyper-saturation, have a tendency to promote opacity in international contexts, for local, topical[,] and nation-specific thematic elements are likely to be only partially comprehensible in other national contexts' (2000: 108). Linking this to the theory presented above, one should consider that film remakes are generally – though certainly not always, as argued above – characterised by their localisation of culturally or nationally specific elements. This localisation circumvents cultural opacity and maintains a socio-cultural verisimilitude for the targeted domestic audience. But, remarkably, the aforementioned culturally specific (and therefore topical) elements in the Dutch *In Orange* were neither omitted nor changed in the Belgian remake *Gilles*. Apparently, the filmmakers of the Belgian remake did not find these elements too closely entwined with the Dutch context, which would make them less comprehensible for a Belgian or Flemish audience. Interestingly, when looking at all of the articles regarding the film that were released in Flemish newspapers, only one small article (aptly titled 'The Original of Gilles') mentioned Marco van Basten and Johan Cruijff. Furthermore, this article was released as a promotion for the Dutch source film, which played that week on Flemish television (Rvg 2006: 40). Hence, neither film critics nor journalists mentioned the link between the background of Gilles' character (the Belgian equivalent of Remco) and van Basten and Cruijff. Indeed, although both names might be familiar to some Belgian people, they are clearly better known in the Dutch context. Consequently, it might be the case that when in the process of remaking *In Orange*, the Flemish filmmakers did not notice the cultural references in the main protagonist's background.

The fact that these at-first-sight 'topical elements' remained unchanged despite the different context (i.e. the remake process) suggests two things: They are perennial and, therefore, not firmly connected to a specific cultural or national context; or, as Hjort would say, they instead qualify as being 'about' the Netherlands. As the surrounding discourse found, the use of two famous Dutch football players in the Dutch source film *In Orange* is indeed highly culturally defined. Thus, it would be incorrect to assert that these elements are part of a perennial theme. Hence, it makes more sense to state that they provide the basis for the film's national quality and do not, 'in and of themselves, constitute a theme' (Hjort 2000: 99). The fact that the biographical background of the main protagonist in the Belgian remake *Gilles* was not changed, as well as the finding that Flemish news articles did not mention anything related to the underlying cultural references, indicate that these aspects cannot really be defined as topical themes. These culturally defined features may be recognised and recalled by Dutch audiences and elicit national sentiments, but they do not, in and of themselves, form an indispensable, central theme of the film. This could, therefore, be seen as an archetypical example of thematic hybridity, whereby the perennial theme of 'dream versus reality' is locally anchored by covering it with national flavour. However, as shown above, it is quite challenging to claim that these nationally specific elements form a separate and self-contained theme.

This finding demonstrates that, when dealing with thematic hybridity, Hjort's theory may be too rigid. Although it is quite reasonable to state that a film can be constituted of different themes, both topical and perennial, it becomes more challenging when the boundaries between topicality and perenniality, and thematisation and 'aboutness', become blurred. This is precisely where the comparative textual analysis of the film remake can be illuminating, given that the defining feature of the remake is its hybrid nature and blurred boundaries. Using the Dutch-Flemish remakes as a frame of reference, it shows that, at first sight, some topical themes were only local interpretations of perennial themes. Moreover, the transformations – or, indeed, the lack of them – in *In Orange/Gilles*, barely affected the general story or the themes of both films. This shows that what is being transformed can hardly be called a theme. Instead, these findings are the perfect example of Hjort's banal aboutness. Consequently, these elements may appear to be inseparable from a specific cultural context, but they are actually quite redeemable and are mainly used to make the film recognisable for a domestic audience. Remco's room, filled with props that refer to the Dutch national football team, the singing of the 'Wilhelmus', and his culturally inspired biographical background aim to create a feeling of familiarity for a Dutch audience. This clearly differs from the full-fledged theme of a particular nation.

Conclusion

Going back to the question of whether the Dutch-Flemish remake phenomenon can be considered a kind of national echo chamber, i.e. including cultural artefacts that are being presented as being inherently national – while actually being hybrid – it seems that there is no simple answer. In order to prove such a fundamentally complex statement (that, as shown, starts from many different assumptions), this chapter argues that, building on existing theories from both the (trans)national cinema debate and the field of remake studies, a similarly multi-faceted approach is mandatory. Therefore, this chapter first zoomed in on the cultural and production context in which these Dutch-Flemish film remakes were produced – acknowledging that many different actors function as intermediaries or gatekeepers standing in between the product and its context. Although these films are largely produced nationally and targeted at domestic audiences in most cases, there are different transnational mechanisms operating simultaneously in the creation of these film remakes. Indeed, a combination of affinitive (because of the cultural affinity and comparable industry), opportunistic (because of the commercial incentives) and even milieu-building (because collaborating structurally may alleviate common obstacles) transnationalism appears to be in play when these film remakes were produced. Hence, on the level of production, the Dutch-Flemish remake practice is, in its core, transnationally defined, but on the surface nationally oriented.

Second, this chapter looked at how film remakes are textually linked with the concept of the nation and the national. More specifically, it considered how and why (Dutch-Flemish) film remakes are national, and emanate, or indeed echo, the nation, national specificity or national sentiments. Applying Hjort's framework to the sample of eleven Dutch-Flemish film remakes, it seemed that most film pairs are characterised by a shared or universal framework (narrative, themes, characters, spaces, etc.) with differing interpretations of these same structures that turn them into (banal) Flemish or Dutch realities. Contrary to the film remake as a national echo chamber thesis, one could assert that the employment of perennial themes in these films might result in mediated cultural encounters with universal norms and values, resulting in a type of banal cosmopolitanism. However, as argued above, these transnationally shared schemas were, at every turn, dipped in a national (Flemish or Dutch) sauce, which complicates these mediated universal encounters. Hence, from a textual standpoint, the films that came out of the Dutch-Flemish remake phenomenon wish to recreate familiar realities for mainstream audiences but also to build on perennial themes and universal values. Indeed, holding the example of *In Oranje/Gilles* in mind, although at first glance it appeared that both films were clearly national, after the analysis, it proved difficult to claim that the films under analysis truly deal with themes of the nation.

As well as analysing the film texts and their surrounding contexts, it is, however, equally necessary to take into account the audiences that eventually watch and interpret these films – reminiscent of Anderson's claim that the nation (but also Europe) only exists in the people's minds. In the case of Dutch-Flemish remakes, one must note that all of these film remakes are actually perceived as 'originally' Flemish or Dutch films, because the audiences are generally unaware of the fact that they are watching a remake of a different source film embedded in a different socio-cultural context. Consequently, even though these films are balanced between the transnational and national, or the universal and the particular, audiences may perceive them to be mainly national and not something coming from a neighbouring nation. In other words, although some of the films' elements are, in fact, transtextually connected to foreign cultures, they may generally not be perceived as such. The comparative analysis shows that even if the Dutch and Flemish are clearly different in some (banal) aspects, they might not be as different as these films want them to believe they are, again pointing to some sort of cosmopolitan potential. Yet from an (implied) audience perspective, one could draw the opposite conclusions, which speak in favour of the argument of the remake as a national echo chamber. Indeed, because of the dual hegemony between the dominant cultural proximity of the US, and the second dominant cultural proximity of the national context, alternative modes of conceivable proximity (linguistic, socio-cultural, or historical ties with other geographically close European nations) are being downplayed or, indeed, diminished. Hence, coincidental with Billig's thesis, what might appear to be banal or superficial on the surface, could, therefore, at its core, be highly ideological.

Notes

1. These are films 'produced or primarily co-produced in one European country, but released in another' (e.g. a French film released in Germany) (Jones, 2020).
2. The Dutch remake of *Madly in Love* is actually directed by the same Flemish director (Hilde Van Mieghem) who directed the source film, also called *Madly in Love*, which makes it an auto-remake.
3. The Dutch and American remakes of the Flemish film *Loft* were both (limitedly) released in Flanders.
4. However, one should note that another reason for this is that the genre of romantic comedy has been very popular in the Low Countries in the past decennium. Many mainstream romantic comedies are produced for a domestic audience, especially in the Netherlands. As these films prove to be attractive and commercially viable, film-makers from across the border want to reproduce these successes in their own market.

References

Anderson, Benedict (1983), *Imagined Communities*, London: Verso.
Berry, C. (2006), 'From national cinema to cinema and the national: Chinese-language cinema and Hou Hsiao-hsien's "Taiwan Trilogy"', in V. Vitali and P. Willemen (eds), *Theorising National Cinema*, London: BFI, pp. 148–57.
Bhabha, H. K. (1994), *The Location of Culture*, London: Routledge.
Billig, M. (1995), *Banal Nationalism*, Thousand Oaks: Sage.
Bondebjerg, Ib, Redvall, E. N., Helles, R., Lai, S. S., Søndergaard, H. and Astrupgaard, C. (2017), *Transnational European Television Drama*, Basingstoke: Palgrave Macmillan.
Buonanno, M. (2002), *Convergences: Eurofiction Fourth Report*, Napoli: Liguri.
Cajot, J. (2012), 'Waarom het Verkavelingsvlaams onvermijdelijk was', in Kevin Absillis, Jürgen Jaspers and Sarah Van Hoof (eds), *De manke usurpator: over Verkavelingsvlaams*, Ghent: Academia Press, pp. 39–66.
Cuelenaere, E., Willems, G. and Joye, S. (2016), 'Reframing the remake: Dutch-Flemish monolingual remakes and their theoretical and conceptual implications', *Frames Cinema Journal*, 1: 10, 1–19.

Cuelenaere, E., Willems, G. and Joye, S. (2018), 'Same same same, but different: a comparative film analysis of the Belgian, Dutch and American "Loft"', *Tijdschrift voor Communicatiewetenschap,* 4: 46, 319–35.

Cuelenaere, E., Willems, G. and Joye, S. (2019a), 'Remaking identities and stereotypes: How film remakes transform and reinforce nationality, disability, and gender', *European Journal of Cultural Studies,* 22: 5–6, 1–17, <https://journals.sagepub.com/doi/full/10.1177/1367549418821850> (accessed 20 February 2019).

Cuelenaere, E., Willems, G. and Joye, S. (2019b), 'Local favors and regional markers: the Low Countries and their commercially driven and proximity focused film remake practice', *Communications,* 44: 3, 262–81.

Harvey, J. (2018), *On the Visual Cultures of the New Nationalisms,* Basingstoke: Palgrave Macmillan.

Herbert, D. (2017), 'The transnational film remake in the American press', in I. R. Smith and C. Verevis (eds), *Transnational Film Remakes,* Edinburgh: Edinburgh University Press, pp. 210–23.

Higson, A. (2002), 'The concept of national cinema', in A. Williams (ed), *Film and Nationalism,* New Brunswick, NJ: Rutgers University Press.

Higson, A. (2015), 'British cinema and the global reach for audiences', In Ib Bondebjerg, E. N. Redvall and A. Higson (eds), *European Cinema and Television,* Basingstoke: Palgrave Macmillan, pp. 127–50.

Hjort, M. (2000), 'Themes of nation', in M. Hjort and S. MacKenzie (eds), *Cinema and Nation,* London: Routledge, pp. 103–17.

Hjort, M. (2002), 'Themes of nation', in M. M. Louwerse and W. van Peer (eds), *Thematics: Interdisciplinary Studies,* Amsterdam: John Benjamins Publishing, pp. 301–20.

Hjort, M. (2009), 'On the Plurality of Cinematic', in N. Ďurovičová, K. Newman, and K. E. Newman (eds), *World Cinemas, Transnational Perspectives,* New York: Routledge, pp. 12–33.

Hjort, M. and Petrie, D. J. (2007), *The Cinema of Small Nations,* Edinburgh: Edinburgh University Press.

Jones, H. (2017), 'Remapping world cinema through audience research', in R. Stone, P. Cooke, S. Dennison, and A. Marlow-Mann (eds), *The Routledge Companion to World Cinema,* Abingdon: Routledge; pp. 467–81.

Jones, H. (2020, in press), 'What makes European films travel? How foreign independent movies can achieve transnational box office success', in I. Lewis and L. Canning (eds), *European Cinema in the 21st Century: Discourses, Directions and Genres,* Basingstoke: Palgrave Macmillan.

Lamarque, P. and Olsen, S. H. (1994), *Truth, Fiction, and Literature: A Philosophical Perspective,* Oxford: Clarendon Press.

Mazdon, L. (2000), *Encore Hollywood,* London: BFI.

Mazdon, L. (2017), 'Disrupting the remake: The Girl with the Dragon Tattoo', in I. R. Smith and C. Verevis (eds), *Transnational Film Remakes,* Edinburgh: Edinburgh University Press, pp. 21–35.

Meir, C. (2018), 'European cinema in an era of studio-building: some artistic and industrial tendencies in Studiocanal's output, 2006–present', *Studies in European Cinema,* 1–17.

Rvg (2006), 'Het origineel van Buitenspel', *Het Volk*, 3 June, p. 40, <http://gpr.me/zj0t9awryb/> (accessed 6 September 2018).

Standard Eurobarometer (2018), 'How "European" do EU citizens feel?' <http://ec.europa.eu/commfrontoffice/publicopinion/topics/fs5_citizen_40_en.pdf> (accessed 15 September 2018).

Straubhaar, Joseph D. (2007), *World Television: From Global to Local*, Thousand Oaks: Sage.

Verevis, C. (2017), 'New millennial remakes', in Frank Kelleter (ed), *Media of Serial Narrative*, Columbus: Ohio State University Press, pp. 148–166.

Verheul, J. (2016), 'Out of many, one: the dual monolingualism of contemporary Flemish cinema', in Tijana Mamula and Lisa Patti (eds), *The Multilingual Screen: New Reflections on Cinema and Linguistic Difference*, London: Bloomsbury, pp. 317–34.

Vincendeau, G. (1993), 'Hijacked', *Sight & Sound* 3: 7 (July), pp. 22–5.

INDEX

ABC (Australian Broadcasting Corporation), 172, 174, 177, 179, 187
AFC (Australian Film Council), 178, 179
alien
 alienated, 38, 76, 79, 131
 alienation, 55, 166
Almodóvar, Pedro, 3, 4, 120–4, 126, 130–7
America/American, 6, 61–3, 75, 91, 93, 102, 119, 143–6, 150, 152–4, 161, 207, 210–12, 215, 217–22, 229, 230, 238, 239
Anderson, Benedict, 230, 237, 238
Anderson, Lindsay, 69, 70, 76, 82
Anna Karenina, 172–6, 178, 180, 182, 186–8
Armstrong, Craig, 58
art cinema, 57, 68, 98, 117
Atonement (film), 50, 51, 62
Australia/Australianness, 3, 5, 46, 172–4, 176–81, 183, 186–8

authenticity, 6, 17, 28, 40, 42, 52, 62, 145, 148, 156, 157, 159, 163, 165, 166, 168, 169, 177

banal aboutness, 231, 232, 236
banal nationalism, 231, 238
Barry, John, 37
BBC (British Broadcasting Corporation), vi, xii, 44, 53, 59, 85, 113, 119, 155–60, 164–6, 169–71, 174, 175, 192, 193, 195, 204, 205
The Beautiful Lie (TV series), 3, 172, 175–7, 179–82, 186
Billig, Michael, 231, 238
Bogost, Ian, 208–10, 218, 220
Bolam, James, 79
Bondarchuk, Sergei, 155, 160, 161, 163–5, 170, 171
Bondebjerg et al., 62, 229, 233, 238, 239
Boyz N the Hood (film), 36

241

INDEX

brand/branding, 40, 60, 155, 158, 159, 169, 173, 177, 186, 188
Brecht, Bertolt, 76
Bright Star (film), 46
British
  costume drama *see* period drama
  countryside, 21, 48, 58, 60
  film industry, 46, 61, 69, 70, 157
  heritage film *see* period drama
  identity, 173
  imperialism, 73
  literature, 46, 47, 57, 58
  New Wave, 67–71, 73–6, 79–81
  period drama, 46, 47, 55, 58, 61
  social realism, 39
Burns, Robert, 101, 102, 116

Campion, Jane, 46, 86
canon/canonical, 21, 47, 57, 58, 60, 69, 75, 80, 142, 157, 172, 173, 177, 179, 184, 186, 217, 218
Caracol TV, 6, 151
Cardwell, Sarah, 58, 60, 156, 157, 160, 164, 165, 185
Cartmell, Deborah, 156, 166
Chan-wook, Park, 3, 191, 194–7, 202, 203
Christensen, Charlotte Bruus, 54
The Claim (film), 61
Clydesideism, 27
Cole, Sydney, 75, 77
Colombia, 6, 141–3, 145–51
colonialism, 145, 146, 207, 211, 212, 214, 215, 217
consciousness
  double, 102, 103, 115
  national, 60
  self, 101–3, 107, 116
The Conversation (journal), 37
cosmopolitanism, 84, 89, 91, 92, 151, 156–60, 162, 163, 165, 237, 238

Cuelenaere et al., 223, 232, 233
cultural proximity, 223, 226, 238

Davies, Andrew, 3, 155–7, 160–5
Dear Wendy (film), 55
Deleuze, Gilles, 208
D'entre les morts (novel), 206, 207, 209–16, 218
Devil Girl From Mars (film), 111
Devine, George, 70
Dexter, John, 75–7
Doctor Zhivago (TV series), 156, 160, 164
Dogme 95, 47, 55
Dutch-Flemish remake phenomenon, 6, 222–34, 236, 237

El Patrón del mal (TV series), 6, 141
An Education (film), 46
The Entertainer (film), 2, 68, 69, 71, 72, 75, 77–9, 81
Escobar, Pablo, 6, 143, 147–9, 150, 152
ethnicity, 92, 165, 228, 233
European cinema, 222, 223

Faber, Michel, 2, 103–8, 110, 112, 113
family, 11, 13–15, 18, 35, 36, 38, 40, 72, 88, 107, 113, 123, 126, 134, 135, 148, 157, 160, 163, 164, 168, 173, 174, 176, 180–6, 200, 202, 217, 232
Far from the Madding Crowd (film), 2, 46–9, 51–6, 58, 59, 61
female protagonist, 84, 85, 87, 89, 93, 94, 96, 97, 115, 122, 123
feminist, 86, 108
Festen (film), 54, 55, 57
fidelity, 120, 132, 134, 136, 165
film noir, 129, 130, 133

The Film Programme (radio), 193, 194
Fingersmith (novel), 192, 194, 195, 203, 204
format (television), 146, 147, 149, 150, 158, 175, 181, 229
France/French, 2, 11, 12, 13, 16–18, 21–3, 39, 46, 50, 54, 55, 61, 87, 89, 91, 92, 133, 164, 167, 203, 207, 210–15, 218, 219, 225, 238
franchise, 193, 218
Free Cinema movement, 69, 70
French new wave, 68
Fukunaga, Cary, 46

gender, xii, 85, 107–9, 111, 115, 116, 121, 122, 127, 128, 130, 136, 174, 225, 233
Glasgow, 107–12, 115–17
Glazer, Jonathan, 2, 4, 101, 103, 105–11, 113, 116, 117
globalisation, 3, 6, 38, 123, 151, 173, 226, 227

The Handmaiden (film), viii, 3, 5, 191–5, 197–201, 203
Hardy, Thomas, 14, 21, 47–58, 61
Harvey, James, 226, 230
hauntological, 39, 42, 43
Hegel, Georg Wilhelm Friedrich, 101, 102, 107
Herbert, Jocelyn, 69, 75, 76, 77
heritage film, 21, 22, 57, 157, 175
Higson, Andrew, 21, 22, 47, 68, 71, 116, 157, 166, 222, 230
Hill, James, 68, 71, 75
Hitchcock, Alfred, 129, 130, 207, 211, 219
Hjort, Mette, 226
Hodge, John, 27, 28, 29, 32, 35, 39, 41

Hollywood, 78, 111, 121, 125, 130, 155, 160, 174, 212, 216, 222, 225, 227, 229, 230
The Hunt (film), 56, 57
Hutcheon, Linda, 5, 102, 103, 106, 172, 186, 194, 198, 199, 206, 213
hybrid, 67, 146, 147, 167, 169, 195, 204, 225, 227, 231, 233, 236

identity, 11, 17, 18, 34, 36, 38, 41, 61, 67, 75, 81, 86, 89–92, 96, 97, 110, 112, 115, 121, 132, 160–2, 165, 166, 172, 173, 175, 177, 179, 180, 186, 196, 197, 200, 203, 225, 227, 230, 232
ideology, 162, 165, 217
Iggy Pop, 29, 37
imagined community, 226, 230
The Imitation Game (film), 46
index (semiological term), 20, 40, 42, 211, 213, 216, 217, 219
intercultural contact, 223
intertextuality, 16, 26, 29, 31, 43, 85, 155, 156, 199, 201, 203
Isadora (film), 69
It's All About Love (film), 54, 55

Jane Eyre (film), 46
Jones, Huw, 222, 226, 238
Julieta (film), 3, 120–34, 136

The Kitchen (film), 68, 75–81
Kneale, Nigel, 72, 73

L'eau des collines, 11–14, 16, 17, 18, 22, 23
La Haine (film), 36, 38
La Jetée (film), 5, 206, 207, 208, 211, 213, 214, 215, 216, 217, 218, 219

243

INDEX

La Movida, 121, 132
La Parabola de Pablo (novel), 6, 141
landscape(s)
  Australian, 179
  cultural, 18, 85, 181
  England and tourism, 48, 58
  hauntological, 42
  Provençal, 15–17
  Russian, 164
  Scottish Highlands, 112–15
  TV, 174
Latvia, 166, 167
letter, 14, 124, 125, 126, 130, 131, 132, 133, 161
Lion Rampant, 114
Lithuania, 166, 167
localisation, 227, 229, 235
Lodge, David, 51
Look Back in Anger (play), 69, 71, 72
Look Back in Anger (film), 79
Low Countries, 223–30
Lust for Life (song), 29, 31, 33, 37

Macdonald, Andrew, 56
magical realism, 142
marketing, 40, 46, 57, 60, 156, 193
Mayle, Peter, 16–17, 23
The Mayor of Casterbridge (novel), 61
Mazdon, Lucy, 225, 229
mediated cultural encounters, 229
melodrama, 122, 123, 126–7, 130, 131, 192, 194
Miller, Jonathan, 79
modernism, 84, 97, 121
modernity, 21, 39, 114–15, 160, 168, 174, 214

monstrous, 86, 132, 133, 134
Moscow, 164, 174
multilinguality, 89
Munro, Alice, 3, 120–1, 123

Napoleon, 161, 162, 164
Narcos (TV series), 141–52
national echo chamber, 237, 238
national identity, 61, 86, 90, 172, 173, 177, 225, 227, 230
nationalism, 112, 156, 157, 161, 162, 230, 231, 237
  transnationalism, 6, 160, 166, 169, 228, 229
nationhood, 111, 161, 163, 173, 176–8
Netflix, 6, 143, 146, 147, 148, 149
New Scottish cinema, 27
Nicholls, David, 56
nostalgia
  analog, 40
  embodied, 27, 34, 35, 39, 42
  reflexive, 27, 38, 40
  spatialised, 27, 32

obscene fidelity, 136
Olivier, Lawrence, 71, 73, 81
ontological security, 31
Osborne, John, 70–2

Pagnol, Marcel, 11, 12, 16, 17, 21
Paris, 86, 87, 163, 209, 211, 212, 214
performance, 67, 68, 70, 71, 73, 74, 79, 81
Porno (film) 4, 26–30, 43
postcolonial 88, 142, 144–6, 151
precarity, 85, 86, 89, 90
Provence, 11, 14, 17, 21, 22, 23
psychogeography, 20

Quartet (film), 85, 86, 89, 90–2, 95, 96

Reich, Allon, 56
remake, 86, 206–207, 215, 223–9
The Return of the Native (novel), 49, 54
Rhys, Jean, 84–97
Richardson, Tony, 68–70, 72
Room At the Top (film), 69
Runaway (short stories), 120–3, 128
Russian
   culture, 165–6, 168–9, 178
   film and TV industries, 160–1, 175
   history, 161, 162, 169, 175
   identity, 175, 161
   landscape, 164
   literature, 155, 160, 169, 173, 179, 186
   tourism, 175, 178

Salazar, Alonso, 141, 145, 147, 148, 150
Saltzman, Harry, 70
Scherfig, Lone, 46
Scott, Sir Walter, 108
Scottish
   cinema, 27
   culture, 36, 108
   femininity, 108, 110, 113
   Highlands, 103, 106, 108, 112–15
   history, 33
   identity, 36, 112
   masculinity, 27, 33–7, 108, 122
   modernity, 114–15
   politics, 112
   urban landscapes, 112–15
Second World War, 209, 211–13, 218
The Secret Life of Us (TV series), 177, 179

Senegal, 209, 212
Sequence (journal), 69
Snowpiercer (film), 191
soap opera, 31, 34, 143, 149
Stannard, Julia, 155, 156, 159, 160, 163, 164, 166–8
Stoker (film), 191
Submarino (film), 56

T2: Trainspotting (film), 26–43
Tagg, Alan, 71
Taste of Honey (film), 76
television
   adaptation, 21, 50, 95, 155, 156
   adverts, 13
   American, 141
   Australian, 178, 179
   British, 158, 165
   Dutch, 229
   European, 317, 320, 321
   Flemish, 235
   French, 21
   markets, 233, 240
   national identity, 172, 177
   Scandinavian, 46
   seriality, 31
   TV series, 173, 178, 179, 217, 218
Tess of the D'Urbervilles (novel), 49, 51, 61
Thatcherism, 35
theatre, 67–73, 76, 77, 78, 80, 81
Their Finest (film), 46
Thornberry, Emily, 112
time travel, 213, 215, 216
Tinker Tailor Soldier Spy (film), 46
Tolstoy, Leo, 155, 160, 161, 163, 165, 172–4
tourist gaze, 47–9, 52, 55, 58
Trainspotting (film), 4, 26–30, 33, 35–40, 43

translation, 5, 7, 91, 150, 198, 199, 203, 206–8, 216, 223, 225
transnationalism *see* nationalism
trauma, 30, 88, 91, 103, 123–5, 127–30, 132, 133
Trishna (film), 61
Tushingham, Rita, 76
Twelve Monkeys (film), 207, 208, 211, 215–17

Under the Skin (film), 2, 101–16

Vertigo (film), 129, 207–18
Vidor, King, 155, 160, 161
Vinterberg, Thomas, 2, 47, 51–60
voiceover, 37, 58, 94, 104, 130–2, 142, 145, 150, 152, 161, 184, 185
von Trier, Lars, 55

War and Peace
  film (1965–7), 160, 161, 165
  novel (1869), 160
  television series (2016) 3, 155, 156, 158, 159, 164–6, 169
Waters, Sarah, 192–5, 197–200, 203
Welsh, Irvine, 4, 27, 30, 36
Wesker, Arnold, 74–7, 79
Whelehan, Imelda, 156, 166
Wide Sargasso Sea, 85, 88, 89, 91, 92, 95, 96, 97
Wittgenstein, Ludwig, 217
The Woodlanders (novel), 49

A Year in Provence (TV series), 16, 17, 18, 23

EU representative:
Easy Access System Europe
Mustamäe tee 50, 10621 Tallinn, Estonia
Gpsr.requests@easproject.com

www.ingramcontent.com/pod-product-compliance
Lightning Source LLC
Chambersburg PA
CBHW071835230426
43671CB00012B/1966